Zichroni v. State of Israel

Zichroni v. State of Israel

The Biography of a Civil Rights Lawyer

Michael Keren

LEXINGTON BOOKS
Lanham • Boulder • New York • Oxford

LEXINGTON BOOKS

Published in the United States of America
by Lexington Books
4720 Boston Way, Lanham, Maryland 20706

12 Hid's Copse Road
Cumnor Hill, Oxford OX2 9JJ, England

Originally published in Hebrew as *Amnon Zichroni: A Different Lawyer*
(Tel-Aviv: Hed-Arzi, 1999).

British Library Cataloguing-in-Publication Information Available

Library of Congress Cataloging-in-Publication Data

Keren, Michael.
    Zichroni v. state of Israel : the biography of a civil rights lawyer / Michael Keren.
      p. cm.
    Includes bibliographical references and index.
    ISBN 0-7391-0315-6 (cloth : alk. paper)—ISBN 0-7391-0316-4 (pbk. : alk. paper)
      1. Zichroni, Amnon, 1935– 2. Lawyers—Israel—Biography. 3. Civil
rights—Israel—History. I. Title: Zichroni v. state of Israel. II. Title.

KMK110.Z53 K47 2001
342.5694'085'092—dc21
[B]

                                           2001048270

Printed in the United States of America

∞™ The paper used in this publication meets the minimum requirements of
American National Standard for Information Sciences—Permanence of Paper for
Printed Library Materials, ANSI/NISO Z39.48–1992.

Contents

Acknowledgments

In the mid-1990s, when the peace process between Israel and the Palestinians was underway, I felt the time had come to tell the forgotten story of Israel's "civil society," the individuals and groups who strive for a degree of autonomy within the state. For reasons that will become clear later, the search for individual and group autonomy has received little attention in Israeli historiography, yet it represents a major battle, perhaps the most important of all, for the public sphere in the country.

While the history of a state focuses mainly on its political leaders, processes, and institutions, the story of civil society gives center stage to the citizen. Thus I decided to throw light on the complex relations between civil society and the state in Israel by tracing the life and career of civil rights attorney Amnon Zichroni, who always seemed to be positioned on the border between the two sectors. Subjecting an active lawyer to a study in the social sciences may be somewhat unfair, as it inevitably emphasizes only one dimension of his life. It also requires that considerable care be taken to adhere to the rules of both academic freedom and legal ethics. I am therefore grateful to many who helped me tread this rocky road, and first and foremost to Amnon Zichroni and his family for their cooperation and openness.

I am also grateful to Mr. Haim Israeli, the Deputy Director General in the Israeli Ministry of Defense, attorneys Dov Khenin and Naomi Stein, journalists Tal Bashan and Hanna Kalderon, and members of Zichroni's family, Eliahu Avital of Tel Aviv and Jerome Levin of Hopkins, Minnesota, for important documents and insights.

In addition, I would like to thank the following archives for their professional and considerate attention to my requests: The Aviezer Yelin Archive of Jewish Education in Israel and the Diaspora at Tel Aviv University; the Tel Aviv Municipal Historical Archive; the archive of the Israel Defense Forces in Givata'yim; the Archive of Immigrants of Latvian Descent in Kibbutz Shefay'im; the information center of the Andrea and Charles Bronfman Center for the Media of the Jewish People at Tel Aviv University; and the information center of the Diaspora Museum in Tel Aviv.

My thanks go as well to all those who agreed to be interviewed for this study for giving me their time and cooperation: Dror Arad-Ayalon, Eliahu and Rina Avital, Uri Avnery, Zalman Breinin, Osnat Cohen, Atara Pchor-Ciechanover, Latif Dori, Yosef Elkes, Bo'az Evron, Talma Geller, Ethan Ha'ezrahi, Haim Hanegbi, Issar Harel, Hanna Kalderon, Ya'acov Katz, Yitzhak Keren, Sara Lipkin, Meir Pa'il, Ya'acov Peri, Yesha'ayu Toma Schick, Gavriel Tzifroni, Shalom Zamir, Sofa Zeligson, Miri Zichroni, Rafi Zichroni, and Zvi Ziv.

I am most grateful to my research assistant, Gabriela Fisman, for her help and advice throughout this study, and to Judy Kraus and Sara Kitai who edited the manuscript.

This study would not have been possible without the inspiration and support of friends and colleagues during my frequent stays at the University of Calgary, especially David Bercuson, Barry Cooper, Roger Gibbins, Rainer Knopf, Ted Morton, Stephen Randall, and David Taras.

Special thanks are also due to Professor Craig Howes, director of the Biographical Research Center at the University of Hawaii, who encouraged me to prepare this study for an international readership.

I greatly benefited from my discussions with numerous people on methodological and substantive aspects of this study, particularly the contribution of biographical research to the social sciences, and I am grateful to them all, especially professors Miron Aronoff of Rutgers University, Alan Dowty of the University of Notre Dame, George Klosko of the University of Virginia, Pnina Lahav of Boston University, Charles Maier of Harvard University, Joel Migdal of the University of Washington, Gershon Shafir of the University of California–San Diego, Leon Sheleff of Tel Aviv University, Russell Stone of American University, and Richard Ullman of Princeton University.

I would like to thank Sage Publications, Inc. and Taylor & Francis Ltd. for their permission to reprint material contained in my articles "Political Perfectionism and the 'Anti-System' Party," *Party Politics* 6, no. 1 (January 2000): 83–92 (http://www.sagepub.co.uk); and "Legal Professionals and Civil Disobedience," *International Journal of the Legal Profession* 6, no. 1 (March 1999): 91–108 (http://www.tandf.co.uk).

Finally, I would like to express my thanks and appreciation to the entire staff at Lexington Books, especially to Serena Leigh, Martin Hayward, and Jason Proetorius for an outstanding publishing process conducted in accordance with the highest professional standards.

CHAPTER ONE

A Day in Court

∞

Nine a.m., the fourth floor of the Tel-Aviv District Court, the first day of the trial of the "Israeli Mafia in New York"[1]—a scene from the movies. Five Federal Bureau of Investigation (FBI) agents, four men and one woman, are there, dressed in gray suits, revolvers showing beneath the short jackets, small earphones in their ears. They scrutinize everybody who enters the room, looking very alert in contrast to the handful of Israeli border policemen who are sprawled in their chairs with their legs spread wide, yawning.

I am seated in the gallery, surrounded by the families of the accused. To my right are two young men, one with smooth skin and the other pimpled, apparently the sons of one of the defendants. They do not say a word, and will continue to remain silent throughout the long months of the trial. Behind them is a large group of ex-Israeli women from New York in narrow tube-pants and heavy jewelry, vulgarly voicing their opinions of the many photographers hounding their loved ones. To my left is the notorious criminal Gad (Shetz) Floom, who will be murdered in a few months. In the meantime, he is present in the courtroom in order to intimidate the prosecution witnesses. This, at any rate, is the assessment of Nathan Zehavi, the articulate crime reporter who sits close by and already knows, at this early stage, everything there is to know about the trial, the judges, and probably even the verdict to be handed down in a year and a half. On the defendants' bench are Joseph Reish and Israel Mizrahi, charged with belonging to an organization labeled by one of the young lawyers in the hall "the garbage team," a group of New York criminals of Israeli origin who go by impressive Hollywood monikers.

Reish is accused of putting out a contract on his business partner because of a conflict over the smuggling of oil between New York and New
Jersey. In his brown jacket and white shirt, he looks like an ordinary busi-
nessman dealing with some temporary inconvenience, occasionally leaf-
ing through documents and passing notes to the lawyers. Mizrahi is
charged with carrying out the murder. He is a brawny man with a dark
complexion who fidgets nervously in his chair, staring warily at the three
prosecutors who maintain poker faces in a somewhat exaggerated manner.
Although it is the 15th of January, it is hot and stuffy in the room, but
when the window is opened, a terrible noise comes in from David Ham-
elech Street. The window is constantly being opened or closed at someone's request. Since the hall is too small to contain all the family members
and their friends, a slim-faced policewoman forces them to rotate every
half hour; each time the door opens to allow a new stream of visitors in,
the trial is disrupted by the commotion in the corridor.

In this dense atmosphere, the figure of Amnon Zichroni stands out—
tall, thickset, he carries a black advocate's robe which, on better days,
hangs on a small hook at the entrance to his office at 57 Rothschild
Boulevard. In the moments preceding the trial he looks more tense
than might be expected of a veteran of so many trials in this hall. During the intermission he will come over to ask how I am enjoying myself
and what I think of it all, his eyes tired and his lips dry. Throughout the
trial, he is seated on a bench that is far too narrow for his big body,
looking like someone who is much more comfortable engaging in corridor intrigues than sitting through the proceedings. When he questions
the witnesses, he stands glued to the right-hand wall, totally ignoring
the two defendants seated close to him, utterly immersed in the papers
covered in yellow markings that he holds in his hands.

Amnon Zichroni represents Reish; Mizrahi is represented by Avigdor
Feldman, who worked in Zichroni's office for many years. Aware of the
conflict of interest that might arise between the alleged killer and the
man who allegedly ordered the murder, the two lawyers hardly exchange a word, although they cooperated in the past in many legal
battles. The first witness for the prosecution, a short bald Jewish–
American lawyer who speaks perfect Hebrew, is questioned by Zichroni,
who remains totally absorbed in the yellow markings on his papers,
forcing the witness to respond without the slightest reaction on his

part, as if the cross-examination were being conducted solely for the sake of protocol. He reads the questions out from the papers, fully dispelling the tension built up by the press before the trial. Zichroni is the only one who remains unimpressed by the massive presence of the legendary FBI agents in the room. Later he will explain to me that they were there to signal to the Israeli court that serious criminals were involved, and that he deliberately ignored them. At this stage, however, I am just bored, as are all the spectators in the room, and it occurs to me that I may have chosen the wrong lawyer for my biography. I sense his fatigue, his impatience vis-à-vis prosecutor Dvora Chen, his restlessness. It is a scene from the movies, but the leading actor is real.

Many years have passed since Zichroni stood before a judge for the first time. Then he was an eighteen-year-old conscientious objector whom the judge called "Smarkatch"—a derogatory Russian term meaning a snotnosed kid. I imagine that his appearance today before the court is probably not very different. He speaks in a measured monotonous voice indicating maturity as well as a certain aloofness characteristic of people with strong convictions. When he sits down, I sense a need for approval in the glances he directs toward the three judges, but the witness can see no sentiment of any kind in his eyes. On the contrary, half an hour into the investigation, the man has been turned from a respected New York prosecutor who arrived in Israel with two fat fish in his net into a small-time rogue. Any attempt on his part to remind the court that he is the representative of the law enforcement authorities of a friendly country is met with a new question that casts doubt on his motives, and any time he invokes American law he comes up against a lawyer who demonstrates considerable familiarity with it. American law, the witness is forced to admit, requires that he seek justice, not a conviction at any price. At this point the entire discussion shifts to a new plane that has the witness sweating and squirming in his chair. During the recess, when he tries to express his appreciation of his colleague, the famous Israeli lawyer, Zichroni responds with a perfunctory smile, the same response he will give his television interviewer that evening.

No lawyer is more familiar to Israeli television audiences than Amnon Zichroni, and no interviewee provides such little information. Zichroni has become a master of the media. His appearances are so frequent, and the information they produce so sparse, that the short interviews he grants every few days sound like coded messages to some secret agent in a remote jungle. "Terezi Will Not be Dismissed from Office" declares a newspaper headline one bright morning, followed by an interview with Zichroni over the question of whether Labib Terezi, the Palestine Liberation Organization (PLO) representative to the United Nations (UN) who was called back to Tunisia for consultations, will be dismissed by his superiors. Zichroni, who spends almost twenty-four hours in his office and always answers the phone courteously, believes that the recall for consultations does not signal dismissal. Question: How did the PLO diplomat impress you? Answer: As a very experienced UN diplomat. End of interview. The newspaper readers have no way of telling whether Zichroni, known for his extensive contacts with individuals and governments in the Arab world, is hiding something, or why he was interviewed on the subject in the first place. But it does not really matter, because they have all gained something: the newspaper a headline, the young reporter an interview with a celebrity, Zichroni his name and picture in the paper, and the readers the sense that they are privy to some secret intrigue.

During the Reish-Mizrahi trial, Zichroni uncharacteristically granted relatively few interviews so as not to fan public interest, a strategy that proved successful; Reish was acquitted. The turning point came during Zichroni's cross-examination of the main prosecution witness; the judge had issued a gag order on publication of his name. On one of those hot stuffy days in the courtroom, Zichroni, in his low monotonous voice, interrupted by incessant coughing, demolished the prosecution's entire argument. Legend has it that Reish, who cannot return to the U.S. because of other charges that are pending against him, cruises the streets of Tel Aviv in his expensive Honda Legend, listening over and over again to a tape of that cross-examination.

Local magazines periodically publish profiles of Zichroni. Most of them resemble each other in providing inaccurate biographical details and emphasizing the lawyer's transformation from a young rebel into a seeming servant of the country's security establishment, an unforgivable crime in the eyes of the bohemian circles Zichroni travels in. It is hard to ignore the perplexity of many of the authors of these profiles, which may have something to do with the smoke screen that literally surrounds the attorney, issuing from the Cuban cigar invariably in his mouth. The pieces tend to focus on his appearance ("tall, heavyset, protruding glassy blue, or green, or gray eyes"), and even experienced investigative reporters have difficulty characterizing him. He has been seen at once as an ideologue of the Left and a liberal defending human rights, a spokesman for the poor and a defender of the rich, and a professional lawyer and a celebrity.

The difficulty of defining the man is accentuated by the dearth of information he discloses about his past, which he hardly ever mentions. He has trouble remembering events, dates, and names from his childhood, and all the family letters and albums were burned by his brother Rafi after the death of their mother Masha. The two brothers' disengagement from the past is so blatant that one gets the impression there is something they are trying to hide. Zichroni claims he is willing to undergo hypnosis in order to discover whether this is indeed so, but his estrangement from the past needs no psychological explanation. All his life he has sought to break away from the factors that determine social and political affiliation, and the past is one of them.

In an article published in 1992, Zichroni voiced his objection to any affiliation that limits a person's free and autonomous thought. Geography, he wrote, determines how we perceive truth and justice. For example, we consider a Palestinian who attacks us to be a terrorist, while in the eyes of his own people he is a freedom fighter. Moral actions, he declared, demand a disregard for the circumstances in which we find ourselves; they require that we transcend our time and place and put ourselves in the role of the other.[2]

This emphasis on individual autonomy has characterized Zichroni's entire career. Although he operates within the central institutions of the state—political parties, the parliamentary system, the courts, the media, etc.—he has always maintained his independence from them. Even when he worked with opposition groups, such as the Third Force, New Force, the Israeli Council for Israeli–Palestinian Peace, and others, he preserved a degree of autonomy. This autonomy in respect to all social affiliations and political groups has made him one of Israel's most articulate advocates of "civil society," a term which may require some elaboration.

Civil society is defined as the plurality of voluntary groups operating in a state with relative autonomy. The term is used not only in reference to this type of activity, but also to characterize societies in which it is prevalent. In both meanings, it refers to activities in which citizens think, talk, assemble, and take action in matters of public significance in a manner that is not constrained by the state. A state in which civil society flourishes can be contrasted to one in which government dictates direct the entire sphere of human activity. The distinction is based on a deep-seated dissent between those who believe that individuals are sinful or erring creatures in need of guidance and manipulation, and those who consider them responsible citizens capable of reasoned dialogue and action.

The term "civil society," coined by Aristotle, has been used to describe civilized constitutional regimes. It became a cornerstone of Hegel's political philosophy, representing a dimension of the state in which legal, professional, and ethical codes are followed. Hegel believed that such civil activity was necessary to restrain both the individual and the government, and could be conducted only in a state that ensures freedom for family, tribe, or church. The term was popularized by the revolutions in Europe in the 1980s and 1990s, especially that of the Solidarity movement in Poland, where it was used mainly to express the demand for free economic and civic activity separate from the state, and reflected deeply rooted suspicions regarding the willingness and capability of the state, with its powerful bureaucratic apparatus, to secure the operation of a civil society.[3]

Thus in modern times, civil society has been redefined to include an element of opposition to the state. John Hall defines it as "the self-organization of strong and autonomous groups that balance the state,"[4] and Michael Walzer emphasizes its autonomy not only from the state, but also from the free market, technocracy, and nationalism. He notes correctly, however, that civil society has no singularity of its own, but complements these forces; the members of civil society do not cease to be citizens of the state, producers and consumers in the free market, or the sons and daughters of a nation.[5] Indeed, once civil activity is assured, prevailing institutions and ideologies do not disappear; rather, they merely have greater difficulty controlling the individual in a totalitarian fashion. This is where the power of civil society lies. By reaffirming the long-neglected role of the self-aware citizen in public life, it serves as a barrier against the absolute control of the dominant political forces in any given place or time.[6]

In *Jihad vs. McWorld*, Benjamin Barber calls for the establishment of civil society on a global scale. Defining it as "a mediating third domain between the overgrown but increasingly ineffective state governmental and the metastasizing private market sectors,"[7] he claims that it grounds democracy as a form of government in which not politicians and bureaucrats but an empowered people use legitimate force to put flesh on the bones of their liberties; and in which liberty carries with it the obligations of social responsibility and citizenship as well as the rights of legal persons. Civil society offers us a single civic identity that, belonging neither to state bureaucrats nor private consumers but to citizens alone, recouples rights and responsibilities and allows us to take control of our governments and our markets. Civil society is the domain of citizens.[8]

The "domain of citizens" has hardly ever existed in Israel. This is not what might have been expected, since Israel was initially conceived by thinkers rooted in the Central European bourgeoisie who believed in civil society. Theodor Herzl, the founder of the Zionist (Jewish national) movement, all but proposed the constitution of an "aristocratic republic" for Jews in Palestine,[9] something like Renaissance Venice, in which virtue, as defined by Montesquieu, would prevail. In his ethical writings, Herzl's associate Max Nordau attributed high morality to societies with a developed set of public institutions where the oppressed were able to appeal to the press and public opinion.[10] Another Zionist leader, Vladimir Jabotinsky, called for the establishment in Palestine of a progressive bourgeois-liberal society. According to Yaacov Shavit, Jabotinsky saw the ideal bourgeois type as

> an entrepreneur with a civic conscience; someone who from a national point of view combined in himself qualities such as republican values, economic and industrial initiative—one who was capable of moving the wheels of industry and civilization through his industrious and innovative qualities, his brains and his capital. This was the idealized image of the French and British middle class which during the nineteenth century had spearheaded the Industrial Revolution and the struggle for political emancipation, as well as the struggle for national independence in various other countries. This republican entrepreneur was an individualist with a natural dislike for the anti-liberal and anti-democratic approach of marxist and socialist collectivism.[11]

The bourgeois–liberal ideology advanced by the early leaders of the Zionist movement had its social base in what are known as the "civil circles"—merchants, shopkeepers, small landowners, industrialists, and professionals who immigrated to Palestine between the two world wars and settled mainly in Tel Aviv. These people established political parties whose liberal platforms resembled those of the middle-class parties in Europe, as well as a variety of economic and social institutions. Nevertheless, they had a minimal impact on public life in pre-state Israel and during the first three decades of statehood when socialism held sway in the country. The socialist movement downgraded the bourgeoisie and fiercely fought its political leaders in the name of "creative pioneering,"[12] a notion that implied that Palestine's future depended not on private initiative and civic conscience, but on a collectivist effort.

In 1920 David Ben-Gurion founded the General Federation of Labor (Histadrut), which controlled a large slice of the country's economy and served as the recruitment base for its political leadership. In 1933 he gained control over the world Zionist movement and coined the phrase "from class to nation," which neatly summed up his ideology: "Private capital was permissible as long as it utilized Jewish labor and increased the prospects for both Jewish immigration and a Jewish economy."[13]

As Israel Kolatt explains, Ben-Gurion did not attack the bourgeois sectors, and particularly Jabotinsky, for establishing themselves through private capital, but for their alleged lack of national solidarity. Indeed, after declaring the State of Israel in 1948, Ben-Gurion invested considerable efforts in enhancing such solidarity, including the establishment of a strong state with working democratic institutions within the economic, political, and ideological hegemony of the socialist movement. An admirer of Lenin, he demanded that the citizenry join in the state-building endeavor in body and mind. Private initiative was restrained by an elaborate system of bureaucratic controls that favored Federation of Labor enterprises, and private affairs were subordinated to the affairs of state through policies that encouraged large families, unified parochial educational systems, instituted a national draft, and so on. In 1949, for example, as part of his attempts to mobilize all of society and its spiritual leaders for the national tasks at hand, he assembled the country's writers and called for the subjugation of their creative talents to the pioneering ideology. What is more, cultural mobilization did not always remain within the realm of rhetoric, but was also manifested in practices such as censorship of the press.

In such a spirit, there was no room for the assertion of a civil society. In the Ben-Gurion era, which lasted until he resigned as prime minister in

1963, the public domain was dominated by an ideology that cherished the collective and was intolerant of any individuals who challenged that collective, whether by conscientious objection or by forming a voluntary group that proposed alternatives. The ideology was reinforced by the experience of the War of Independence, as well as by the massive tasks of security and immigrant absorption in the 1950s, as a result of which the country's intellectual elites aligned themselves with the mainstream discourse. As Shlomo Sand states: "Most cultural creation in the first decade of the life of the state consisted in committed nationalistic works that reveled in the birth of the state. The intellectual classes quickly completed the process of conformist integration within the new cultural establishment, and thereby contributed greatly to erasing the borders between state and civil society. Indeed, reducing the separation between the state and civil society was necessary for continuing the rapid consolidation of a new national culture."[14]

Amnon Zichroni was a lone wolf who declared himself a conscientious objector at a time of intense security tensions, challenged the definition of citizenship according to nationalist or religious criteria, opposed the construction of settlements in the West Bank when the country was in a state of euphoria over Israel's victory in the Six Day War, and engaged in other unpopular activities, such as defending freedom of the press, association, and religion not only for Jews but also for Arabs in Israel and the occupied territories, protecting the right of minorities to run for elections, and providing legal aid to persons accused of espionage and treason. As such, he may be seen not as an ideologue, but as the protector of civil society under the most inauspicious of circumstances.

Zichroni was a lone wolf long before he took upon himself the role of advocate of civil society. "He would come to see us, he was such an urban type coming from the city to the country, one of those who never walk barefoot,"[15] relates his cousin Osnat Cohen from the rural community of Herzliya. In the eyes of the healthy, tanned youngsters growing up in rural Israel of the 1940s, Amnon was a strange phenomenon when he came to visit them in the summer from the city of Tel Aviv. He was an intelligent, serious, quiet boy who played the violin and read books in the lavatory. The scar he still bears on his cheek was caused by a fall from a tree during one such vacation in Herzliya, after which he had to walk around with a "kalabra," a device used in the 1940s to protect the jaws. In a society that venerated collectivism, Zichroni was never one of the gang. When his peers joined the pre-state youth movements in the 1940s, debating the issues of socialism, nationalism, and statehood long into the night, Zichroni did not join up. Instead, every Saturday, on his own, he traversed the many kilometers on foot to the Amishav *ma'abara* (a temporary tent and hut camp in which newcomers were housed) in Petach Tikva, where he taught the new immigrants Hebrew.

In later years, when he defended the poor and weak he did not do so because he was a socialist; when he defended the rich and famous he did not do so because he identified with them; and when he talked with PLO activists two decades before they were recognized as negotiation partners by Israel, he did not do so because of any affiliation with the "peace camp." Over the years, Israeli peace movements developed rituals—singing sad songs in a soft voice, holding hands during demonstrations, lighting candles, etc.—as well as shared notions, such as their self-definition as the sane citizens fighting irrational right-wing forces. But Zichroni never became part of this subculture. So when peace activists committed acts of civil disobedience, Zichroni restrained them in order to enable their defense in court, and yet when delicate international negotiations were required to release captured soldiers and those missing in action (MIAs), it was this sober attorney who was called upon.

This special quality of maintaining autonomy from established political frameworks without becoming estranged from them warrants explanation. It is not enough to attribute unique psychological traits to Zichroni. However determined his attempt to distance himself from the past, his autonomous mind and behavior can be traced back to growing up in civil circles. Although this sector is largely ignored by the history books that describe the birth of Israel, it has left a legacy of which Zichroni is a prime example. It is the refusal to yield to the imperatives of the collective.

Notes

1. *Ma'ariv*, January 30, 1995, 6.

2. A. Z. "Assirei Ha'makom" [prisoners of their location], *Ma'ariv*, January 2, 1992.

3. See Dominique Colas, *Civil Society and Fanaticism: Conjoined Histories* (Stanford: Stanford University Press, 1997).

4. John A. Hall, "In Search of Civil Society," in *Civil Society: Theory, History, Comparison*, ed. John A. Hall (Cambridge: Polity Press, 1995), 15.

5. Michael Walzer, "The Civil Society Argument," in *Theorizing Citizenship*, ed. Ronald Beiner (Albany: SUNY, 1995).

6. See Robert D. Putnam, *Bowling Alone: The Collapse and Revival of American Community* (New York: Simon & Schuster, 2000).

7. Benjamin R. Barber, *Jihad vs. McWorld: How Globalism and Tribalism Are Reshaping the World* (New York: Ballantine Books, 1996), 284.

8. Barber, *Jihad vs. McWorld*, 285.

9. Theodor Herzl, *The Jewish State* (New York: Herzl Press, 1970), 99.

10. Max Nordau, *Morals and the Evolution of* Man (London: Cassell, 1922).

11. Yaacov Shavit, *Jabotinsky and the Revisionist Movement 1925–1948* (London: Frank Cass, 1988), 285.

12. David Ben-Gurion, *Israel: A Personal History* (New York: Funk & Wagnalls, 1971), 229.

13. Israel Kolatt, "Ben-Gurion's Image and Reality," in *David Ben-Gurion: Politics and Leadership in Israel*, ed. R. W. Zweig (London: Frank Cass, 1991), 25.

14. Shlomo Sand, "Between the Word and the Land: Intellectuals and the State in Israel," in *Intellectuals in Politics*, eds. Jeremy Jennings and Anthony Kemp-Welch (London: Routledge, 1997), 110.

15. Interview with Osnat Cohen, November 7, 1994.

CHAPTER TWO

The Civil Circles

One day in 1924, a young unemployed *halutz* (pioneer) named Zvi Avital came to Tel Aviv from the *moshava* (a rural settlement). As he was walking down the street, he ran into Mrs. Levin from his hometown of Uman in the Ukraine. Thirteen years had passed since he had arrived in Palestine, and in all that time he had hardly thought of his hometown, for he had started a new life here in the Land of Israel. Like other *halutzim*, he preferred to forget the past and focus on the problems of the present: the climate was so harsh, the land so arid, and the new farmers so unskilled. Moreover, the British, who ruled Palestine by a mandate from the League of Nations, were determined to make the country a market for the Australian flour that competed with local grain production. How could the Jewish immigrants be productive, and how could they compete with the far more experienced Arab workers for the few jobs available? Preoccupied with these thoughts, Zvi heard from Mrs. Levin that the Nipomnichi family, acquaintances from Uman, had arrived in Tel Aviv. So he went to visit them and was stunned. In their home he found a culture he had not expected to see in the Land of Israel: here were merchants who had not come to build the land in the pioneering spirit, but to make a living. As he wrote in a letter to his parents in Uman, people like the Nipomnichis were opening stores all over the place; there were as many stores in Tel Aviv as there were houses, and soon the shop owners would be living off each other.[1]

This was the typical attitude of the *halutzim* to the civil circles. Beginning in 1882, modern Jewish immigration to Palestine arrived in a series of waves, known as *aliyot* (singular: *aliya*) literally meaning "ascents." The first three *aliyot* (1882–1903; 1904–1914; 1919–1923) consisted mainly of young people from Russia and other parts of Eastern Europe, many of whom left their families behind and built rural settlements that were first supported by Jewish philanthropy abroad and later by the World Zionist Federation founded in Basle in 1897. The second and third *aliyot* are known for the experimental forms of collective settlements they developed, especially the kibbutz, as well as for the infrastructure of socialist economic and political organizations they established, culminating in the General Federation of Labor (Histadrut), founded in 1920. The Histadrut became the main organ for promoting the development of a Jewish working class, and it controlled the economic and political life of the *Yishuv* (pre-state Jewish community in Palestine) for many years.

The ethos of the *halutz* evolved during the second and third *aliyot*. In an analysis of the term, Gideon Shimoni stresses its double meaning in Hebrew, referring to "pioneer" and to "avant-garde." In both senses, it is used for people who consciously strike out ahead of a larger mass of followers to carry out a commonly conceived social project. Shimoni demonstrates an interesting paradox, namely, that the fulfillment of the *halutz* ideal was to be achieved through *hagshama*, roughly translated as "self-realization." Contrary to present-day understanding of this term, however, it did not refer to individualistic self-fulfillment, but rather implied the conscious decision to fuse one's own search for personal fulfillment with national objectives. *Hagshama* thus involved the acting out of one's convictions by personally immigrating to the Land of Israel and undergoing the transformation into a laborer.[2]

No one has ever expressed the contradiction between this pioneering ethos and the civil circles better than the first secretary general of the Histadrut, David Ben-Gurion. Later waves of immigration were less exposed to the notion of the *halutz*, and so for them, individualism did not necessarily entail devoting oneself to a life of labor as conceived by socialist thinkers. The fourth *aliya* of the mid-twenties from Poland, and the fifth *aliya* of the thirties from Germany, consisted largely of merchants, artisans, and professionals who opened the sort of businesses that had been typical of the middle classes since the late Middle Ages. Yet whereas the middle classes are generally admired for their enterprise and entrepreneurship, those who settled in Palestine encountered an extremely hostile environment. The self-proclaimed pioneers dubbed them "soft drink vendors." For

Ben-Gurion, being a merchant in Tel Aviv was a true aberration. Those who sought the means to make a living for their families, rather than reading Lenin's *What is to be Done?*—or for that matter Ben-Gurion's own *From Class to Nation*—were looked upon as capitalists still tied to the traditional roles that had been forced on the Jews throughout history, such as money lending, and were accused of failing to join in the modern Zionist revolution. Ben-Gurion, whose own farming experience, incidentally, was quite limited, extolled the image of the farm worker holding a scythe in one hand and a gun in the other as the symbol of the new Jew building modern Israel, in contrast to the urban merchant, depicted as unproductive and worthless.

In his many writings, Ben-Gurion praised the youngsters of the second *aliya* (to which he belonged) and the third, "who came to the Land of Israel having, as their sole asset, a deep faith in the responsibility and capacity of creative and daring Man, and the aim of whose life was working defense, as the most certain way to redeem the Homeland and the nation."[3] In the eyes of Ben-Gurion: "A new human type appeared in Jewish history; one marked for great things. This type aimed at personal, individual implementation and pioneering—what is known in Hebrew as Halutziut—which does not reject any task, great or small, does not flinch at any difficulty or danger, and demands everything from itself before it demands anything from others."[4]

There was no doubt in his mind that those who did not believe in the possibility of going from town to country or from schoolbook and profession to physical labor, were simply misguided. He often spoke out against diaspora Jews, who not only lived a life of exile, dependent on the mercy of strangers, but whose economy and social structure could not be compared to those of any independent people living in their own land and controlling their own destiny. Diaspora Jews were landless and did not work in any of the primary branches of the economy on which a people's survival depends. And this applied, as well, to the civil circles who resembled Diaspora Jewry in their failure to work the land. He declared: "Without a return *en masse* to the soil and to labor, without a fundamental transformation in the economic and social structure of the Jewish population of the Land of Israel, we should never have achieved a Jewish State, for no state is conceivable in which the majority of the people neither till the soil nor do all the other work of hand and brain required for its survival."[5]

Shmuel Almog offers an explanation for the harsh treatment doled out to the civil circles by the champions of pioneering. He claims that the term *"halutz,"* referring to the avant-garde preparing the soil for the Jews who would come to Palestine in the future, came into use between the two world wars, at a time when *aliya* to Palestine did not seem an immediate answer to the needs of Jewish existence abroad. It was used to distinguish that part of society which was willing to sacrifice itself to achieve future values, and involved an ambivalence toward those who were not *halutzim*, including the immigrants from Poland and Germany who arrived in the 1920s and 1930s. According to Almog, this ambivalence toward "Diaspora Jews" stemmed from the mixed feelings of the pioneers. Although on the one hand they were proud to have left home, on the other hand the difficulties awaiting them in the new land—scarcity, unemployment, and skirmishes with the local Arabs—endowed their life back home with a certain appeal. The way these youngsters coped with the ambivalence, Almog suggests, was by stressing their own self-sacrifice in striving to build a new society and a new race of man, as opposed to people like their parents, who were preoccupied with the petty matters of raising families and pursuing petit-bourgeois hopes.[6]

The letter sent by unemployed Zvi Avital to his parents was written in just this spirit. Not surprisingly, he wrote, the Nipomnichis had not struck roots in the country. Working the land requires sweat and blood, which can be expected only from a special breed of pioneers, not from people in pursuit of the American dollar. For anyone coming to Palestine to make money, the land is a disaster, and they are disastrous for the land. Avital used particularly harsh language when he spoke of the daughter, Shifra Nipomnichi, who worked in the Lieber candy factory. Although he appears to have been smitten by the woman he would later marry, for the moment she represented everything he despised. Her personality, he wrote, is "symptomatic of the young generation that is growing up over there in the Diaspora in the Ukrainian savannas. . . . She works in a private candy factory, earning 2.5 shillings a day. Obviously, such work cannot provide any satisfaction, but only oppress the spirit in a horrifying way."[7] The city factory owner, he was convinced, demanded that the exploited workers devote their whole selves to the job, leaving them no time to alter existing patterns of life or to build new forms of settlement, like the kibbutz. Zvi expressed his anger at the beautiful, intelligent young

Shifra who looked down on him, the pauper, with the arrogance typical of those who lived in the cosmopolitan city of Tel Aviv. He blamed her lack of proper values on his parents, and rebuked them by saying that if young people like her, with no nationalist spirit, were growing up among them in the Ukraine, they could consider themselves solely responsible for the corruption of the Jewish soul.

Uman, located at the meeting point of the Uman and Kamenka Rivers in central Ukraine, was first settled in the Middle Ages, and belonged to Poland since the sixteenth century. In 1648, Bogdan Chmielnicki led a rebellion of Cossacks, who were subjects of the king of Poland but enjoyed a certain autonomy as warriors, in a rebellion. Departing their camps along the Danube River, they established a short-lived independent Ukrainian state that soon became part of the Russian Empire. When Poland was divided up in the late eighteenth century, the Russian Empire took over all the regions of the Ukraine west of the Dnieper, save for Galicia, which was turned over to Austria. The nineteenth century saw the emergence of a Ukrainian national movement that flourished mainly in Galicia, and was fiercely persecuted in the regions under tsarist rule. During the civil war that followed on the Bolshevik revolution of 1917, Ukrainian nationalists were defeated by Soviet forces, and in 1924 the Ukraine became a republic of the Soviet Union.

Each of these events in the history of Ukrainian nationalism had dire implications for the Jews of Uman. Chmielnicki, for example, is known as one of the worst slaughterers of Jews in history because of the pogroms committed by the bands of Cossacks under his command, and every new wave of Ukrainian nationalism took a similar toll. In 1749, Uman was conquered by the Haydmaks, who butchered the Jews; in 1768, Maxim Zaliznyak, the leader of a peasant rebellion, oversaw a massacre of Jews, as well as of Polish refugees who had fled to Uman; in 1919, during the civil war, Ukrainian nationalists committed even more terrible atrocities against the Jews. The pogrom of 1921, which forced the Nipomnichi family to flee the city and head for Tel Aviv, was the worst ever. In its effort to mobilize the countryside, the Ukrainian nationalist intelligentsia took advantage of age-old anti-Semitism, which led to the murder, rape, and looting of Jews. Here is an eyewitness account of those events:

It was on the twenty-ninth of June, at dawn. In the streets inhabited by Christians, the Polish girls and ladies got up and went out, dressed in white an carrying bouquets of flowers to welcome the three-man gang of Sokol, Stizura and Nicholski, who entered Uman greeted by music and the shouts of the crowd, as was common in those days. The moment the gangsters entered town, a terrible silence fell over it. In the empty streets, in the bright sun, Commander Nicholski rode, erect and imposing, on a fattened horse, white gloves on his hands and a white flower in his lapel. In the terrifying silence, under the brilliant sun, the echo of his powerful voice was heard: kill them by the multitudes, my brothers . . . kill them by the multitudes! And again the terrible silence took over, broken only by the screams of the tortured and the raped periodically filling the air, while at the same time, music wafted from the house of the Polish doctor, whose genteel educated sons were playing the piano.[8]

Uman is known for the Hassidic Rabbi Nachman of Bratslav, who was buried there in 1810, but its Jewish community was influenced most by the Enlightenment movement initiated by Moses Mendelssohn in eighteenth century Germany. Mendelssohn called upon the Jews to break down the ghetto walls and seek a general education, which he considered the key to the emancipation of the oppressed Jews of Europe. In 1822, Zvi Dov Horowitz founded a school in Uman in the spirit of Mendelssohn's ideas. The small community, numbering 5,000 at the beginning of the nineteenth century and 28,000 at the beginning of the twentieth, was also known for the large number of musicians it produced.

Most of the Jews of Uman were engaged in commerce, among them the head of the Nipomnichi family, Michael Halevy, who owned a hardware store. His wife Leah Kalika also came from a family of merchants. As was customary in those days, Michael Halevy, a tall, good-looking, bearded gentleman, was an observant Jew, and when he fled the pogroms and landed in Tel Aviv, he brought with him his Bible in its splendid leather cover. Until his death from old age, he continued to pray in a synagogue established by the Hassidic followers of Rabbi Nachman. But he also made sure that his children got a good education in general, as well as religious, subjects.

Michael Halevy and Leah had three sons and three daughters whose life stories encapsulate modern Jewish history. Rivka, the eldest daughter, married a devout Communist who believed in the redeeming vision of Karl Marx, stayed behind in the Ukraine, and was murdered by the Nazis in the massacre of Babi Yar. Her daughter Dora found refuge in Alma-Ata in Kazakhstan, where she gave birth to Rita, who came to Israel during the Gulf War in 1991. The second daughter, Nadia, married an architect named Zvi Tabechnik and came with him to Palestine, where he erected many houses in Tel Aviv. Some time later, because of some long-forgotten dispute, they moved to the United States. We have already met the youngest daughter, Shifra. She eventually married the impoverished Zvi Avital and settled with him in the countryside in order to realize the socialist dream. The youngest brother Haim, the least educated of the six children, came to Palestine where he opened a bicycle repair shop. The two remaining brothers, Shalom and Tuvia, had been sent to Palestine by their father in 1912 in advance of the rest of the family. They went to high school in the country and were partners in several business enterprises. Shalom married Mania and had one daughter named Adina. Tuvia married Masha and had two sons, Amnon and Rafi. When he came to Palestine, Tuvia changed his name from Nipomnichi to Zichroni. In Russian, "nipomnichi" means "I forgot." As Jews were customarily given derogatory names, this one was probably assigned to a forefather of the family who forgot the answer to some question posed by a Russian clerk. In Hebrew, "zichroni" means just the opposite: "my memory." Thus Tuvia was the father of Amnon Zichroni, and Shalom his uncle.

Shalom and Tuvia were typical of the civil circles. In a picture from their early days in Tel Aviv, the older brother Tuvia is dressed in a suit and tie, narrow-framed glasses, and heavy boots, looking very different from the socialist newcomers who discarded their European clothing, preferring instead short khaki pants and a worker's shirt. This proletarian dress code was one way in which the pioneers distinguished themselves from the bourgeois civil circles. But it was not only his clothes that set Tuvia apart. Although he and Shalom arrived in Palestine during the pioneering era, they never participated in the pioneering saga of draining swamps, paving roads, and making the desert bloom. The only connection between Tuvia's life and the description of that heroic era found in history books was his membership in a group known as "Chevre Trusk," a collection of young bohemian types who were known for the carnival parades they organized in Tel Aviv in honor of the Purim holiday, and the parties at which they danced the "sinful" European tango rather than the collective hora circle dance. Although some members of the "Chevre Trusk," such as Nathan Alterman, Alexander Penn, and Avraham Shlonsky, became quite famous as writers and poets, this was not so of Tuvia Zichroni. He lived the life of a building contractor and merchant who saw ups and downs in his business endeavors. His neighbors remember him as an elegant man and his sons as a good father who took an interest in their studies and was active on the school board. His primary business was the sale of eggs. While the story of Tel Aviv's egg merchants receives virtually no attention in the history books, the historical archives provide some information.

Tuvia and Shalom were the first to import eggs to Palestine. As Jewish rural settlements such as Beit Hanan and Ramot Hashavim could not supply the entire demand for eggs, the two brothers established "The Egg Center." Shalom served as the accountant and Tuvia traveled to Syria, Lebanon, Turkey, Iraq, and Egypt to purchase eggs and arrange for their transport in padded straw boxes by truck or ship. The eggs were stored in a large warehouse on Merchavia Street in Tel Aviv, and were held up to the sunlight one by one before sale to a retailer. The system was later improved, and each egg was placed in a small tin box with an electric light labeled "Roentgen" after the discoverer of the x-ray. The importers of eggs, meat, fish oil, grains, vitamins, and other basic commodities played a crucial role in the survival of the *Yishuv*, especially in war time. Nevertheless, the documents relating to their activities reveal the arrogance of the *Yishuv*'s socialist leadership toward them. During World War II, when there was a shortage of basic foodstuffs, the leaders called upon the private egg importers to help in supplying eggs to hospitals and pregnant women, and in 1947, at the beginning of the War of Independence, when the country's roads were blocked because of the fighting, the private merchants were again asked to increase their imports in order to stave off hunger. Yet despite this obvious dependency on the private sector, the appeals to Tuvia Zichroni and his fellow merchants were clearly made begrudgingly. In a letter from May 1949, Zichroni and his colleagues complained that the eggs they imported at great risk were being left to rot in the warehouses because the authorities gave precedence to the distribution of eggs by collective farms: "We have also earned the right to sell our merchandise and receive appropriate help from our government. In times of crisis, we have demonstrated our concern and undertaken considerable risk to supply the population—at the explicit request of the import authorities."[9] The new State of Israel, however, promoted cooperative enterprises over private initiatives, and in the early 1950s, the brothers went bankrupt. Tuvia tried his hand at several other businesses, but from this time on he was forced to live mainly off his savings. When Amnon became a lawyer, Tuvia used to help out in the office, always making sure nobody left the lights on at the end of the day.

Masha, a young woman from a well-to-do family in Latvia, seemed the perfect match for him. In a picture from the 1920s, she is seated on a bench on a Tel Aviv boulevard in a fashionable hat and fur coat with a diamond ring on her finger. She was elegant, well-educated, and foreign. Masha was born in the small town of Friedrichstadt, seventy-three kilometers southeast of Riga, the capital of Latvia. The town was established in the late seventeenth century and served as a commercial depot through which rafts carried merchandise from White Russia and Poland to Riga. At the end of the eighteenth century, it came under the control of Russia, and lost its commercial importance when the Riga–Dvinsk railway was opened in 1861. Friedrichstadt became part of Soviet Latvia after World War I.

The first Jews settled in Friedrichstadt at the end of the eighteenth century, and by 1863 accounted for three-quarters of its population. Many of them were members of the Wasserman family; in the mid-nineteenth century, the register of the town's 542 Jews included 71 Wassermans. In 1915, the Jews were exiled to the interior of Russia, leaving only a tiny Jewish community in place. Under the Soviet regime, established over Latvia in 1940 as a result of the Ribbentrop–Molotov pact, the community's institutions were dismantled and the Jews were again exiled to the Soviet interior. Those who remained were assassinated by Latvian fascists during the retreat of the Red Army in World War II.

Masha was the daughter of Yitzhak–Yosef Wasserman, a traveling salesman who sold Singer knitting machines. She was one of five sisters, all of whom were well educated. Three of the sisters, Yeti, Anya, and Genia, perished in the holocaust. Masha went to high school in Riga, where she became fluent in German. She was sent to Palestine by her father, possibly in order to find a Jewish husband, but never developed a Zionist consciousness, never learned Hebrew properly, and never abandoned the dresses and jewelry she had brought from Latvia, especially her fancy hats. Unlike her sister Dora, who also came to Palestine and lived on a kibbutz, Masha spent her afternoons in Tel Aviv's lively coffee houses, where tea was served to British soldiers, bohemian artists, and society women from the civil circles. Her niece Osnat remembers her fox fur coat, with the poor animal's head hanging over her shoulder and its tail stuck in its mouth.

Tuvia and Masha were married in 1934. The following year, on September 22, 1935, their eldest son, Amnon, was born at the Freud Maternity Hospital in Tel Aviv. Their second son, Rafi, was born eight years later in January 1944. The family lived in an apartment at 8 Hevron Street, in the center of Tel Aviv. Their home contained many items to remind them of their life in the past: a round living room table, an ancient clock, a huge radio, and a heavy glass-fronted buffet displaying decorative plates, candlesticks, embroidered tablecloths, and the tall wine glass from which the family had drunk at Amnon's Bar Mitzvah. In the children's room were two beds covered in colorful spreads, and above Amnon's bed, a bookshelf.

The couple lived a harmonious life. Despite the frustration Tuvia suffered when his egg business failed, Masha remained supportive. Having studied accounting in high school, she took charge of the family finances, making sure they could maintain a reasonable standard of living and socialize with their friends in the bourgeois circles of former Latvians, including such wealthy people as the Frumchenko family, owners of the Elite chocolate factory. The couple went for walks on the Tel Aviv beach, visited friends and had them over for afternoon tea, listened to the radio, and raised their two children. Relatives recall the delicious Eastern European food Masha cooked, particularly the special Passover dishes. They also remember her as always feeling somewhat rootless; throughout her life, she longed for her parents' home in Latvia. This may be why she maintained a religious lifestyle, keeping a kosher kitchen with two sets of dishes to separate meat from milk and occasionally attending services in a small synagogue nearby. On one occasion, when the entire family drove to a birthday party on the Sabbath, she chose to walk. Even in her later years, Masha remained a vibrant woman. She collected stamps and coins and bought a lottery ticket every month, always holding on to the old tickets so that if she should ever win, she would be able to calculate whether it had been worthwhile. After Tuvia's death, she was cared for devotedly by Rafi, who had gone into advertising. Since his business required a great deal of driving in the busy streets of Tel Aviv, where parking has always been a problem, his elderly mother would wait in the car, waving a small stick at any traffic cops who dared try to give him a parking ticket.

When Amnon was two, Masha sailed with him to Latvia to show him off to her family. Amnon remembers standing on the top bunk in their cabin and looking out the porthole at the sea. At the age of three he was sent to nursery school, and his parents hired a young lady, Nurit Rainowitz, to take him on walks in the afternoons. She would take the child to movies like "Nikita" and "Tarzan," eventually turning him into a true film buff. He started school at the age of six. His blonde teacher, Esther, was very fond of him, but was also concerned that he was so quiet, a characteristic of his to this day. Once he had learned his letters, he became an obsessive reader, a quality demonstrated today in a weekly talk show he presents on Israeli television. In the 1940s, considerable effort was made in Palestine to translate the world's literary treasures into Hebrew. Thus, despite growing up in a small Hebrew-speaking community (numbering only 600,000 in 1948), Amnon was exposed at an early age to many of the same books that young people throughout the world were reading: *Robinson Crusoe, Alice in Wonderland, Gulliver's Travels, Don Quixote, Treasure Island, Quo Vadis, Anna Karenina, Crime and Punishment, Madame Bovary, For Whom the Bell Tolls*, and so on. Although his home lacked the socialist literature one could find at the time on the shelves of most Histadrut members, Amnon spent many afternoons in the public library, named for the national poet Chaim Nachman Bialik, where he was introduced to a variety of thought-provoking books, such as Erich Maria Remarque's pacifistic *All Quiet on the Western Front*.

Both of the Zichroni children were sent to a private school—which was quite rare in those days. They attended the School of Commerce, most of whose students came from well-to-do families. The school was established in 1920 by the Tel-Aviv Merchants' Association with the aim of "preparing the students for practical life and training them for commerce and clerical work in the Land of Israel, while at the same time providing them with a solid high school education."[10] In a statement issued a few years after the school's founding, the administrators expressed their satisfaction that the first graduates were, in fact, working in commercial and clerical jobs and earning the praise of their employers. They also asked to be contacted whenever "a clerk proficient in English and Arabic, accounting, correspondence in the three languages, typing and commercial skills"[11] was needed. Providing both an elementary and a high school education, the school started out in a rented building, but in 1925 moved to Ge'ula

Street, where it is still located, and soon came to be known as the Ge'ula School.

Although the school suffered from financial problems in its early days, and indeed almost had to be shut down, it was restructured as a stock company in 1930 under the auspices of the Commerce Lodge, the City of Tel Aviv, and the parents. It then came under the pedagogical supervision of the education departments of the city and the Zionist Executive Board (which served as the executive branch of government in pre-state Israel), and consequently was accredited by the Hebrew University in Jerusalem. In 1941, when Zichroni entered first grade, it had 700 students. The school was associated with the political parties of the civil circles, particularly the General Zionists, who controlled the city council of Tel Aviv at the time, and was featured in their campaigns before each municipal election in an effort to garner the votes of the Tel Aviv merchants. It was hailed as the institution providing their sons and daughters with a general education and, in contrast to the orientation of other schools, preparing them for a future in commerce and industry.

In an article that appeared in the liberal newspaper *Haaretz* in 1932, David Ismuzik complained that the Jewish society in Palestine had built an education system to meet the needs of a cooperative socialist economy, while neglecting universal education:

> Our small country is mostly an agricultural land, but small and medium-range industry is beginning to develop fairly rapidly. . . . The most modern machines are now being introduced into all industrial fields, from the smallest machine for the manufacture of socks to the greatest turbine for the cement industry. There are quite well-developed railways and other modern means of transportation in the country. The country has taken a great leap all at once, from the camel that plods its way to the most sophisticated automobile, without leaving in place the intervening stages that block the fast development of other countries. This is a country whose moving power is going to be electricity—lighting, creating, and also generating movement.[12]

In a country that could not be based solely on agriculture, he wrote, and in which even agriculture itself would eventually be industrialized, high schools had to train the necessary manpower for the emerging industrial sector.

It would appear that the school did indeed prepare its students for jobs in the commercial and industrial economy that was developing in Israel, despite the dominant socialist ideology. A report on its graduates prepared in 1932 reveals that of the 280 students who graduated in the first 10 years, only 19 were working in agriculture. Twenty-four were employed in the civil service, 32 in public institutions and banks, 12 in industrial plants such as the electricity company, 78 in private enterprises such as lawyers' offices, and 23 in family businesses. Fifty-one pursued a higher education in Jerusalem, Beirut, Europe, or the United States, 13 were teachers, 14 women were married and did not work outside the home, and the fate of 16 was unknown.

It is no wonder that the school, operating in accordance with market demands but not in line with prevailing ideology, suffered chronically from a lack of financial support from the national institutions of the *Yishuv*. In fact, it was often the object of sanctions. In a letter to the Teachers' Association in 1933, the principal complained that his students had been forced to march at the tail end of the parade of schools during Hanukkah.[13] In a letter to the city education department in 1937, he reported bitterly that when a mother had tried to register her son at a high school on the basis of the school's report card, she was told that they would not accept it because grades were bought and sold there.[14]

However unfavorable the treatment of the school as a stronghold of capitalism may have been, its curriculum in the 1930s bears testimony to an admirable emphasis on civic, liberal values, as opposed to the narrow ideological education offered by most institutions at that time. Analysis of the curricula of *Yishuv* schools reveals an obvious dissonance between the values they aspired to instill and the actual environment in which the children lived. As Shimon Reshef has shown, schools controlled by the labor movement sought to educate children to be pioneers, and thus teachers were not necessarily chosen for their professional skills, but rather for their ideological orientation. This often led to conflicts between the school and the parents, who sensed that the values disseminated by the school were irrelevant to their children's real lives.[15] The School of Commerce's curriculum, on the other hand, suited the interests of the parents in the civil circles mainly because of its emphasis on a general education.

The curriculum of 1933 illustrates the school's liberal approach.[16] In the first grade, emphasis was placed on storytelling by the children themselves (as opposed to indoctrination), along with activities such as painting, singing, ceramics, and gymnastics, adapted to correspond with these stories. In second grade, the main theme was the observation of gardens and orchards, fruits and vegetables, house pets, the street, and the beach. The study of reading and writing, math, the Bible, the prayers, and the various crafts were all related to the child's observation of the environment. In higher grades, geography lessons focused on the real (not the ideal) environment in which the child lived: the town's quarters, public buildings, historical sites, roads, and railways. While textbooks from that era generally painted pastoral pictures of the homeland, here emphasis was placed on the inhabitants of the city, as well as on its public institutions—hospitals, the post office, the city hall, or the school itself.

In the fifth grade, English was taught through conversation on subjects such as class and school activities, the human body and nutrition, the home and the family. Geography lessons dealt with the Land of Israel and the region, but also stressed general principles of physical geography. Hebrew language studies aimed at enabling the students to master the language and express themselves accurately and logically. In order to achieve that aim, the children were exposed to a variety of literary styles, not only in Hebrew literature and the Bible, but also in world prose and poetry. In the eighth grade, for instance, the syllabus included such literary treasures as *The Ideas of Marcus Aurelius*, *Wilhelm Tell*, and *Crime and Punishment*. While the curriculum placed considerable stress on Jewish history, it was taught within the framework of world history. In fact, the express objective of the study of history was to afford acquisition of knowledge about the history of the world so as to enable the student to recognize the spiritual and material treasures produced by humanity from the beginning of civilization to the present.

In addition, the school provided practical skills in the realm of commerce, such as correspondence, the preparation of contracts, advertisements, authorizations, complaints and appeals, the terms, form and organization of commercial letters, and the specific features of documents concerning the purchase and sale of goods, debt collection, banks, notes, and checks. Even in chemistry lessons, the emphasis was on the production of materials of practical value for agriculture and industry. In the higher grades, the students were offered a choice among several courses of study. The economics course, selected by Zichroni, included economic theory, accounting, commerce, and law. Here students were taught the concept of the law, public and private law, international law and the

British mandate system, the legal system in the Land of Israel, the origins of British and colonial law, land laws, city ordinances, civil procedures, rules of arbitration, etc.

The adjustment of the curriculum to the norms and demands of the civil circles contributed to the appreciation that many of its graduates still express for the school today. In pre-state Israel and in the early years of statehood, students were often troubled by the disparity between the pioneering norms they were taught in school and their experiences at home. The sons and daughters of doctors, engineers, merchants, and storeowners were confronted with collectivist ideals that were unrelated to the urban environment in which they were growing up. Nevertheless, Ge'ula did not disdain a patriotic education, and its students were actively involved in current events. They demonstrated against the British mandate, held long debates about the resolution of the Palestine problem, distributed fliers on behalf of the underground movements (with Zichroni's class distributing fliers of the mainstream Hagana while he gave out those of the revisionist Irgun), danced the hora, worked as volunteers on kibbutzim, and so on. Yet the school also managed to provide the students with a universal education, and its teachers, many of whom held doctoral degrees, combined patriotism with broader humanistic values.

Zichroni's classmates remember him as a loner. Tall and handsome, he had a blond forelock and bright blue eyes that made him seem remote, as if he existed in a different world. When most of his age group joined the pre-state youth movements, he did not. He played football but had little interest in the sports news, and refused to take part in the school's drama productions. Despite his good looks, he had little success with the girls, who, like Edna, the "queen bee" of the class, sensed his remoteness, maturity, and introversion. He had an inner serenity that might have aroused curiosity, but did not allow people to get close to him. The teachers noted his serious character, as well as his delight in intellectual debates, where he often took the role of devil's advocate. Although he was not particularly eager to share his views with other students, when asked a political question, he would take out a brown notebook and in a voice that was monotonic, yet filled with conviction, would read out long, carefully explicated ideas that he had written down. He generally walked around with his eyes lowered, but when greeted would lift his face and direct a penetrating gaze and a gracious smile at the other person.

Amnon Zichroni always loved politics. His classmate Atara Pchor-Ciechanover still keeps a note he passed to her during some boring lesson in which he promised that when he became prime minister, he would appoint her minister of labor. "Keep the note," he wrote, "because one day it will be worth a thousand pounds."[17] In the eleventh grade he displayed his political skills working behind the scenes when his friend Rami Levtov, a very talented boy who could quote Scottish ballads by heart and died at a young age in a car accident, decided to run for the student council. Although Amnon did not take much interest in the elections, he lobbied successfully among the tenth and eleventh graders, convincing them that the twelfth grader who was running against Rami was too busy cramming for the matriculation exams to devote time to the council. Two years earlier, in the ninth grade, Rami had edited a class newspaper which printed articles about the need for the students to stand united against the teachers when one of their number was expelled from class, a report about the new Knesset (Israeli parliament) which had just been formed complaining that the representatives came and went and did not sit still, a few elegant literary pieces—among them an accusation of God for abandoning his people during the Holocaust—and a heated debate over the recruitment of school children for pre-military training programs. Zichroni's contribution consisted of a short feature expressing his opinion of Prime Minister Ben-Gurion's decision to declare Jerusalem the capital of Israel.

On December 10, 1949, by a vote of 38 to 14, the United Nations General Assembly passed an Australian resolution, backed by the Vatican, that made Jerusalem an international city. The proposal had the support of the Moslem countries, the Communist bloc, Nationalist China, and the Catholic states of Europe and South America. Ben-Gurion, acting swiftly, engineered a government decision declaring Jerusalem the Israeli capital, and Zichroni concurred:

> In Jerusalem, the Jewish nation's spiritual, religious, and political image was shaped. In Jerusalem, the Jews created their culture. After being exiled from their land, many of the Jews assimilated into foreign nations. It was Jerusalem that reminded them that they belonged to our nation and of their ties to the homeland. Ever since, Jerusalem has symbolized the Jewish people's independence. . . . Let us hope that Jerusalem remains forever ours and ours alone.[18]

Not surprisingly, Tuvia and Masha loved Amnon dearly. He was a good son and good brother to Rafi, who received his first bicycle from him. Amnon was an intelligent child who devoured books, showed an interest in public affairs, and wrote patriotic articles for the school newspaper. The whole family was proud of him. Cousin Zalman Breinin remembers how a lawyer who hired Amnon shortly after he completed law school once told him: "This boy will be a great man one day."[19] And Tuvia once said to Breinin that had Amnon joined the ruling Mapai party, he could have gone a long way. But he did not join the ruling party. On the contrary, when he graduated high school in 1953, he almost lost his life in the first celebrated case of a conscientious objector in Israel.

Notes

1. Zvi Avital, letter from 1934, kept by his son Eliahu Avital.

2. Gideon Shimoni, *The Zionist Ideology* (Hanover, N.H.: University Press of New England; Waltham, Mass.: Brandeis University Press, 1995).

3. David Ben-Gurion, "Jewish Survival," in *Like Stars and Dust: Essays From Israel's Government Year Book* (Sede Boquer: The Ben-Gurion Heritage Center, 1997), 131.

4. Ben-Gurion, "Jewish Survival," 131.

5. David Ben-Gurion, "Israel and the Diaspora," in Ben-Gurion, *Like Stars and Dust,* 203.

6. Shmuel Almog, "He'halutz Ha'metaphori Mul 'Ha'zikna Ha'galutit'" [the metaphorical pioneer against 'diaspora-driven old age']. In *Idan Ha'zionut*, eds. Anita Shapira et. al (Jerusalem: Shazar Center, 2000), 91–108.

7. Zvi Avital, letter from 1934.

8. Rachel Feinberg, *Megilat Dubova: Toldot Ir Sh'e'avra U'vatla Min Ha'olam* [The tale of Dubova: history of a town that disappeared from the face of the earth] (Tel-Aviv: La'am, 1940).

9. T. Zichroni and others to Moshe Shlush in the matter of "distribution of imported eggs," letter, May 18, 1949. Tel Aviv Municipality, Historical Archive, Section 5, file 98.

10. Memo, November 2, 1926. Tel Aviv Municipality, Historical Archive, Section 4, file 1580.

11. Memo, November 2, 1926. Tel Aviv Municipality, Historical Archive, Section 4, file 1580.

12. D. Ismuzik, "Ein Do'eg" [Nobody takes care]. In *Haaretz*, 19 Nissan, 1932. Aviezer Yelin Archive of Jewish Education in Israel and the Diaspora, Tel-Aviv University, Container 4.59.

13. Dr. S. Urbach, letter, February 15, 1933. Tel Aviv Municipality, Historical Archive, Section 4, file 1581.

14. Dr. S. Urbach, letter, July 20, 1937. Tel Aviv Municipality, Historical Archive, Section 4, file 1582.

15. Shimon Reshef, *Zerem Ha'ovdim Ba'hinuch* [The workers' educational stream]. (Tel-Aviv: Ha'kibutz Ha'me'u'had, 1980).

16. In Aviezer Yelin Archive of Jewish Education in Israel and the Diaspora, Tel-Aviv University, Container 8.103.

17. Interview with Atara Pchor-Ciechanover, October 10, 1994.

18. Class 5\3's journal. Aviezer Yelin Archive of Jewish Education in Israel and the Diaspora, Tel-Aviv University, Container 3.153.

19. Interview with Zalman Breinin, October 14, 1994.

CHAPTER THREE

Conscientious Objection

∞

If You Force Me to Eat—I Will Commit Suicide

Amnon Zichroni, a young Tel-Aviv born man who refuses to serve in the military for conscientious-ideological reasons, has been arrested by the military authorities on the charge that he refused to obey orders by his superiors.

When Zichroni was drafted into the IDF [Israel Defense Forces], he refused to take the oath, was detained and sentenced to 21 days in prison. He declared a hunger strike, arguing that his arrest is illegal because he did not take the oath and is not a soldier. Zichroni announced that if he were forced to eat—he would commit suicide. After fasting for 4 days he was moved to a mental institution in Acre for psychiatric observation.

A few days ago, Zichroni was returned to prison and the military authorities announced that he will be placed under court-martial. The day before yesterday, Zichroni contacted attorney Mordechai Stein and asked him to prepare his defense brief. Zichroni's father visited his son and tried to convince him to change his mind but to no avail. (*Yediot Ah'aronot*, May 11, 1954)

The conscientious objection affair that first came to the public attention in this item was to constitute one of the most complex and important chapters in the history of Israeli democracy during the early years of the State of Israel. An understanding of the affair, of the various points of view voiced during it, and of its significance requires a brief introduction to the subject.

Conscientious objection, which means disobedience of a law due to an individual's conviction that a higher moral law bans obeying such a law, refers mainly to cases in which military service required by law is perceived by individuals or groups as contrary to their religious or moral convictions.[1] This is one of the knottiest issues in democracies because democratic government is based on the principle of an equal distribution of rights and duties. Any democracy, therefore, has difficulty allowing certain groups to avoid fulfilling their military duty. Several eighteenth-century democratic thinkers, however, allowed certain personal religious convictions to be taken as justification for exemption from fighting for the state. Philosopher Michael Walzer attributed this thinking to the Protestant belief in personal conscience as signaling a link with the divine, alongside the minimal danger posed to the state at that time by religious conscientious objection. Claims for exemption existed within a limited Protestant historical tradition, involved no political judgment of the state, and were put forward by a small number of people.[2]

Once claims by conscientious objectors were no longer grounded in religion, however, legislators found it more difficult to justify exemption. The secularization of conscience in the modern era made it impossible to distinguish between genuine and false claims for exemption, or between claims based on moral conviction and those aimed at making a political statement. Moreover, even when conscientious objectors functioned as part of broader ideological groups, these groups' involvement in defending individual objectors usually began when the individuals had already confronted the authorities on their own. Moreover, conscientious objection is a phenomenon that is difficult to fit into a framework of group action because, as Sibly and Jacob have shown, non-religious groups of conscientious objectors have a tendency to split apart and disintegrate.[3] Also, as pointed out in Carolyn Moorhead's study of conscientious objection in England, the United States, Germany, and Japan, objectors often avoid predictable patterns of group behavior and come up with surprises in their dealings with the conscription boards. Military authorities all over the world have had difficulty defining conscientious objection and its limits, delimiting it to specific political groups, or classifying and understanding the objectors' arguments, even when the authorities were not exceptionally hostile towards them.[4]

The incident discussed here is perhaps even more complex than those described in the literature. When on a night in May 1954 Sergeant Major Levi Chibutero, during a routine check of soldiers about to begin night guard, found himself face to face with canteen aide Amnon Zichroni who was holding a stick instead of a rifle and quoting Henry David Thoreau, had no frame of reference whatsoever with which to relate to this event. Neither did any of the ranks above him. The Israeli army then was at one of its lowest points. It had witnessed a grave drop in morale after the War of Independence of 1948, reflected, inter alia, in soldiers brawling in military camps, a low level of training, failures of military operations beyond the country's borders, poor relations within the officers' ranks, and widespread desertion from the camps. This atmosphere was vividly described by Moshe Dayan who, taking over as chief of staff in December 1953, noted in a report that many of the infantry soldiers were "hashish smokers, criminals and thieves ('graduates' of prisons), pimps, etc."[5] His report also referred to the deficient level of lower rank officers and their inability to cope with difficult welfare problems discovered among the soldiers. Ten percent of the draftees found ways of getting released from the army in the first month of service for health reasons. In this atmosphere, a soldier declaring conscientious objection would easily be viewed as a draft dodger.

Not only did the military lack a frame of reference to deal with Zichroni's stance but so did society at large. Conscientious objection was a phenomenon quite unknown in Israel then. Moreover, it totally negated the norms in Israel, a society of consensus over its moral foundations. Less than a decade after the Holocaust when Jews had been totally defenseless, and six years after the establishment of a sovereign Jewish state fiercely defending itself against enemies who threatened to liquidate it, a conscientious objector had risen. This was considered not only unforgivable from a normative point of view but treasonous from a practical point of view. As Prime Minister David Ben-Gurion had declared in 1953, "We need a maximal quantity, and must draft the maximum of our manpower. In this war, no man or woman can be exempt. This is Jewish law and it is necessary for the survival of the State of Israel."[6] The entire affair, which involved eighteen-year-old Zichroni, his commanders, military judges, the security establishment, his family, his lawyer, and eventually support groups, decision makers, intellectuals, the press, and public opinion both in Israel and abroad, must be viewed against this background.

Zichroni was not, in fact, the first conscientious objector in Israel, although he was the first to gain widespread attention. Conscientious objection had been noted already during the conscription of Jewish soldiers in Palestine to the British army during the Second World War.[7] Several cases of conscientious objection occurred during Israel's War of Independence (1947–1949) as well, including the refusal of the son and daughter of Zichroni's lawyer, Mordechai Stein, to serve in the army, the demand by Moshe Elimelech of Kfar Galim to serve in a civilian rather than a military role, and the objection of violinist Joseph Abileah of Haifa to contribute to the war effort even in a civilian role.[8] During 1949–1950, eight draft dodgers were registered in the Defense Ministry and fourteen reserve soldiers refused to serve. Until the Zichroni case, however, most of the objectors had been classified in the Defense Ministry files as "special cases, individualists, the product of an education given to children at home by cloistered parents, secluded from reality and the world around them."[9] Although this was not necessarily true in every case, the idea of conscientious objection was considered marginal and a foreign import.

In 1945 a local branch of the War Resisters International (WRI) was opened in Jewish Palestine. Most of the founding members of the branch—Avraham Lissod, Nathan Hofshi, Joseph Abileah, Meir Lissa'i, Moshe Elimelech, and several others—were mostly members of the Brith Shalom and the I'hud peace movements that called for Arab Israeli reconciliation. The mentor of the branch was Nathan Hofshi, of the veteran settlement Nahalal, a thinker, strongly inspired by Tolstoy, who linked religious pacifism with utopian socialism. Hofshi, who believed that war is a crime against humanity, accepted the position of the International Association of War Objectors established in 1921 opposing national wars allegedly fought to defend a homeland, bourgeois wars favorable to the rich, and proletarian wars. Hofshi spread Tolstoyan ideas at a time when the bearing of arms seemed unavoidable. He wrote in 1955 that the State of Israel suffered from a duality—on the one hand it considered itself to be the fulfillment of the vision of the ancient prophets, but on the other hand it had been established "in blood and fire and by robbing the Arab inhabitants of the land. One sin leads to another. Now the stolen property must be guarded by means of the total militarization of all Israelis in the land of Israel, man and woman, boy and girl, fire burning around us and under our feet."[10]

Hofshi was known in certain circles, but most of the members of the branch were quite unknown, far beyond draft age, viewed as eccentric and insignificant. Their voice was not heard at all in the country's public discourse. Once Zichroni came on the scene, however, things changed. He was the first objector whose views could not be ignored as foreign or displaced, and who could not be easily classified as obscure. He was a Sabra— Israel-born, Hebrew-speaking, rooted in the country's culture, and yet expressing refusal to serve in the IDF. To this, Israel in 1954 had no ready response.

The country's entrenched political leadership then, rooted in socialist traditions, left almost no room for autonomous individual or group activity in Israel, exercising strong control over both the distribution of material resources and over educational and cultural life. It was able to operate in this manner for an extended period that started long before the formation of the state, as a result of a strong sense of togetherness which it fostered. Conscientious objection had little place in such a collectivist milieu. Although the Zichroni affair occurred during the brief period when Prime Minister David Ben-Gurion, the towering figure, had resigned from office (1953–1955), the public sphere was still largely determined by collective values. The challenge to these values by a single individual, therefore, caused real surprise.

Zichroni was drafted on July 20, 1953, given a soldier's number, and sent to the Golani (an infantry brigade)12th regiment for basic training. He had developed pacifistic feelings toward the end of high school but did not dare to voice them to his parents, who assumed that he would join the army as did every other young Israeli. Shortly after arriving in the military camp, however, he began to rebel. Some of the details about his behavior are still a matter of controversy. According to his testimony in his trial, he had refused to take the IDF oath, yet the defense ministry manpower department insisted that he had signed a form on October 23, 1953, in which the oath was included. Still, why and how he was made to sign a form that contained the oath a full three months after being drafted is not explained. The anti-establishment weekly *Ha'olam Ha'ze* reported he was given a weapon on the first night of his service but refused to carry it,[11] while the military insisted that he trained with weapons up until November 1953.[12]

Events that began on November 10th are clearer. According to his unit commander, Colonel Eliezer Amitai, Zichroni argued that as a pacifist he refused to train with weapons and was therefore sent that day to the unit's headquarters. A few days later, Amitai discussed his pacifist views with him and decided to move him to the regimental medical center, but there too he refused to perform his duties and in particular refused to hold a weapon in his hands.[13] On March 18, 1954, a complaint was filed against him for holding a stick rather than a gun when assigned to guard duty. On March 24 another complaint was filed over his absence without leave for three days (when he made contact with members of the WRI). The two complaints were investigated and Zichroni was to be put on military trial on April 28, but on April 23, after another refusal to obey orders, he was placed in detention for twenty-one days. That day, he dictated the following note to his guards, which was delivered to Colonel Amitai:

> To the commanders of Regiment 12:
> I consider my arrest an absolute denial of my human and civil rights. I am not a soldier, I cannot be a soldier because I did not take the IDF oath. Hence I have decided to conduct a hunger strike.[14]

According to Amitai's testimony, Zichroni then tried to escape from detention but was caught and was transferred to Camp 396 to complete his sentence. He continued his hunger strike there and was then transferred to the mental hospital in the city of Acre. The trial scheduled for April 28 did not take place because he was confined to hospital that day. On May 5, Israel's Independence Day, all military prisoners, including Zichroni, were pardoned. However, on May 11 the press item quoted before appeared in *Yediot Ah'aronot* stirring the military to action. A trial was scheduled for June 1. During the month that passed between the pardon and the beginning of his trial, Zichroni began a series of hunger strikes, was sent to military hospitals, was returned to his unit, and so on. During one hunger strike he was forced to eat by a lieutenant but refused, leading to yet another complaint filed against him.

On June 28, five days before a scheduled court-martial, Zichroni announced a hunger strike that was to last 22 days, nearly causing his death. His announcement took the form of an open letter to the president of Israel, published in bold type in *Ha'iton Ha'demokrati* (the Democratic Newspaper) edited by attorney Mordechai Stein:

> An Open Letter to the President of the State of Israel:
> Sir, I inform you with due honor that ever since Friday, May 28th, I have been refusing to eat. Sir, consider my fast as proof of my explicit

objection to the ongoing restriction of free conscience common in Israel. I am being held in a military unit despite the fact that I totally reject—for reasons of conscience and morality—the very existence of the institution of the military in this country and in the world. Holding a war resister in military units—sometimes also in military prisons—stands in full contradiction of the United Nations Declaration of Human Rights and the founding proclamation of the State of Israel, which guarantee freedom of conscience!

With greetings of peace,
Amnon Zichroni[15]

The commotion and embarrassment concerning what came to be known as "the Soldier Zichroni affair" was felt at the highest decision-making echelons as soon as the May 11 story appeared. Since Israel lacked any policy toward war resisters, the policy was devised in a brief, undated note sent by Minister of Defense Pinhas Lavon to his office chief, Efraim Evron:

To Efi, it is advisable to find a general arrangement
   a. to nominate comptrollers who will advise the Minister of Defense
   b. determine alternative forms of service. P. L.[16]

On February 18, 1954, probably as a result of this note, Evron requested the ministry's legal adviser to prepare a document describing how other countries in the Western world treated war resisters. The response he received, dated April 1950, showed that approaches to the issue varied greatly. According to Anglo-Saxon law, the document said, a judge may take into account any argument deemed reasonable to reduce the sentence for disobedience, including disobedience for reasons of conscience. In European continental law, reasons of conscience do not appear as part of admissible reasons for the reduction of a sentence. In the Russian criminal code, although reasons of conscience are considered relevant in certain offenses, the judge is not permitted to consider such reasons in the case of a military command given legally. Additionally, the Russian code does not allow exemption from military service for reasons of conscience, as is the tradition in England, the Commonwealth, the United States, and the Scandinavian countries. In the United States, the Supreme Court had ruled that conscientious objection is justified only when it is based on a world view objecting to all bloodshed, yet even so there can be no exemption from a specific war, as in England. Canadian law recognizes conscientious objection only if it is based on religious belief. Every country, the document pointed out, determines its own criteria for evaluating the arguments raised by war resisters, and the alternative forms of service demanded of them. The document concluded by presenting the decision-makers with three options: (1) To exempt conscientious objectors from military service; (2) To oblige them to participate in alternative forms of national service that do not require the bearing of arms; and (3) To exempt them only from participation in combat units. The first two options, the document noted, demand parliamentary legislation, while the third could be instituted administratively within the military.[17]

A few days after receiving the document, Evron notified the chief of staff and the director general of the ministry that an arrangement is to be found in the matter of conscientious objectors without exempting them fully from military service. He asked them to nominate representatives to a committee that would determine the alternative forms of service in each case. The response he received from the chief of staff's office was quite harsh. No changes in the law ought to be made, said a letter attributed to the head of the manpower division of the army. "The special security position of the State of Israel demands, in our opinion, treating the war resisters problem very severely, and in any case treatment must be on an individual basis and not as a recognized group."[18] Even with individual consideration, the letter went on, exemptions could not be considered, but at best the occupation of the soldier in such units as the medical corps or logistics. Moreover, the army refused to send representatives to any committee and demanded that any solutions be found within the army's manpower department. Following a series of meetings on this matter, the army's position was accepted by the minister of defense.

This, then, was the background to the opening of Zichroni's trial on June 1, 1954, the fifth day of his latest hunger strike. A report sent that day to the chief of staff mentioned "the above [Zichroni] appeared, accompanied by lawyer Mordechai Stein of Tel Aviv, dressed in civil clothing, without a beret and making a most sloppy appearance."[19] The charge was refusal to stand on guard duty with a weapon and desertion from the camp for four days. The trial took place in the Nazareth regional military court before Judges Major Iro Drucks, Lieutenant Eliahu Klein and Private Meir Rosenkranz.[20]

The trial began at 11 a.m. with a question by Major Drucks as to whether the prosecutor and defendant had any objection to being tried before him. The prosecutor answered "No objection," while Zichroni used a longer sentence: "I have no objection, I have nothing against the present composition of the court." Throughout the trial, Zichroni tried to use civilian language rather than the legal terminology of the military court. When asked whether or not he admitted his guilt, he replied that he did not consider himself guilty, refraining from the more legal "not guilty." His arguments occasionally infuriated the three judges. He stated that he objected to the very existence of the army, complained that he was not treated in accordance with the principle of "absolute justice," and observed that he considered himself the prosecutor rather than the defendant. He insisted that he had not taken the IDF oath, claimed that he had filed a request to be released from the army, which had been denied, and explained his four-day desertion as a reaction to an unjust attack by the Israeli army on a Syrian village at that time, which made him realize he could never be a soldier. He did not "escape" from the barracks, he said, because, by definition, a pacifist never escapes but simply leaves.

His testimony, as recorded by the court clerk, Private Dina Gershon, contained the following observations:

> I am a war resister and as a war resister I oppose the use of arms, because in my opinion there is no need to bear arms. It is a negative element that regresses reality. . . . Despite the fact that a stick is a weapon that does not harm actively, it is a weapon. The moment I was dismissed from the formation, I threw away the stick out of mental abhorrence. . . . When I was drafted, I was a person with pacifistic convictions. . . . I said to myself I cannot be drafted and I will not be drafted. I don't know why I agreed to be drafted, maybe I wanted to be correct. Despite the fact that I was drafted, I wasn't ready to take the oath because I couldn't. I found the solution to my pacifism over time. The starting point of my thinking is the individual. I consider the individual to be the anchor of all social phenomena. I consider the individual as the end [rather than the means].

Zichroni's lawyer, Mordechai Stein, presented a line of defense that attempted, as draft evaders during the Vietnam War a decade later would, to place his client within a larger group of conscientious objectors. Stein requested that members of the Israeli branch of the WRI be called to the witness stand in order to demonstrate that the defendant's behavior was consistent with their position, which had been recognized as legitimate in the enlightened world. Although the request was denied by the court, Stein brought up this point again in his summary. He claimed that the defendant was not the only war resister in the country, referring to Hofshi and his group, and submitted a document indicating that a pacifist had been released from the army in the past, with "pacifism" given as the official reason. He pleaded that even if Zichroni were found guilty, he be recommended for a pardon because his actions stemmed from deep conviction.

Neither the lawyer's reference to the obscure WRI nor Zichroni's sermon on the individual as an end rather than a means convinced the unsympathetic court, which found his disciplinary offenses to be subversive and sentenced him to seven months in military prison. His argumentation that the refusal to bear arms and deserting camp were manifestations of conscientious objection was found by the court to be an unacceptable reason to relieve him of his responsibility as a soldier. In the verdict the court wrote that Zichroni seemed of higher intelligence than the average high school graduate, but it considered him "a bit confused and willing to assume the role of a hero fighting for his convictions and suffering from the world in which he lives." In Israel of 1954, a more considerate approach toward a conscientious objector would have been difficult to expect. When the defendant was given the opportunity to say a few words before the reading of the sentence, the following dialogue took place, according to Private Gershon's minutes:

The defendant's final comment:
I know I am being put on trial before a military court. I know that my very standing here is somewhat paradoxical. I oppose the military [and] in applying [the criteria of] absolute justice to me, I am not treated justly. I know the domain of the army is very limited. I am no defendant. I consider myself to be an accuser of the army, an accuser of the very existence of the army. My parents in Tel Aviv—
Chief Judge to defendant:
I am a judge in Israel and a citizen of the State of Israel, and you are nothing but a big smarkatch [A derogatory Russian term meaning a snot-nosed kid].

Curiously, years later, when Major Drucks had become a judge in the traffic court, a traffic violator appeared before him accompanied by a young lawyer, Amnon Zichroni. Drucks was so stunned that he immediately acquitted the offender of any charges. However, back in the stuffy courtroom in Nazareth on June 1, 1954, Zichroni, the conscientious objector, was led away to prison by military policemen. It was the fifth day of his hunger strike and he was so weak that as he was leaving the courtroom he fell and broke his right elbow and right knee. Hospitalized in a military hospital, he refused to accept any food and would drink only water. On June 4 he was transferred to the internal medicine department where he spent the next two weeks, during which time the entire country followed the reports of his deteriorating health. Throughout his twenty-two-day hunger strike, his daily nutrition consisted of 2.5 litres of tea in which the amount of sugar was gradually increased to about 250–300 grams. After a severe deterioration in his condition, on June 12, this was supplemented by a one hundred gram food supplement containing vitamins, iron, and phosphorus, which amounted, in the last days of his fast, to 1,400 calories. Zichroni lost 18 kilograms during the hunger strike.

The reports on his behavior during the hunger strike highlighted his resolute stand:

> We met him walking on the road in the military hospital grounds in a white robe that emphasized his dark facial complexion. Although he looked weak and thin . . . his cheeks were reddish. Occasionally he moved a bony hand over his eyes, as if to dispel dizziness . . . indeed, this agitated kid's world view—a somewhat blurry philosophical view seeking to embrace the entire world and revolutionalize ancient values—stood in total contradiction to his calm and quiet demeanor.[21]

The correspondent from *Dvar Ha'shavu'a*, a weekly belonging to the ruling party Mapai, described Zichroni's stark hospital room. She noted that a military policeman was stationed in it and that Zichroni had developed good relations with him. She also reported that Zichroni intended to study philosophy and history once he was released, and had told her that "the State of Israel must turn into a model for pacifism for the entire world."[22] He admitted that he felt hungry, especially between two and five in the afternoon, but overcame his hunger by lying on his bed and looking at the green Carmel mountains from his window and contemplating.

Such reports could not hide the fact that a young man was dying in military confinement and, as the hunger strike progressed, a public debate emerged over the difficult issue raised by the conscientious objector. For the first time since its formation, Israeli society was forced to consider whether its fundamental norms, over which there was little disagreement, ought to be maintained even at the cost of an individual's life. Put differently, in a collectivist society, did a conscientious objector, however despicable, and however disruptive to the social order his behavior seemed, deserve a death sentence?

The extensive discourse carried on in the country's press, in the defense ministry, and in declarations by politicians essentially reflected three theoretical approaches to conscientious objection. The first view, identified mainly with the American 19th century writer Henry David Thoreau, is that right and wrong are not the product of decisions by governments or even by majorities, but rather of conscience, and should therefore be given greater weight than the law.[23] The second view, identified mainly with philosopher of law Ronald Dworkin, calls for a degree of tolerance toward conscientious dissent based on pragmatic policy considerations that ought to be kept separate from the question of whether the act of dissent is perceived as morally wrong by the community.[24] The third view, developed by philosopher John Rawls, bases the justification of acts of conscientious objection on the degree of agreement in principle that can be expected in a community toward such acts. In this view, the justification of conscientious refusal consists mainly of an appeal to violations by the state of principles applying to the conduct of war.[25]

Zichroni's argumentation throughout the affair instinctively followed Rawls's approach. Zichroni dissociated himself from the state as a result of behavior conducted by the state he could not agree with in principle. Using this argument instead of Thoreau's was understandable in light of the difficulty to place in Israel of 1954 a moral principle above the jurisdiction of the state. Significantly, those who came out on his behalf during his hunger strike also refrained from referring to a higher moral law. They mostly followed Dworkin's reasoning, dissociating themselves from the morality of Zichroni's act yet demanding tolerance for it. Philosophers, educators, poets, columnists, and others who dealt with the issue were explicit in expressing their disagreement with Zichroni's act, yet they insisted on the right of the individual in a democracy to act upon personal convictions—so long as this did not endanger the state—without incurring the death penalty. As the hunger strike progressed, demands mounted that an enlightened society must recognize an individual's right to think differently, even to err.

In an open letter to Prime Minister Moshe Sharett, three noted intellectuals—theologian Martin Buber, philosopher Hugo Bergman, and educator Ernst Simon—closely followed Dworkin's reasoning. Averring that their approach was not politically motivated and that they did not belong to any war resisters group, they argued that despite their sincere wish for peace, the tragic nature of human history must be recognized. Even nations reluctant to fight were not spared involvement in bloody struggles. At the same time, they pointed out, the right of others to think differently and condemn all wars, including a war perceived as just, must be recognized. The three assured the prime minister that in light of present attitudes in Israel and in the world, there was no chance that the pacifist mood would spread and endanger Israel's or any other country's security. Conscientious objectors would remain a very small minority everywhere. Moreover, conscientious objectors are plainly distinguishable from mere defectors. Hence, the prime minister was obliged to find an honorable way out of the dead end in which both the young objector and the authorities found themselves. The letter ended with yet another pragmatic argument, hinting that if Zichroni's hunger strike ended in his death, Israel's reputation would be jeopardized.[26] Significantly, even a thinker of Buber's status, while unwilling to grant government exclusive power to determine an individual's life and death, was unwilling to defend conscientious objection in reference to a higher law.

The situation seemed like a dead end because officials in the Ministry of Defense, however anxious to find a solution to the embarrassing affair, held firm to the traditional perception of conscientious objection identified with Thoreau. They were willing to excuse conscientious objection as long as it was linked to esoteric conviction, especially stemming from religious sources, but were unwilling to reconsider the very foundations of the social contract, as Zichroni's Rawlsian statements essentially demanded, or negotiate the right to refuse to serve, even with eminent intellectuals. Actually, the Dworkin argument demands of governments not only to make decisions about war and peace but to grade them by degree of importance and tolerate exceptions to them. The Rawls argument actually obliges governments to engage in theoretical disputes over political obligation. The Thoreau argument, by contrast, puts the burden of proof on the objector, who must demonstrate moral consistency and sincerity.

Defense ministry officials argued in letters, declarations, official statements, and press conferences that Zichroni's behavior was not based on a consistent normative system that contained the category of conscientious objection in the usual sense of the term. They claimed that he did not refuse to enter into the army in the first place, and he signed the IDF oath, yet he committed common disciplinary misdemeanors and refused to cooperate when offered alternative forms of service. Minister of Defense Lavon was particularly harsh, referring to Zichroni as a "moral parasite"[27] and claiming that any attempt to compare his act to that of famous conscientious objectors of the past was erroneous:

> Dodging the duty to defend the existence of our country and state is a public crime, and there is no foundation to references in this context to great persons such as Gandhi, who considered passive resistance as the appropriate way to defend his nation of hundreds of millions of backward and oppressed people, yet didn't say a word against [the establishment of] an Indian army when that country achieved its independence.[28]

Lavon argued that the law in every country defines a conscientious objector as a person who prior to induction announces his objection to serve in the military. Once drafted, every soldier is bound to the rules of the army, which meant that if Zichroni persisted in his objection, he would have to remain in prison. "This fellow is possessed with willpower and positive qualities, but this does not reduce the damage and the negative effect of his act, and there is no way to avoid handling him harshly."[29]

With every passing day, the public was updated about the worsening condition of the hunger striker. Despite their marginality in Israeli society, the members of the WRI were effective in keeping the issue in the headlines, as shown in the following examples:

The War Resister's Hunger Strike—Reaches its Thirteenth Day
WRI Center Has Been Contacted
Israel's War Resisters' secretariat sent a telegram yesterday to the world center of war resisters in Anfield, Middlesex, England, requesting it ac-

tivate all war resisters associations throughout the world to express their protest to Israeli embassies throughout the world over the arrest of Amnon Zichroni whose hunger strike is in its thirteenth day, Ha'aretz's correspondent in Haifa has learned. A group of war resisters in Haifa announced that the military authorities have refused for several days to allow his relatives to meet with the striker, who is being held in a hospital. Zichroni's condition has worsened lately, the source said.[30]

Zichroni's Hunger Strike Enters Its 15th Day
The hunger strike by Amnon Zichroni, the war resister who was sentenced to 7 months in prison and is being held in a military hospital, is entering its 15th day today. Yesterday, during a visit by his father, the youngster could no longer move from his bed on account of dizziness. Zichroni told his father during the visit that he informed the doctors he would resist being fed by force and said: 'Either I am released from miliary service or the military gets my corpse. This was made known to Haaretz's correspondent by the war resisters group. The same source conveyed that a petition has begun to be circulated in Jerusalem demanding the release of Amnon Zichroni from the army. The petition has already been signed by Professors Martin Buber, A. E. Simon and H. Bergman, and dozens of students.[31]

Zichroni's Fast Reaches Its 20th Day
Tel Aviv, Wednesday—The doctors warn that war resister Amnon Zichroni, who is in the twentieth day of his fast, may at every moment succumb to a state of total collapse with no prior warning and no possibility thereafter of recovery said Nathan Hofshi of Nahalal, chairman of the Association of War Resisters in Israel, in a press conference this morning. Attorney M. Stein, Zichroni's defense counsel, stated that "a slow and deliberate murder is being carried out here against a 19-year-old pure-hearted, conscientious youngster, and the chief culprit is Defense Minister Pinhas Lavon, who a few years ago was himself a pacifist and a disciple of A. D. Gordon, a peace advocate." M. Stein added that the entire government was responsible for the affair in that it was allowing Lavon a free hand in this matter.[32]

Zichroni's Hunger Strike In Its 22nd Day
War resister Amnon Zichroni's hunger strike is entering its 22nd day today. Yesterday the Chief Rabbis of Tel Aviv–Jaffa sent a telegram to the minister of defense, requesting him to act on Zichroni's behalf. Zichroni

received a letter signed by Professors M. Buber, H. Bergman and A. Simon begging him to stop the hunger strike. He declined the professors' request and said that stopping the fast without being released from the army "would be a betrayal of myself." Yesterday, Zichroni was visited by his mother. She found him weak and tired.[33]

Although Hofshi, Stein, and their comrades were able to keep the issue in the headlines, and made efforts to get internationally known pacifists such as Albert Einstein and India's President Rajanda Parassad involved, their effectiveness in gaining public sympathy for the cause of freedom of conscience seemed to have been minimal. The Zichroni family found itself in a dilemma, as they could not comprehend their son's position. His parents were of course less interested in the ideological issues than in saving their son's life, and tried various avenues to achieve this. During one visit to the hospital they announced that they too would begin a fast if their son did not desist from hunger strike, but Zichroni simply asked them to leave the room. Relatives tried to help by approaching individual defense ministry officials, despite the relatives' own rejection of Zichroni's behavior, expressed in interviews forty years later.

An interesting aspect of the affair is the extent to which public discourse over it lacked ideological components, despite the handful of war resisters who attempted to focus debate on ideological principles. Clearly, the intellectual community of the time would not allow a serious ideological debate over the issue of refusal to serve in the military. Most of the discourse centered on technicalities, such as the role of the oath in determining a soldier's commitment to the army, or what exactly the practice in other countries is. Internal correspondence in the defense establishment indicates a wall-to-wall rejection of the war resisters and their stance. A note by a defense ministry official who was approached by the Ministry of Justice to supply the actual text of the IDF oath in light of a request by the WRI evoked the response: "Are you engaged in public relations with those?"[34] The government in effect launched a war against "those." When Shalom Zamir, one of the WRI activists, demonstrated at the Knesset against the alleged violation of the UN declaration of human rights in the Zichroni affair, he was arrested by the police. The president of Israel refused to discuss the matter with a representative of WRI. Military spokespersons insisted repeatedly that Zichroni was inconsistent in his behavior, implying he was no genuine pacifist. Psychological warfare was waged through the press, with supporters of releasing Zichroni from the army emphasizing his deteriorating condition and the prime minister insisting that his life was not in danger. Another arena in which the discourse took place was England, where the WRI approached the Israel embassy, resulting mainly in an internal debate between representatives of the foreign ministry and the defense ministry in the embassy.

At a certain point it became clear that continued discourse would simply lead to Zichroni's death, but then another element evolved: admiration for the young man's determination. If initially the Israeli public accepted the defense ministry's position that Zichroni was merely a confused youngster who deserved to rot in military prison, as time went by his unshakable stand against not only the defense establishment but the entire normative system in the country began to be perceived as impressive. The press defined the choice faced by Israeli society as one between acceptance of the young man's position or sentencing him to death. The young man who defied every plea by his parents, and by the country's eminent intellectuals to break his fast evoked admiration alongside implacable opposition. Uri Kessari, writing on the twenty-second day of the strike in the daily Ma'ariv, a paper associated at the time with right wing circles, called Zichroni's hunger strike a form of blackmail, and described such suffering from pangs of conscience as requesting psychological treatment—treatment, he believed, that could turn the young fellow from a war resister to a "loyal soldier."[35] With this, Kessari expressed positive feeling for a person who at the age of eighteen was not drawn to soccer players or movie stars but to putting the world aright.

On the same day, Zmanim, a newspaper associated with the Progressive Party, devoted a long editorial to the affair. The release of the "naive youngster" from his duty to serve in the military, or even his release from combat duty only, the article began, would constitute a precedent that others—less naive—might exploit. "Can the State of Israel, whose fundamental problem is security, and one of whose most crucial tasks is the strengthening of its defense force . . . create such a precedent?" The answer, according to the editorial, was no. "Every progressive person in Israel would bless a situation in which a permanent peace with our neighbors would allow us to treat war resisters for reasons of conscience with patience and generosity. Apparently, however, such a situation is still remote from us." The editorial described

Zichroni as having violated the laws of military discipline by disobeying orders and deserting his unit without permission, which showed irresponsible behavior. However, it acknowledged that Zichroni's stubborn and consistent stand since his arrest proved that his actions were not the product of superficial thinking, evil intentions, or fear. "Both his energetic refusal to continue to serve even in a non-combat unit, and the strength of soul that allows him to persist in the physical effort of a three-week fast that he has imposed on himself out of his free will—prove that strong and deep ideological motives are at work in him." Opposing the defense ministry's claim that Zichroni signed an assent form along with the IDF oath, the newspaper argued that reasonable adults can undergo a spiritual crisis at a certain moment in their lives that changes their world views, which is definitely a possibility in the case of a nineteen-year-old. Therefore, Zmanim concluded, a humane view of the Zichroni case demands, in addition to condemnation of his undisciplined behavior, recognition of the purity of his motives and the acknowledgment of his refusal to serve as stemming from a genuinely humanistic conviction.[36]

An editorial in Ha'aretz concurred: "Since the problem has now entered the sphere of public discourse, the government must investigate it—examining the laws and practices of other enlightened nations—and bring the results of its investigation to the Knesset in the near future in the form of legislative proposals. As for Amnon Zichroni—we hope the minister of defense uses his prerogative to release him from obligatory service and thus halt the hunger strike. Amnon Zichroni undoubtedly has given sufficient proof that his refusal stems from deep convictions for which he is willing to sacrifice even his life."[37] Whether or not one accepts the objector's views, Ha'aretz concluded, they have gained an emotional persuasiveness that is beyond debate.

Zichroni's stubborn demand that society either accept his position or in effect sentence him to death for it, was to impel a significant change in the treatment of the issue of conscientious objection. It was transformed from an esoteric matter dealt with on occasion by a hostile or indifferent clerk in the defense ministry to an integral part of public discourse in Israel. As summed up years later by the leader of the war resisters movement, Yeshayahu Toma Schick, the Zichroni affair brought fundamental issues concerning the attitude toward war in Israeli society "to the street." It enabled the consideration of refusal to participate in any war, or in selected acts of war, as a public issue. Although actual cases of refusal continued to be treated by the defense ministry on an individual basis until 1980, Zichroni paved the way for discussions on the fundamental questions involved, particularly the question that was so easy to ignore in a collectivist society of the value of a single human life.

Interestingly, the strongest expression of the dilemma between society's tendency to perpetuate its entrenched norms versus the value of the life of a single individual who defies these norms was articulated in a poem written by none other than Nathan Alterman, the acclaimed national poet closely identified with the ruling establishment. In a poem appearing in his weekly column in *Davar*, the organ of the dominant Mapai Party, on the twenty-second day of Zichroni's hunger strike, he wrote that a community that permits a war resister to sacrifice himself for an ideal that all consider to be wrong may be justified in letting him die, but if this is the collective wisdom, it must be stated explicitly. This brave young man, Alterman wrote, deserves an answer that must be given with the same courage and conviction that he has shown. Significantly, Alterman used the plural "we" throughout the poem, a reflection of the strong sense of togetherness characteristic of Israel at the time. There was no question in his mind, or in that of his readers, that the ideals held by Zichroni were wrong. The poet even expressed understanding for the urge to take revenge on the young man for breaking Israeli society's strongest code. However, he also stressed Israel's responsibility to behave as a sovereign state. Alterman, the poet laureate of the emergence of Jewish sovereignty, would not permit the new state to behave in the manner of an irresponsible mob, for example by state officials allowing a young man to die and then shifting responsibility away from themselves. Moreover, Alterman made a connection between sovereignty and truth, mocking attempts by the prime minister to suggest that the hunger striker's health was satisfactory or the defection of the discourse to technicalities such as Zichroni's signing of the army oath. Sovereign states operate by law, not by glib spokespersons, he pointed out. Zichroni, he concluded, must be released and a clear policy toward war resisters must be formulated.[38]

Alterman's entry into the discourse could not be ignored. Defense Minister Lavon, under pressure as well by the Zichroni family, made a decision to release him from prison and grant him a month's leave after which he was required to return to military service. On June 20, the twenty-third day of the hunger strike, Zichroni's father arrived at the hospital at 9 a.m. to pick up his son. Before his release, Zichroni was given a large amount of vitamins and instructions for the gradual halting of his fast, beginning on the first day with only one glass of orange juice and followed by a gradual increase of nutritional intake thereafter. The crowd of journalists awaiting the famous war resister at his family's home in Tel Aviv found a weak but fully energized Zichroni who announced that he viewed the leave he was given as the first step in finding a "fair and principled solution to the problem."[39] His father, conceivably dismayed by the son's obvious intention to pursue his incomprehensible course, assured the journalists that he himself was no pacifist and regretted that he had so little influence on his stubborn son. The younger Zichroni, meanwhile, addressed the journalists at length about the negative effects of war and the need to eliminate them by not engaging in war. He vowed he would devote his whole life to his ideas, although he still did not know how. He thanked the civilian doctors who treated him during the hunger strike. He discussed a letter he had received from a group of intellectuals who urged him to refrain from extreme behavior that negated his own view of the sanctity of life, but he explained that he could not accede to the request because strongly held convictions must be defended by extreme means.[40]

Zichroni regained his strength during his month-long leave and continued to preach his ideas to anyone willing to listen. What he was probably unaware of was that his ideas were being noted not only by those he spoke to directly. The combination of mounting pressure on Israel's borders during the mid-1950s, mainly along the Gaza Strip; economic and social tensions stemming from the large influx of immigration into the country; intrigues in the corridors of power, especially in the defense establishment; and the effects of the cold war resulted in an atmosphere of paranoia in the country's ruling circles and the Shin Bet, the security services headed by Isser Harel collected information on everyone who could be associated with the Soviet Union. A file on Zichroni was amassed showing that he established contact with the Israeli branch of WRI during his month-long leave but did not join the organization because he was critical of its passivity; he believed that only street activity would attract adherents to war resistance. Agents who encountered him reported that he objected to the concepts "army," "state," and "nation," rejected the Bible not only as a religious document but even as historical evidence, objected to the IDF's retaliatory activity beyond the borders, believed in internationalism (since statehood leads to bloodshed), and did not think the IDF would be truly effective at the moment of need. Over time, he was reported to have thought that the Arabs, by their sheer quantity, would be able to liquidate Israel. Therefore, the only hope lay in disbanding all its military forces, which would turn Israel into a symbol that would be imitated by the entire world.

Based on the information gathered on Zichroni, the army's manpower department submitted an evaluation to Chief of Staff Moshe Dayan that "Zichroni intends to keep up these disgraces until his release from the army or until the bitter end."[41] The easiest way for the army to rid itself of the issue, it advised, was to declare him mentally ill. Summoned to the neuro-psychiatric department of Tel Hashomer hospital on July 8, Zichroni was examined by Professor Julius Zelermayer. However, the professor, in a letter to the chief military medical officer's headquarters, wrote that he could not detect any signs of mental illness. The examination, he reported, revealed a person with higher than average intelligence and although personality attributes bordering on schizophrenia and introversion were identifiable, there was no indication that the world view he espoused stemmed from them. His behavior, the professor concluded, seemed to be prompted by his absolute and unshakable convictions, and most definitely not by egoistic motives such as a desire to desert the army.

Ultimately, it was Chief of Staff Moshe Dayan, the military hero with sharp political instincts, who decided that the army had no interest in continuing to deal with Zichroni and ordered that a way be found to postpone his return to service. The arrangement that was finally concluded between the minister of defense and the Zichroni family was that he be released from the army in several months' time, and in the meantime be occupied in preparing civil defense materials. The Israeli population during the Sinai campaign of 1956, instructed to cover the windows of their homes and their car headlights with blue cellophane paper, would have been surprised to learn that the explanatory brochures distributed to them were written by war resister Amnon Zichroni.

Notes

Unless otherwise noted, all the documents in this chapter are located in the "conscientious objectors" file, Archive of the Israel Defense Forces, Givata'yim, Israel.

1. Joseph Raz, *The Authority of the Law: Essays on Law and Morality* (Oxford: Clarendon Press, 1979).

2. Michael Walzer, *Obligations: Essays on Disobedience, War and Citizenship* (Cambridge, Mass.: Harvard University Press, 1970).

3. Mulford Q. Sibley and Philip E. Jacob, *Conscription of Conscience: The American State and the Conscientious Objector 1940–1947* (Ithaca, N.Y.: Cornell University Press, 1952).

4. Caroline Moorhead, *Troublesome People: The Warriors of Pacifism* (Bethesda, Md.: Adler & Adler, 1987).

5. Quoted in Moshe Dayan, *Avney Derech* (Tel Aviv: Dvir, 1976), 111.

6. David Ben-Gurion, "Hok Sherut Bita'hon (Misspar 2), Tav Shin Yod Bet," *Hazon Vaderech* 4 (Mapai Publication, 1953).

7. Yoav Gelber, *Toldot Ha'hitnadvut*, vol. 2 (Jerusalem: Yad Ben-Zvi, 1981), 11.

8. Anthony G. Bing, *Israeli Pacifist: The Life of Joseph Abileah* (Syracuse: Syracuse University Press, 1990).

9. Y. Amir to Director General, letter, July 4, 1960.

10. Nathan Hofshi, *Belev Va'nefesh* (publication by the author's friends, undated), 171.

11. *Ha'olam Ha'ze* 865, May 20, 1954, 12.

12. *Ne'hemya Kin*, letter, June 8, 1954.

13. Colonel Eliezer Amitai to Northern Command Headquarters\Attorney, letter, May 20, 1954.

14. Attachment to Ne'hemya Kin's letter, note 12.

15. *Ha'iton Ha'demokrati*, May 28, 1954.

16. Undated note, Conscientious Objectors file.

17. Attorney, Prime Minister's Office to the Prime Minister, Document, April 9, 1950.

18. Major Y. Bassman, letter, March 26, 1954.

19. Ne'hemya Kin, letter, June 8, 1954.

20. All quotations are from Tik Bet-Din [Trial File] 181/54.

21. Ari'ela Re'uveni, "Lisbol? Ken Ach Lo Bi'sde Ha'krav" [Suffer? Yes, but not on the battlefield], *Dvar Ha'shavu'a*, June 24, 1954.

22. Re'uveni, "Lisbol?"

23. Henry D. Thoreau, "Civil Disobedience," in *Civil Disobedience: Theory and Practice*, ed. Hugo Adam Bedau (Indianapolis: Pegasus, 1969).

24. Ronald Dworkin, *Taking Rights Seriously* (Cambridge, Mass.: Harvard University Press, 1977).

25. John Rawls, *A Theory of Justice* (Oxford: Oxford University Press, 1973).

26. M. Buber, S. H. Bergman, A. E. Simon, letter to Prime Minister Moshe Sharett, June 10, 1954.

27. "Lavon—Al Sarbanut Ha'milh'ama" [Lavon—on war resistance], *Davar*, June 23, 1954.

28. "Lavon," *Davar*, June 23, 1954.

29. "Lavon," *Davar*, June 23, 1954.

30. *Ha'aretz*, June 10, 1954.

31. *Ha'aretz*, June 11, 1954.

32. *Al Ha'mishmar*, June 15, 1954.

33. *Ha'aretz*, June 18, 1954.

34. These lines were added in handwriting to an undated letter by M. Shalgi to the defense ministry's attorney general.

35. Uri Kessari, "Shovtey Ra'av [Hunger strikers], *Ma'ariv*, June 18, 1954.

36. "Sarban Milhama" [War resister], *Zmanim*, June 18, 1954.

37. *Ha'aretz*, 8 Sivan, 1954.

38. *Davar*, June 18, 1954.

39. *Davar*, June 20, 1954.

40. See *Ma'ariv*, June 21, 1954; *Zmanim*, June 21, 1954.

41. Havat Da'at [Evaluation], July 11, 1954.

CHAPTER FOUR

The Third Force

∞

In September 1954, Zichroni, still working for the civil defense authority, enrolled in evening classes in law at the Upper School for Economics and Law in Tel Aviv. As the bus he rode to school each evening passed through Petach Tikva Road, he could see the graffiti that pacifist Shalom Zamir had scribbled in red on a wall during his hunger strike. It remained there for years: "Let the name of Israel not be stained by Zichroni's blood." Zichroni finished law school, was married in 1959 to Miri Mendleberger, who opened a public relations office, had two children—Tivona born in 1960 and Sharon in 1967—and began his career as an attorney. Yet for several years he continued to be in close contact with the small group of war protesters who had supported his struggle. Totally ignored by Israeli historiography, these people were eccentric political activists who advocated pacifism, universal peace, national brotherhood, Arab–Jewish coexistence, world disarmament, world citizenship, naturalism, vegetarianism, and what not. More than anything else, however, they were a headache to the opposition groups whose demonstrations they sometimes joined, as their ideas were considered outlandish even to critics of Israeli society at the time.

In point of fact, some of their ideas actually appeared in the platforms of established political parties: the Communist party called for a world fraternity of workers, and Mapam (United Workers' Party) believed in reconciliation in the Middle East. But these parties participated in the mainstream discourse over the questions on the national agenda in the 1950s: immigrant absorption, the Sinai campaign, the role of the Histadrut, and the like, while Zichroni found himself in the company of "street aliens"—

strange people in shabby, ill-fitting suits clasping old-fashioned satchels overflowing with leaflets they would distribute to anybody willing to take them (although few were). Most of their activity took place in the streets. They demonstrated, were arrested, declared hunger strikes, debated long into the night, formed organizations that soon split up over obscure ideological differences, preached incomprehensible notions to anyone who happened to pass them on the street corners where they handed out their fliers typed on old typewriters, and cursed Stalin, John Foster Dulles, and David Ben-Gurion. Zichroni's wife Miri, a very down-to-earth woman, recalls how, as a newlywed, she had to put up with visits from such types in their small apartment at all hours of the day and night. Once she caught sight of a mental-hospital gown under the coat of one man who arrived in the middle of the night to debate pacifism with her husband.

Until such time as the archives of Israel's security services are opened, probably the only place where the activities of these "street aliens" are recorded, their story will remain untold. Zichroni's affiliation with them, however, affords a rare glimpse into their world. Particularly intriguing is the story of Mordechai Stein, Zichroni's trial lawyer. Stein arrived in Palestine on his own as a child from Russia on the eve of World War I. He attended the Herzliya School in Tel Aviv (where Tuvia and Shalom Zichroni also studied), and joined the Communist party. In 1925, he became co-editor of the party organ Ha'or (the light), but later found himself at odds with the party leadership because of his criticism of Stalin. When these disputes escalated into fundamental ideological differences in 1945, he started his own paper, Ha'iton Ha'demokrati (the Democratic Newspaper), a biweekly that offered him a forum for his independent opinions. Stein wrote the articles, printed the paper, and distributed it by himself for over twenty-five years. He would deliver it to Tel Aviv kiosks on Saturday nights, when there was no competition from other newspapers, but all the copies were often confiscated by the security service.

In 1951, Stein established the "Third Force," a small movement calling on Israel to remain neutral in the Cold War. The movement's charter boasts six signatories—Yosef Golumb, plumber, Petach Tikva; Shalom Zamir, laborer, Tel Aviv; Arie Livne, teacher, Ramat Gan; Mordechai Mani, owner of a translations office, Tel Aviv; Ze'ev Re'e-Ze, clerk, Tel Aviv; and Mordechai Stein, attorney, Tel Aviv[1]—and its membership apparently never grew much beyond these six men. The movement was answering the call issued at a conference held that year in Rangoon under the sponsorship of India's Prime Minister Nehru and Yugoslavia's President Tito, who appealed for the establishment of a bloc of nations in South Asia, the Middle East, North Africa, Latin America, and parts of Europe that would maintain neutrality and thus serve as a buffer between Western imperialism and the Stalinist dictatorship. The idea became popular among Western intellectuals who were disillusioned by the form Communism had taken.

In his desire to create a better world, Stein contacted similar movements abroad, such as the Independent Socialist League and the Association of Pacifists in the United States, and sent hundreds of letters to Rangoon, Tokyo, Delhi, London, and New York. In 1963, for instance, he wrote to Bertrand Russell urging him not to accept the Freedom Prize he had been awarded by the City of Jerusalem in order to protest against Israel's policies toward its Arab minority and the Palestinian refugees. Russell was not swayed by the letter.[2] He also corresponded with Arnold Toynbee, who expressed his support for the principles of the Third Force and his hope that a solution to the problems in the Middle East could be found along these lines.

Although known as a communist, Stein strongly criticized the Communist parties in Israel and other countries for selling out their ideology in order to toe the Soviet line at any given point in time. He supported Trotsky's internationalist policy against Stalin's "socialism in one country," but did not refrain from criticizing Trotsky as well in the name of his independent social–liberalism.[3] Above all, however, Stein was an anti-Zionist. Zionism, he wrote in his paper, was a national movement that focused on the past and served exploitative imperialistic forces, and he believed that true socialists had no choice but to oppose it. On the other hand, he approved of the 1947 UN partition resolution dividing the land between Jews and Palestinians, claiming that he did so not because the Soviet Union had supported the resolution, but because "the Zionist movement and the Arab national movement, with their stupid and evil policies on the one hand, and the Palestinian Communist party, with its prevaricating and dishonest policy on the other, are eradicating any sign of international fraternity and true Arab–Jewish coexistence in this country."[4] He maintained that a genuine socialist movement could be established in Palestine only after both the Jews and the Arabs had achieved independence and each side was free to handle its affairs according to its own will and understanding.

Stein supported the partition because he realized that the Jewish state would be able to accommodate the Jewish displaced persons who had survived the Holocaust, and could invest its resources in providing a better life for them and for the local inhabitants. After the war and the proclamation of the State of Israel, he continued to support the Jewish state, but believed that its fundamental objectives should be the return of the Palestinian refugees who had fled in the war, the return of their property, the abolishment of the military rule imposed on the Arab residents remaining in Israel, and an intense effort to achieve peace. He strongly opposed affiliation with either side in the Cold War. The Western countries, he claimed, would not defend the Middle East, but bring about its total destruction, and the Soviet Union would not liberate but oppress it. The Jews in the region, he wrote in *Ha'iton Ha'demokrati*, could expect the worst possible fate: they would live like rats in a trap. Those who did not lose their lives as a result of the "help" they expected from their Western allies would be uprooted by the false "liberators" from the East. The Third Force called for a united Middle East that would defend itself from the embrace of both the West and the East, and would cooperate to bring prosperity to all its people.

Stein feared the arms race between the superpowers. He felt the world had become too small to accommodate both capitalist and communist regimes, not necessarily because of their differences, but because of their similarities. In both, the masses were being exploited by a small minority that enjoyed special privileges. As both were oppressive regimes seeking power and expansion, they were standing in each other's way and would ultimately collide. Stein believed it inevitable that the Middle East would be at the center of a future war between the two superpowers. The Soviet Union was geographically close by, the region was rich in resources that both sides were in need of, and it had strategic geopolitical importance. Moreover, the superpowers could easily get away with the total destruction of the Middle East, as they could not do in Europe. In 1951, Stein wrote that the only chance to prevent the region from becoming the primary victim of a war between the two blocs was for the countries in the Middle East to unite and join with their great neighbor India. This would not only reduce the danger of annihilation in a future war, but would serve as the start of the unification of the entire colonized Eastern world, a reference to what was later to be known as "the third world." These countries, which contained most of the world's population, were not looking to replace colonial suppression with another form of slavery to either of the sides in the Cold War. The emergence of the East as an independent force would bring about a fundamental change in the balance of power, and could prevent another world war. The unification of the Middle East was the first step.

Stein did not consider the Arab threat to Israel significant. The Arab states were militarily and industrially weak, they did not get along with each other, and their leaders had more serious concerns than war with Israel, he believed, especially since no superpower would allow the victory of either side in the Arab–Israeli conflict. According to Stein, the dangers Israel faced were of a different kind. His main worry was a world war which would lead to starvation. Israel, he claimed, was a small country that produced only a fraction of the food it required. The closest and cheapest markets were closed to it, and it did not have the resources to import the necessary quantity of basic commodities. In addition, he expected the hostility he sensed among newcomers to Israel to explode as soon as an economic crisis took hold. The country, he wrote in the Third Force platform,[5] was populated by people who did not comprehend each other's language and did not understand each other's culture. The new immigrants, who came in the hundreds of thousands in the early 1950s, mainly from Arab-speaking countries such as Morocco, Iraq, Yemen, and others, were doomed to a life of suffering and stagnation. Housed in temporary tents and huts, they realized the country was trying to help them, but also saw that it was prospering while they were not. In a crisis, all their feelings of anger, frustration, and hatred would erupt.

He believed the only solution was peace between Israel and its neighbors. Israel had to cease to be a foreign element among the countries of the Middle East, and had to become their friend and ally. Stein refused to consider the improbability of this vision. The Arab masses, he contended, had no interest in perpetuating the conflict that was the main cause of the corruption and oppression in their countries. Peace had to come from the heart, and the only way to achieve it was by a willingness to pay the price it demanded. He believed that the primary condition for peace between Israel and the Arab states was the return of the Palestinian refugees, and never ceased to regard this as a just demand. Moreover, in his opinion, once Israel accepted the principle of the right of return of the refugees, the international aid that would be forthcoming to implement it could also be used to provide adequate housing for its own immigrants, who had also arrived as refugees. As the platform of the Third Force framed it, justice and democracy were indivisible, and a state that acted unjustly and undemocratically toward others could not survive as a democratic state.

These intriguing ideas seemed extremely marginal at the time, and gained little notice when they appeared in Stein's paper or in the leaflets distributed on street corners by Stein and his young disciple, Amnon Zichroni. In 1959, Stein registered the Third Force as a party of both Jews and Arabs, with Zichroni listed as secretary. The party ran in the Knesset elections held that year, and received 594 of the 969,337 qualified votes. Let us not be misled, however, by this level of electoral "success"; movements like the Third Force did not expect to win elections. Participating in them, and being heard, was enough in and of itself, and was only one of the hundreds of activities organized by Stein, whose entire life was devoted to street politics. He fought the forces of darkness in the world by publishing articles, organizing meetings, joining demonstrations, and, when necessary, running for election. This figure of the lonely, courageous, irrepressible champion of justice emerged the world over against the background of the grand ideologies that prevailed between the two world wars, and seems to have disappeared from the face of the earth today. No wonder that a meeting held in 1994 to commemorate Stein failed to characterize the man, as he did not fit into any known category. Some indication of who he was and the influence he had on others on the margins of society can be found in Fauzi Al-Asmar's *Being an Arab in Israel*:

> I could stay with Stein when I had no place else to go, and I also helped him prepare the Arabic edition of his newspaper. Stein, also known as 'a lone wolf,' was a special personality. Yet many people came to consult with him on all kinds of issues, and sometimes even to ask for his legal help, and when he saw that they did not have the means, he did not ask them for a dime. Despite his sense of humor and the gentleness of his character, when he was convinced of some just cause, he would fight for it fearlessly. Several times he went out to demonstrate with a couple of associates or even alone. I recall once he loaded signs on his back and went to Dizengoff Circle, where he sat on the ground and dis-

tributed fliers against military rule. He corresponded with noted world figures like Bertrand Russell, and many foreign correspondents came to hear his opinions on political questions. Had I not known him personally, I would not have believed such a person really existed.[6]

Stein was a small man with a big white mustache who lived in two spare rooms. One of them, crowded with piles of papers, law books, and Lenin's writings, served as his office, while the other was bedroom, living room, and press center. He drank herbal tea with honey for breakfast, and had an onion, a potato, and a slice of bread fried with a spoonful of oil for lunch. When Zichroni convinced him to see a movie for the first time in his life, assuring him it was a political film, he sat there in the dark theater asking why the pictures on the screen kept moving all the time. On another occasion he was invited to a coffee house, and did not have the slightest idea how to order. Married twice, both his wives left him on the grounds that he was a terrible husband whose entire life was devoted to saving the world.

This, then, was Zichroni's mentor, a man who proposed a third way in a world in which only two ways—capitalism and communism—seemed possible; who, as a lawyer, took on lost causes (such as defending Zichroni in the military tribunal); who never tired of preaching his ideas and founding organizations to advance them, among them the Committee to Promote Civil Marriage, with Zichroni, of course, as committee secretary. Stein and the handful of other political activists on the fringes of Israeli society in the 1950s and 1960s were seen as aliens whose presence on the streets of Tel Aviv or Jerusalem contributed to street folklore more than to any substantial political debate. Consequently, some very interesting ideas, such as those propounded by the Third Way, were disregarded. Nevertheless, these people fulfilled an important function, however unrecognized it was at the time: they preserved in the public memory ideas that were all too easily ignored, but that reemerged when the time was ripe. The man with the thick mustache distributing fliers on a street corner, the poet muttering ethical pronouncements to passersby, the self-made ideologue spending his last pennies to publish a newspaper nobody read, or the lone demonstrator carrying a sign—these people do not allow mainstream discourse to numb individual consciousness. On the whole, in the 1950s and 1960s the Israeli public was convinced that the military rule imposed on Arab citizens was necessary, and it was quite willing to take the issue off the public agenda and leave it to those in charge, i.e., the security forces. This, however, was not allowed to happen, largely as a result of the relentless activity of those "street aliens." For the most part, their efforts had no political impact, and as long as the public is not alert, political leaders can do as they like. But there are times when even marginal figures like Stein and young Zichroni can shake the earth. Such a time was the Kfar Kassem affair.

Kfar Kassem is an Arab village in central Israel close to the Jordanian border. In 1956, it had about 2000 inhabitants under Israeli military rule who supported themselves by agriculture and blue-collar work in nearby Jewish towns. In October 1956, the Sinai War broke out, and a curfew lasting from five in the evening to six in the morning was imposed on the Arab villages whose residents, although citizens of the State of Israel, were suspected by some of being fifth columnists. A large group of villagers, unaware of the curfew, were returning to Kfar Kassem from their work in the fields when they were shot down in cold blood by border guards, leaving forty-nine people, including fourteen women, dead, and thirteen wounded.

On December 7, the satirist Dan Ben-Amotz, a Holocaust survivor known for his vulgar language, published a piece in the evening paper *Ma'ariv* in which he described a fictitious conversation between himself and a German. They were discussing theater and music, international relations, and, of course, the Holocaust. He asked the German how he had reacted when he learned about the killing of Jews in World War II, how he had slept at night when millions were being imprisoned in concentration camps and sent to the gas chamber, whether he had been making love to his wife or playing with his children at the time. The German claimed to have known nothing of the atrocities. The German then asked the Israeli intellectual how he had reacted when he learned that a massacre had taken place a month earlier in Kfar Kassem—whether he had slept well at night, whether he had been kissing his girlfriend or reading poetry at the time. Now it was the Israeli's turn to say: "I heard nothing about it."[7] Ben-Amotz insisted that although he read the newspaper every day, there had been no mention of the events in Kfar Kassem.

This was not entirely accurate. A keen-eyed reader might have found a hint in the Israeli press that something terrible had happened on the first day of the Sinai Campaign, but newspaper readers in those days did not have particularly keen eyes. The Israeli public was enthralled by the glorious victory: the army had conquered the entire Sinai Peninsula in a few short days. The extraordinary military achievement even forestalled serious debate of the political implications of the campaign, in which Israel had joined forces with Britain and France, two colonial forces in retreat who hoped to restore their control over the Suez Canal. As a result, Israel became identified as a colonial power at a time of de-colonization, generating unusual joint condemnation by the two superpowers—the United States and the Soviet Union. When matters of such global importance were being ignored, the Israeli public could hardly be expected to take notice of sporadic indications of some crime committed on the margins of a spectacular military victory, especially when the victims were members of a population suspected of collaborating with the enemy.

But the government did not ignore the massacre. On November 1, Prime Minister Ben-Gurion appointed a committee to investigate the affair, and when the committee submitted its report, a government press release was issued. It announced that on October 29, in the wake of increased terrorist activity, a curfew had been imposed on several villages on the eastern border in order to protect the lives of their inhabitants. A unit of border guards was detached to implement the order, and the villagers dutifully obeyed the curfew from five in the evening to six in the morning. In certain villages, a few inhabitants returning home after inception of the curfew were hurt by the border guards. When this came to the attention of the prime minister on November 1, he appointed a commission of inquiry, headed by District Judge Benjamin Zohar, to determine the circumstances, the degree of responsibility of the border guards, and the appropriate compensation by the government to the families of those who had suffered as a result of the behavior of the soldiers. The commission had heard evidence from representatives of the villages, the border guards, and the military authorities, and on November 6 had submitted its report. Subsequently, the commander of the unit was to stand trial, as were several of his subordinates who had executed an illegal command. The government had also decided to pay each family who had suffered the immediate sum of 1,000 Israeli pounds, and had charged the Zohar commission with determining the appropriate amount of compensation for each family as soon as possible. An additional sum would be paid in accordance with the commission's decisions.[8]

This was a fast and effective response by a government aware of the minimal public interest in the affair. The official statement enabled the population to feel pure and just, knowing that crimes were not covered up in the State of Israel. The people could be duly impressed by the swift action taken by the government, and could continue to admire its newly cleansed military forces, including the border guard. The statement placed the entire event in the familiar context of terrorist attacks on Israel, and maintained total anonymity as to the identity, gender, or location of the victims. It indicated that the curfew had been imposed on "several villages" located on the "eastern border," strengthening the impression that it was all part of war, and also possibly the association of the villages with a fifth column in view of their proximity to the border. The curfew was imposed, of course, to protect the villagers themselves, and as a result of this humanitarian act, "a few inhabitants" were "hurt" and their families had "suffered." But the suffering would not last long, for the government had decided, out of the goodness of its heart, to pay an "immediate sum" to any family that "had suffered," that is, had suffered in the past tense, since now that compensations were being paid, they would suffer no longer. The statement made no mention of anyone dying, to say nothing of Israeli citizens being murdered in cold blood. Not surprisingly, it was quite effective in averting any potential protest that might have been expected from rabbis, judges, doctors, university professors, or other free-thinkers.

This is precisely the point at which a "third force" comes into play between the government spreading half-truths and the public accepting them as givens, and it is what makes the "street aliens" who operate on the fringes of the public discourse so significant, because their political sensitivity never sleeps. The framers of democracy have devised a set of institutions and procedures aimed at ensuring political justice: the separation of powers, freedom of speech and association, the state comptroller, a free press, and so on. Ever since the Dreyfus affair in the late nineteenth century, many have put their faith in intellectuals using these protections to cry out "J'accuse" when blatant violations of justice occur. But because of the actual conditions in which democracies exist, and especially because of security concerns, such procedures do not always succeed in restraining governments. At time of war in particular, the separation of powers is blurred, the press is silent, and many intellectuals subordinate moral considerations to "realpolitik." Moreover, even when security pressures are not an issue, it is easy for a society to ignore atrocities committed in its name if the government makes a concerted effort to cover them up. It takes a lot of work to uncover the truth—collecting information, confirming testimony and evidence, convincing witnesses to sign written statements, and the like. And this is what Mordechai Stein did. He sent the young law student Amnon Zichroni to Kfar Kassem, and he returned with the evidence.

It is hard to assess the exact role played by what became known as "the odd couple," Stein and Zichroni, in the Kfar Kassem affair. When dealing with such a marginal group, more established opposition organizations have a tendency to minimize their importance, both at the time, when they shy away from cooperating with these eccentrics, and after the fact, when it comes time to take credit for exposing the truth. But their exact role does not really matter. The Third Force was undoubtedly part of a process that revealed the truth of the massacre and made it known to the public in fliers illegally pasted on walls throughout the streets of Tel Aviv. Shalom Zamir recalls how he would hold a bucket of glue while another activist brushed it on the flier and stuck it on the wall, with Zichroni serving as lookout, watching for police cars. Dissemination of the facts about the massacre strengthened the appeal by Arab Member of the Knesset (MK) Touffik Toubi to the Israeli public not to let the government shift responsibility for the killing of forty-nine innocent citizens away from itself and onto the commander of a border guard unit and a couple of soldiers. The ones to blame, he proclaimed, were not only the men who pulled the triggers, but the entire apparatus responsible for the military rule that had been imposed on Arab citizens since 1948. Stein joined in the demand of theologian Martin Buber's I'hud movement for a public trial of the border guards, rather than one conducted behind closed doors.

On December 12, Prime Minister Ben-Gurion made a statement about the affair in the Knesset. Several weeks after the event, he now declared it to be "horrible" and expressed deep concern that such acts could undermine the very foundations of human morality established in the Torah. The Jewish people, he stated, along with the best of the human race, have always been justifiably proud of cherishing human life. "Thou shalt not kill" was an imperative handed down to us on Mount Sinai, and no other nation revered life more than the Jewish people.

Moreover, Jewish tradition did not abide with discrimination on the basis of gender, race, religion, or nationality. The Arabs in Israel were citizens deserving of equal rights, and their lives were sacred.[9] Like many other speeches delivered in the 1950s, this one too was phrased in eloquent language, but had little connection with reality. The emphasis on the importance of humanistic values hid a very sad situation in which the Arab minority not only lived under military rule, lifted by Ben-Gurion's successor, Levy Eshkol, only in 1966, but were forced to listen to clichés extolling the greatness of the Jewish people at a time when they had suffered severe affliction at the hands of that very nation. From the perspective of fifty years, invoking the moral imperatives handed down to the Jews on Mount Sinai in the same breath as when he acknowledged the appreciation of the heads of the Arab villages involved and the families of the deceased for the swift government action to compensate them, may sound somewhat ironic. At the time, however, few people saw it that way.

Among those who did were Stein, Zichroni, and their associates, who rather than closing their eyes to the condition of the Arab citizens, made it their primary concern, and were infuriated by the combination of an evasive government report together with declarations of the moral superiority of the Jewish people. In an article in *Ner*, Nathan Hofshi protested against the disparity between Ben-Gurion's eloquent speech and reality. He rejected the claim that the state did not discriminate against people on the basis of race or nationality at a time when Arabs were subject to rules imposed by military commanders, were open to administrative detention and exile, were convicted in military tribunals with no right of appeal, suffered collective punishment, were discriminated against in terms of the confiscation of land and civil status, etc.[10] In another article in the same issue, R. Benyamin, a member of I'hud, criticized the lack of sincerity in Ben-Gurion's speech, demanding that he forgo fancy words about the Ten Commandments when a murder had been committed. "What is the face of a nation that repeatedly commits murder and then all of a sudden remembers the commandment 'Thou shalt not kill' and sings hymns of praise to it?"[11] he asked.

Israeli intellectuals in the 1950s were quite willing to engage in the public discourse dominated by Ben-Gurion. Like other state builders in Asia and Africa in the post–World War II era, the Prime Minister developed an ideology that stressed the messianic meaning of the endeavor and considered the harsh reality in the present to be the fulfillment of the messianic vision of the Jewish people and the restoration of a glorious past. As he once declared:

> The tales of the Patriarchs four thousand years ago; the travels, deeds and life of Abraham; Israel's wanderings after the Exodus from Egypt; the wars and acts of Joshua Bin-Nun and the Judges who followed him; the life and deeds of Saul, David, and Solomon; the achievements of Uzziah, King of Judah, and Jeroboam II, King of Israel—all these are nearer and more timely, more instructive and alive, for the generation born, raised, and living in Israel, than all the speeches and debates at the Basel Congresses.[12]

This link between the present and the mythological, rather than historical, past of the nation had a functional value in a society composed of thousands of new immigrants to whom the Zionist ideology that came out of Basel meant very little compared to the messianic promise of Psalms 69:36: "For God will save Zion, and will build the cities of Judah." The messianic ideology, however, required mobilization of the country's intellectuals, e.g., of philosophers, archeologists, and Bible scholars to establish the connection between the modern people of Israel and their biblical past.

For Ben-Gurion, this was more than mere rhetoric. In March 1949, when the War of Independence was barely over and the state-building effort had just begun, he assembled the country's literary elite in his office to explain the importance of the intellectuals' contribution to the national goals. In later public appearances, he often called upon them to uphold the messianic vision and lend their support to the state. And they did. Most intellectuals in the 1950s seemed to revel in the stature they were afforded, and participated willingly in the dissemination of messianic ideology. Bible scholars were particularly cooperative: inspired by Ben-Gurion, they devoted major efforts to the study of the Book of Joshua, which deals with the conquest of Canaan.[13]

At the Ideological Congress, for instance, held in Jerusalem a few months after the Kfar Kassem massacre, foremost professors debated at length the relationship between the Jewish return to Zion and the messianic vision of the Bible. These were not stone-hearted people; they believed in peace, in equal rights for the Arab minority, in the abolishment of military rule, and in other high-minded principles. Many of them expressed views that were not that different from those of Mordechai Stein, who put the individual at the center of his philosophy and was willing to renounce political ideologies, such as Communism, as soon as he became aware of their oppressive nature. The only real difference between the majority of Israel's intellectuals and the "street aliens" lay in the latter's endless political activity—the fliers, demonstrations, newspapers, and so on—which did not allow them to be lulled by the messianic rhetoric that could so easily divert attention from the evils committed by the state.

The story of Israel's intellectuals reveals a complex dynamic. In the early 1960s, after a decade during which they had been willingly mobilized by the country's towering leader, many of them, especially Hebrew University professors, rebelled against Ben-Gurion, to whom they now attributed authoritarian tendencies. During the Six Day War in 1967, some came to regret this stand, calling upon Ben-Gurion, now eighty years old, to resume captaincy of the ship of state. All this time, however, the "odd couple," Stein and Zichroni, and their associates had operated outside the sphere of influence of these dynamics. They were unimpressed by Lenin, Trotsky, Stalin, or Ben-Gurion for that matter. Nor were their views vis-à-vis the Arabs affected by passing intellectual trends or fads. They never abandoned the autonomy of their opinions of the events and processes taking place in the country, nor were they swayed by the rhetoric that accompanied them.

Zichroni was admitted to the bar in 1960. He had studied at the Tel Aviv Law School, established in 1935, which later became part of Tel Aviv University. In the 1950s, the school suffered from a lack of prestige, largely because it catered to relatively older students, government officials, accountants, military personnel, and others who chose to study law in evening classes. Its library was quite sparse, and it was looked down upon not only by the British mandatory authorities but also by the Hebrew University in Jerusalem. Yet despite its poor image, some of the best Israeli jurists of the time lectured at the school. Zichroni studied contracts with Judge Ze'ev Zeltner, civil law with Judge Joel Sussman, Hebrew law with Professor Elisha Scheinbaum, and English law with Judge Eliezer Malchi. The common denominator shared by this group of jurists was their emphasis on formal procedure. Sussman, for example, associated natural justice with correct procedure, and was known for his insistence on formalities and his demand to resist the tendency to abuse procedure in the service of a client. On the whole, they admired English and European law, but were not averse to criticizing those statutes, especially British mandatory regulations, that seemed inappropriate. But Zichroni did not limit his studies to law alone. He also took courses in accounting and philosophy at an institute located in Abu Kabir, on the outskirts of Jaffa, where he was introduced to Greek philosophy, modern European thinkers, and aesthetics.

This was his first encounter with some of the intellectual and social trends that were starting to take hold in Israel in the 1960s. As in other Western societies, that decade saw a liberal modernism begin to pervade cultural life, reflected in literature, philosophy, and the arts. Writers pegged as the "War of Independence generation" because of the influence of that formative event on their work were now writing about the individual; philosophers were beginning to explore universal themes, such as "the eternal silence" of Pascal's infinite spaces, Kierkegaard's religious existentialism, and Erich Neumann's "essence of evil"; and playwrights were venturing into personal, often surrealist experimental realms. Many of the figures associated with these trends, among them actor Ili Gorlitzki, filmmaker Uri Zohar, and journalist Boaz Evron, also studied at Abu Kabir at the time, and Zichroni, who was younger than most of his fellow students in law school, now found himself in a compatible setting in which anti-establishment political views could be exchanged, and where his anti-war reputation was not a hindrance.

But the same was not true for the early days of his legal career. Zichroni interned in a law office where his father had connections. In 1948, during the War of Independence, Tuvia Zichroni had tried to import a shipload of eggs from Turkey. The Turkish crew, well-aware of the war raging in Palestine, used the opportunity to sell the eggs in Greece, so that the ship arrived in the port of Haifa empty. When the owners refused to compensate Zichroni, the ship was seized and offered at auction, but nobody was interested in buying a ship that seemed to have less value than its original cargo, and it was eventually sunk. The matter had been handled by a lawyer named Ben-Zion Barkai, who agreed to take Zichroni in as an intern. However, in September 1960, after successfully passing the bar exams and looking forward to receiving his license in a ceremony to be held on September 17, his past as a conscientious objector almost got in the way again. The chief military advocate, Meir Zohar, objected to Zichroni being given a license to practice law because of his conviction by a military tribunal, and the committee of the Legal Council (later to become the Israeli Bar Association) went along with him. There was no way Zichroni could appeal this decision in time, since the council did not have a meeting scheduled until after the ceremony. Unwilling to accept the situation, Zichroni went to Jerusalem and presented himself at the office of Minister of Justice Pinhas Rosen, demanding to see the minister. Rosen, recognizing the young man's name, called him in, listened to his plea, and ordered a special session of the council to be called immediately. The council reversed its decision and allowed Zichroni to participate in the ceremony.

And so Zichroni began his career as an attorney, but with his reputation as a conscientious objector, clients were not beating a path to his door. A young man with a wife and baby, he did not have the money to open an office of his own, and his parents were not in a position to help him out financially. He thus began his career by renting space in the law office of a religious lawyer named Mordechai Stern in return for legal services. From 1960 to 1964, Zichroni saw to the needs of Stern's clients, suffering the disillusionment of many law school graduates whose dreams of the glorious profession are transformed in the real world into countersigning contracts and shuffling papers. Zichroni's own first clients were members of the Tel Aviv bohemian circles who were less put off by his past. In 1963, for example, they included two Israeli youngsters charged with inappropriate behavior in a public place during a demonstration against nuclear testing in front of the American embassy. They had been carrying a sign with the words: "Americans, go fuck yourselves with your H-bombs." Appearing for the defense, Zichroni, argued that in English the four-letter word "fuck" meant "go to hell," and called to the witness stand such bohemian figures as the English professor Arie Sacks and the theater director Peter Frei. Not surprisingly, the conscientious objector turned inventive lawyer soon attracted the attention of Uri Avnery, editor of the opposition newspaper *Ha'olam Ha'ze*.

Notes

1. Haviv Cna'an, "Tnu'at Ha'ko'a'ch Ha'shlishi Be'israel" [The Third Force Movement in Israel], *Ha'aretz*, May 26, 1954.

2. Haviv Cna'an, "Bertrand Russell Da'ha Pni'yat Ha'koa'ch Ha'shlishi" [Bertrand Russell Rejected Appeal by the Third Force], *Ha'aretz*, September 4, 1963.

3. See Dan Miodownik, MA thesis on Stein's political thought, written under the author's supervision, Tel-Aviv University, 1996.

4. *Ha'iton Ha'demokrati*, April 10, 1948.

5. Published in *Ha'iton Ha'demokrati*, January 16, 1954.

6. Fauzi Al-Asmar, *Li'hiot Arvi Be'israel* [Being an Arab in Israel], (Jerusalem: Dr. Israel Scha'hak Publication, 1975).

7. Quoted in Al-Asmar, *Li'hiot Arvi Be'israel*, 58–59.

8. Published in *Ner* (November–December, 1956), 16.

9. Published in *Ner* (November–December, 1956), 15–16.

10. Nathan Hofshi, "A'ye Ha'emet?" [Where is the Truth?], in *Ner* (November–December, 1956), 20.

11. R. Benyamin, "Kfar Kassem Be'sha'arey Ha'knesset" [Kfar Kassem at the Knesset's Gates], in *Ner* (November–December, 1956).

12. David Ben-Gurion, "Worlds and Values." *Jewish Frontier* 24 (December 1957), 15.

13. Michael Keren, *Ben-Gurion and the Intellectuals: Power, Knowledge and Charisma* (DeKalb: Northern Illinois University Press, 1983).

CHAPTER FIVE

Political Perfectionism

∞

In 1950, two veterans of the War of Independence, Uri Avnery and Shalom Cohen, purchased a weekly called *Ha'olam Ha'ze* (This World), and turned it into a major organ of social criticism. The two editors became the voice of the young people disillusioned by the older generation who had sent them to fight for a state they felt did not deserve their sacrifice, not an uncommon feeling after any war. The paper became very popular among the youngsters who were frustrated at the failure of the leadership to solve the Arab–Israeli conflict. It propounded the position that the founders of Jewish nationalism, who had come from the ghettos of Europe, were unable to acknowledge the existence of an Arab national movement, while the younger generation, who had fought in the War of Independence, had a different perspective. The editors wished to awaken Israel's youngsters, untouched by the dross of 2,000 years of Jewish life in the Diaspora, to the discrepancy between the model-state they had dreamed of during the War of Independence and the corrupt state emerging in reality. Thus every week *Ha'olam Ha'ze* published exposés, printing outsize sensational headlines on red paper long before the days of the tabloids. It revealed wrongdoings by corrupt officials, called for the separation of religion and state, and raised human rights issues. The vanguard of a combative press exposing corruption, inefficiency, and other ills, it portrayed the entire social and political "establishment" as corrupt.

A militant newspaper needs a lawyer, and Zichroni spent many years of his life in the service of Avnery. His association with Avnery differed fundamentally from his relationship with Stein. Although in a very real sense he was still operating on the fringes of society, he was now fighting battles for the freedom of speech within the institutional system. This, however, did not make those battles any easier. Despite the cultural renaissance of the 1960s, strong government controls were still in effect, most particularly military censorship instituted under British emergency laws. The government controlled the information conveyed by the mass media, both by means of the party press—notably *Davar*, which belonged to the Histadrut, affiliated with the ruling party Mapai—and through the direct intervention of the prime minister's office in the content of national radio (Kol Israel) broadcasts. An opposition newspaper that exposed the wrongdoings of the government and bashed its members—particularly Ben-Gurion and his young aide Shimon Peres, who became the paper's Public Enemy Number One—could not be tolerated.

The government was not the paper's only target. It attacked the army, coming out against Unit 101, under the command of Ariel Sharon, which was engaged in acts of retaliation against Arab villages and military installations across the border, exposed cases of espionage in high places, and published innumerable scoops about the private lives of politicians such as former chief of staff Moshe Dayan. Not surprisingly, it acquired many enemies, and its staff was the object of several instances of harassment and worse from sources still unknown. In December 1952, a bomb placed on the window of the newspaper offices exploded, injuring one employee; in December 1953, the two editors were attacked at midnight by a group of hooligans whom they identified as members of Ariel Sharon's unit; in December 1957, the chief correspondent was kidnapped under mysterious circumstances; and in January 1958, the national theater Habima produced a play entitled "Throw It to the Dogs" in which a newspaper editor was not averse to lying in order to further his vendetta against the political establishment. Opening night was attended by the prime minister, most of the members of his government, the leaders of the ruling Mapai party, and the upper echelons of the police and security service, who occupied the front rows of the theater and applauded enthusiastically at the climax of the play when the editor's bones were broken. At one point the General Security Service made a failed attempt to underwrite a newspaper meant to compete for the readership of *Ha'olam Ha'ze*, and in 1962, the Ministry of Justice began preparing an anti-defamation act which Avnery perceived as specifically targeting him and his operation.

Zichroni's activities as attorney for *Ha'olam Ha'ze* were far from routine. Avnery and Zichroni became known as an adept team that not only assured the newspaper's freedom of speech, but turned it into an effective weapon in their war on corruption. They often walked a very thin line, as in the case of the fierce battle they conducted against MK Menachem Porush, one of the leaders of the ultra-orthodox Agudat Israel party. Although the affair ended with their public apology, it changed the way a whole generation viewed the ultra-orthodox leadership in Israel. The story involves a lawsuit filed against *Ha'olam Ha'ze* and its editors in 1969 which, on the face of it, appeared to be a ploy by Porush to win votes in an election year. The newspaper was charged with defamation of character for publishing a photomontage of a naked woman alongside a TV reporter in conversation with Porush. The picture was part of a satirical piece deriding the ban imposed by the Broadcasting Authority on interviews with political figures during the final days leading up to the elections. The naked woman was saying that in her condition, she was not banned from expressing her views on any issue.

Porush hired one of the country's top lawyers, Michael Caspi, who argued that the picture had dishonored his client and could damage his position as a distinguished member of the Knesset and political secretary of Agudat Israel. Ignoring the fact that the picture was obviously a photomontage, he claimed that it might be deduced that this ultra-orthodox man would agree to be interviewed by a naked woman. Porush demanded compensation of 240 thousand liras, a huge sum which, as *Ha'olam Ha'ze* understood, was meant to bankrupt the paper.

In anticipation of the legal battle, the weekly printed an apology for any distress it might have caused the MK. When Porush still did not withdraw his suit, the paper characterized it as a nuisance complaint filed for political reasons and asking for damages in excess of any normal standard. Zichroni argued that any damage had been aggravated by Porush's repeated reference to the lawsuit in the media, and that the juxtaposition of the ultra-orthodox leader and a naked woman was so far-fetched that nobody could take it as anything but satire. Its intention was not to vilify Porush, but to make a point about political censorship on television, which was in the public interest. The relations between a newspaper and the public made it incumbent upon it to publish such articles. If Porush was harmed in any way by the publication, no more than token compensation should be awarded him.

The affair soon came to involve more than a routine legal defense, turning into what was to become one of the most controversial cases relating to the power of the press in the history of the country. Porush rightly hoped that few Israelis would support the freedom of press of a newspaper many despised for its anti-establishment views, as well as for its penchant for adorning its back page with sensational and semi-pornographic materials. Yet for Avnery and Zichroni, this was not only a battle over freedom of speech, but a political struggle between secularism and clericalism. As part of the litigation, Zichroni submitted to the district court a questionnaire for Porush containing hundreds of items whose publication in *Ha'olam Ha'ze* revealed to the Israeli public the wholly different world in which the ultra-orthodox political circles, still held in respect by most secular Israelis, allegedly operated. In light of the fact that the newspaper was ordered to apologize later, it is hard to say how much of the information conveyed in the form of questions phrased in legalese was true, but the questions definitely raised a lot of eyebrows at the time.

The questions were designed to prove that the feature about Porush could not have caused him any damage. Among other things, he was asked if it was true that after filing his complaint, he was praised in an Agudat Israel newspaper for his impressive visit to South Africa. He was then asked whether the article had been written by him, and if not, by whom, thereby allegedly exposing the journalistic practices of the religious parties' press (and perhaps that of other political parties as well). Another swipe was taken at Porush, addressed in public as "rabbi," by the question asking whether it was true that he called himself "rabbi" and whether he had ever been officially granted that title. From the numerous questions on this subject, based on information that Zichroni apparently got from Porush's political rivals in religious circles, the reader was led to understand that he had been expelled from yeshiva because of some prank that had sullied the name of the legendary Rabbi Cook, and that even within his own political sets there had already been objections to his use of the title "rabbi."

Most of the questions concerned inappropriate fundraising practices for party institutions, practices that the public was quite unaware of at the time. The questionnaire hinted at tax evasion, as well as at the possibility that the fundraisers received a percentage of the amounts they collected. By presenting these allegations in the form of innocent questions, the newspaper could not be accused of libel, even if some of the information it had gathered contained inaccuracies. The phrasing, however, did not detract from the public responsibility the paper had undertaken. *Ha'olam Ha'ze* tied Porush to activities nobody had ever attributed to ultra-orthodox circles. By way of illustration, here is one set of questions posed by the questionnaire:

> Have you ever visited Las Vegas?
> Is it true you raised money in Las Vegas?
> Is it true you accepted donations from gamblers?
> Is it true you visited gambling casinos there?
> Is it true you accepted donations in gambling casinos?
> Is it true the gamblers there asked for your blessing as a "rabbi"?
> Did you grant blessings to the donors in Las Vegas?
> Have you also visited gambling casinos outside of Las Vegas?
> Have you asked for donations from gamblers in other parts of the world?
> If so—where?
> Is it true you once accepted a donation from the actor–singer Frank Sinatra?
> If you have accepted donations from Frank Sinatra:
>
> > i. What was the purpose of his donation?
> > ii. What was the amount of his donation/s?
> > iii. Where were his donations conveyed by you?
> > iv. In what way were his donations conveyed?
>
> Are you aware that in the United States, Las Vegas is considered a town of lawlessness and gambling?

In this affair, as in many others, *Ha'olam Ha'ze* took it upon itself to change the face of Israeli society by debunking its central myths. In this instance, for example, a respected ultra-orthodox politician who enjoyed the halo of a rabbi was presented with a questionnaire that hinted not only at inappropriate behavior on the public level, but at hypocrisy on the personal level as well. He was asked about business relations with a doctor who performed abortions, about the mysterious circumstances surrounding the death of his first wife, about his acquaintance with his second wife while his first wife was still alive, etc. *Ha'olam Ha'ze* similarly slaughtered many other sacred cows. It depicted the revered Ben-Gurion as a dictator, and labeled the security services "the apparatus of darkness." It exposed local political bosses who operated under the umbrella of the

Labor movement as bullies running Tammany Hall-like political machines, and cooperated with the lawyer Shmuel Tamir, who had bashed the entire Mapai establishment in the Kasztner trial.

Israel Kasztner, the spokesman for the Ministry of Commerce and Industry, had been a Jewish official in Hungary during World War II, and was accused in a pamphlet written by a man named Malkiel Gruenwald of collaborating with the Nazis. Kasztner sued. Tamir, an ambitious young attorney associated with the right-wing circles that despised the Labor establishment, took on Gruenwald's case and turned Kasztner's libel suit into one of the most sensational trials in Israeli history. The sensationalism was fanned by the cooperation between Tamir and *Ha'olam Ha'ze*, which bombarded the country with endless headlines denouncing Kasztner. When Kasztner was assassinated, Avnery and Tamir were seen to have incited the frenzy that led to the murder. Obviously, such uses—or perhaps we should say abuses—of the power of the press were no longer the work of "street aliens" operating on the fringes of society. What we have here is the use of a powerful tool in the service of "political perfectionism," a term whose meaning and implications will become clear below.

In 1962, the Ministry of Justice framed the draft of an anti-defamation bill which was enacted several years later. According to this bill, any individual, including a journalist, who destroyed another person's reputation and could not prove the truth of their allegations was subject to severe punishment. From the beginning, *Ha'olam Ha'ze* perceived itself to be the direct target of the law. Indeed, Avnery said so explicitly. If previously the political establishment had tried to silence his paper by breaking it financially, such as by forbidding public sector entities to take out ads, the anti-defamation law was seen as a frontal attack. "They threw bombs and broke our bones," Avnery wrote. "They imposed on us an economic boycott and tried to suffocate us by administrative means. They tried to block us from getting to sources of information, arrested the editors, and kidnapped the chief correspondent. But they always discovered that truth will win out. . . . Now the establishment is preparing for its final battle against the truth-sayers. They are trying to harness the wagon of justice to their terrorist cart, and impose on Israel's judges the implementation of the anti-defamation act—a fascist law inspired by Dov Yosef [then Minister of Justice] and Juan Peron."[1]

In order to combat the law and evade its consequences for the newspaper's freedom of speech, Avnery made the strategic decision to run for election to the Knesset. As an MK, he would be immune from prosecution. In the elections of 1965, a movement calling itself "Ha'olam Ha'ze–New Force" (NF), headed by Avnery, won one seat in the Knesset. Zichroni, who had also been on the slate, served as Avnery's parliamentary aide, and was soon dubbed "the 121st Knesset member" because of his extreme visibility in the house. In the next elections in 1969, NF won two seats and hammered out a rotation agreement whereby Shalom Cohen would be the party's second MK for the first half of the term, after which he would turn his seat over to Zichroni. When the time for the switchover came, Cohen refused to budge, causing a serious rift in the small party. Nevertheless, it was mainly the team of Avnery and Zichroni who conducted the parliamentary activity of NF during the eight years of its existence.

NF's visibility in the Knesset is particularly interesting because it was way out of proportion for its small size—one Knesset member out of 120 in the first term (1965–1969), and two in the second (1969–1973). For eight years, NF proposed legislation, posed queries, challenged rules, changed procedures, introduced innovations, sparked anger, raised public awareness, and contributed to the gradual transformation of the Knesset from a forum controlled by and legitimizing the policies of ruling coalitions to an arena of wide-ranging political discourse.

Students of Israeli politics were confounded by NF because it did not lend itself to any traditional classification on Israel's "political map." Attempts to portray it in terms such as "left of center but anti-Communist"[2] could hardly capture its essence. It was neither left-wing nor right-wing, neither authoritarian nor democratic, neither elitist nor populist, neither liberal nor radical. Although it was clear that the party represented a new phase in Israeli politics long before the term "new politics" was coined, there were no means available for analyzing its unique features and resolving its apparent contradictions: a peace agenda together with an excessive use of militaristic rhetoric; anti-poverty campaigns alongside support of the free market; an empathy for underprivileged sectors and a touch of elitism; and most particularly, anti-establishment attitudes and an unprecedented devotion to democratic and parliamentary procedures.

The scholarly literature thus referred mainly to episodic aspects of the party's activities, and refrained from any attempt to analyze its goals, strategies, and political role. NF was explained away as the outgrowth of Avnery's personal ambitions, and its ideology as "a personal and idiosyncratic amalgam of libertarianism, anti-corruption crusades, and a pro-Palestinian rights perspective."[3] Small parties, it was commonly agreed, "lend local color (and at times comic relief) to Knesset deliberations, but their political role is insignificant."[4]

First and foremost, however, NF was an "anti-system" party, a concept which may require some explanation. In a classic article on Germany, Otto Kirchheimer distinguishes between two forms of opposition, the "loyal opposition," which pursues its goals in harmony with the constitutional requirements of a given system, and the "opposition of principle," which exhibits "the desire for a degree of goal displacement incompatible with the constitutional requirements of a given system."[5] This distinction was called for by the European experience, in which fascist parties on the extreme right and communist parties on the extreme left, as well as some regional separatist parties, played the parliamentary game with the aim of destroying parliamentarism itself. Thus the "opposition of principle" consisted of those parties and movements whose challenge to the political system exceeded conventional goal differences and threatened the very existence of the system.

This, of course, raises the question how one measures such a threat. While principled opposition refers to the transformative nature of a party's ideology, as Gordon Smith explains, there may be difficulties in agreeing on just what that ideology is, especially when it consists of a hazy collection of contradictory ideas. There may also be a genuine ambivalence as to the degree to which a party aims to abolish the existing political institutions and the socioeconomic system, or whether it is only interested in replacing one or the other.[6]

The concept of an "anti-system party" was designed to provide a partial solution to these analytical problems by focusing not on an opposition party's ideology, but on its success in undermining the legitimacy of the regime it opposes, on its "delegitimizing impact."[7] This, however, is an overly demanding measure. The Nazi party was no less "anti-system" before the crisis it triggered than after it. Moreover, the measure may reflect the initial strength of the regime as much as the nature of the anti-system party. Consequently, it is generally agreed that "the term 'anti-system' is one of the less satisfactory ways of classifying parties."[8]

Nonetheless, the term could not be abandoned, as political reality, especially in the 1980s, gave rise to an increasing number of political parties that played the democratic game while pursuing transformative goals and strategies aimed at encouraging a crisis of legitimacy. In the European context, this was seen as no less than a "silent counter-revolution,"[9] but the phenomenon exceeds the boundaries of Europe. In his discussion of the "anti-political-establishment parties" of the 1980s, Andreas Schedler lists an array of parties ranging from Jean Marie Le Pen's Front National in France and Franz Schonhuber's Republikaner in Germany, to Preston Manning's Reform Party in Canada and Ross Perot's United We Stand America in the U.S., all characterized by a populist rhetoric that presents the party as champion of the people in their struggle against the ruling elites.

This lumping together of fascist, populist, and radical parties suggests that the "anti-system" category, whatever name we give it, may be too broad, but it also brings to light the common denominator that indicates the direction for its refinement—the disgust with politics expressed by anti-system parties. This is the same attitude detected many years ago by Bernard Crick among what he called "non-political conservatives," "a-political liberals," and "anti-political socialists."[10] In its updated version, the attitude is manifested by political parties that take an active part in the political process in pursuit of a wide variety of goals whose achievement would entail the demise of politics itself. As Schedler states: "In a truly anti-political perspective, politics would be replaced by operating principles of other societal spheres of action, for instance, by divine commandments ('religious anti-politics'), by the invisible hand of the market ('liberal anti-politics'), by the unitary and self-evident will of the people ('communitarian anti-politics'), or by science, technology or administration ('technocratic anti-politics')."[11]

NF represented a refined version of the "anti-system party" model. Its parliamentary conduct reveals not only what an anti-system party takes a stand against, but also what it stands for. NF acted on behalf of an imaginary, rather than a real, civil society. As noted in the introduction, the term "civil society" refers to the plurality of social groups operating in relative autonomy from the state. Political parties have traditionally been classified by the social groups they represent. The group NF catered to, however, was an imagined one; it was committed primarily to the memory of Avnery's fallen comrades in the War of Independence. In everything it said and did, the party sought the standard of perfection worthy of what

Mosse has labeled "fallen soldiers,"[12] those who gave their life for the establishment of the state. And nothing fell shorter of that standard than politics-as-usual, with its wheeling and dealing, coalition alliances, party intrigues, and parliamentary debates, all of which NF both participated in and expressed revulsion for.

NF's unique political behavior may thus be labeled "political perfectionism." The idea of perfectionism, the attempt to maximize human virtues,[13] has been applied to politics since Aristotle, who believed that politics did not encompass all spheres of life, and thus ought to include provisions for the enhancement of inherently valuable human qualities. But such provisions have become problematic in modern societies where the intrinsic value of human qualities is less clear, and even when there is a consensus on the subject, it cannot easily be incorporated as a political principle. In A Theory of Justice, for example, John Rawls does not ignore the need "to maximize the achievement of human excellence in art, science and culture,"[14] but finds no room for a perfectionist principle in his theory, which regards a just society as one that approximates the consent of hypothetical individuals negotiating behind a veil of ignorance, that is, without knowledge of their initial status in the negotiations. These individuals may agree on an index of primary virtues as a basis of interpersonal comparisons, but not on the restrictions on their liberty which derive from that index. According to Rawls: "While justice as fairness allows that in a well-ordered society the values of excellence are recognized, the human perfections are to be pursued within the limits of the principle of free association."[15]

The difficulty of incorporating standards of perfection into modern democratic theory has not prevented political parties with perfectionist agendas from pursuing them in democratic regimes to the extent that they jeopardize the political principles underlying those regimes. In his discussion of "perfectionism and utopia," Sartori associates the perfectionism of such parties with "bad idealism,"[16] the flip side of "bad realism,"[17] i.e., the perception that politics involves nothing but force, fraud, and the ruthless wielding of power. Like the bad realist who relates to power in its most literal form, "the perfectionist is precisely someone who takes ideals for something they are not, who pays little attention to the necessary *declage* between ideals and practice and, by the same token, who does not know how to turn, or how to apply, prescriptions to reality. The perfectionist characteristically attends to the maximization of ideals—his foot is always on the accelerator—without being in control of the ideals that he propounds."[18] Sartori warns that we endlessly hear talk of ideals being betrayed, but since ideals are, by definition, destined not to be realized, the perfectionist will always and easily find anybody else to be a traitor to ideals. Yet by the same token, the perfectionist, too, is a traitor to ideals: "By sticking to their letter, the perfectionist betrays their intent. Ideals can be betrayed in many ways, and the most insidious one consists of ignoring that the meaning-function of ideals changes as their real-world environment changes. There are not only many ways of betraying ideals, but also of being betrayed by ideals. One of them, and probably the surest one, is the way of the perfectionist."[19]

The saga of NF almost precisely fits this theoretical model in the way it set perfectionist goals, lost track of the sense of the impossible when choosing strategies, and oriented its political behavior toward the excessive realization of democratic ideals. Let us begin with the goals, as spelled out quite clearly in Avnery's autobiography:

"My name is Biblical, Uri, meaning light. Avner, or Abner, was the field marshal of King David, a figure I always liked. I was not born with this name. I gave it to myself. Like most of my age group in what was then Palestine, I changed my name immediately on reaching age eighteen. With this one act we declared our independence from our past; we broke with it irrevocably. The Jewish diaspora, the world of our parents, their culture and their background—we wanted nothing more to do with. We were a new race, a new people, born the day we set foot on the soil of Palestine. We were Hebrews, rather than Jews; our new Hebrew names proclaimed this."[20]

These words are symptomatic of the repeated attempt by the founder of NF to replace the real with the imagined. The most striking feature of the excerpt is the fact that Avnery's real name, Helmut Oystermann, is never mentioned. Avnery was born in 1923 to a Jewish middle-class family in Germany that immigrated to Palestine after Hitler's rise to power. Yet like other members of his generation, he invented a new identity for himself, the identity of a "new Hebrew," the son of a nation whose origins could be traced back to the ancient Middle East, and was thus free of the detritus of 2,000 years of Jewish exile. Since childhood, Avnery had been involved in diminutive political groups that carried this torch and "felt we were the wave of the future, the authentic new voice of Hebrew youth."[21] While the search for a new identity was common in pre-state Israel, and was sanctioned by none other than the country's founder David Ben-Gurion, Avnery's version of the new Hebrew nation was unique in that at its core it included provisions for the peaceful coexistence of Jews and Arabs in Palestine.

In October 1947, one month before the United Nations resolution partitioning Palestine between Jews and Arabs, young Avnery published a pamphlet entitled "War or Peace in the Semitic Region." It was described as the statement of Hebrew youth, which found itself on the eve of a terrible war wrought by the failings of the older generation. Avnery objected to the partition of Palestine, claiming that an independent Jewish state in the region would eventually become a regional superpower that sought to control the area economically and militarily. Such Jewish imperialism would only strengthen Arab nationalism, unacknowledged by the framers of Jewish nationalism who had grown up in the ghettos of Europe as that which was won by the sword could not be preserved. His solution: a "Semitic" national movement which would prevail over the narrow-minded attitudes of Jewish and Arab nationalists alike, and would provide a framework for cultural, political, and historical cooperation for the peoples in the Fertile Crescent, specifically Iraq, Syria, Lebanon, and Palestine.

The pamphlet, which explained in detail the process by which the new Semitic nationality would be formed (as part of the creation of a united East Asia led by Nehru's India), stressed the importance of cultural factors in the history of nations, an approach reminiscent of Herder's nationalism. It all but called upon both Jews and Arabs to give up their history for the sake of a new historical model in which they would become the descendants of the glorious nations that had lived in the region in ancient times, like the Assyrians and Babylonians. Thus, while the establishment of an independent Jewish state in Palestine was viewed as contrary to the geopolitical logic of the region, the envisioned Semitic community was not.

Shortly after publication of the pamphlet, the UN General Assembly passed the partition resolution, and Avnery found himself a soldier in Israel's War of Independence. His service in an elite unit known as "Samson's Foxes," which he referred to in his writings time and again, was undoubtedly the formative experience of his life. He never lost the sense of being betrayed by the older generation. His entire political career may be seen to be anchored in the mind of the soldier compelled to fight for a state whose leadership had diminished it. The recurrent motif in his war diaries, in the several books he wrote, and in the hundreds of articles he published as editor of *Ha'olam Ha'ze*, was the disparity between the pure desires of young soldiers "in the field, around campfires and between cactus hedges,"[22] and the corrupt state emerging on the home front, with its failure to ensure the separation of religion and state, its dependence on foreign aid, its party machines, its spoils system, and its helplessness to resolve the Arab-Israeli conflict.

On a variety of occasions, including in the speech in 1965 in which he announced the founding of NF, Avnery recalled how, as an injured combatant in a military hospital in 1948, a nameless soldier, his face covered in bandages, lay dying beside him throughout the night. As he stated in that speech:

> When in the morning I saw his dead body in the bed across from me, I made a vow to myself. I swore that if I came out of that room alive, if I regained my strength, I would devote the rest of my life to two goals. The first: that there would be no more war, that youngsters like him would no longer have to go to the killing fields, that we would no longer have to kill and be killed for the survival of our state. The second goal: to fight for the character of the state, so that the state which was established at such a high price would be deserving of this sacrifice. That it be pure, clean, and free, seeking justice and truth.[23]

Avnery's vow to a dead soldier in a military hospital in 1948 was instated as part of NF's program, and affected every move it made. This was not a one-man party pursuing contradictory goals, but a well-defined operation, often compared by its leaders to a commando raid, aimed at purifying the political system. As Avnery promised in his speech, NF would not be just another party of distinguished politicians drinking tea in the Knesset cafeteria, but a "political commando."[24]

Israeli scholars, misled by the small size of the party, have failed to recognize its unique features. This was an anti-system party which, unlike the European fascism that preceded it, was committed to democracy, and unlike the Greens who were to follow, had a patriotic agenda. The first clause in the party's program pledged allegiance to the sovereignty, security, and independence of the state, and called for the reinforcement of the

Israeli Defense Forces. As part of its patriotic aims, the party promised to unify the citizenry in an open democratic struggle to take over the government and build a perfect regime whose parameters seemed, at times, to be derived from pesticide advertisements. NF sought the "fundamental purification" of the government machine, the "dismantling" of compulsory institutions, the "removal" of political parties from pubic sector activity, and a fierce battle to "clear out" corruption.

The aphorism that history is a series of impossibilities made possible is heard quite commonly in Israel, whose leaders have often portrayed the country as a cemetery of realized utopias. Thus, NF's pledge to clean up an entire country with one Knesset member in the first term and two in the second does not seem extraordinary in the cultural context in which it was offered. Even in that context, however, NF represented an extreme attempt to combine utopia and politics. The party was utopian in the fullest sense as defined by Sartori—it imagined an "impossible reality" with the purpose of realizing it, and, most importantly, that reality was to be realized solely by political means. The party leadership, however far-reaching its goals and however fierce its criticism of "politics-as-usual," was always intensely involved in Israeli power politics. As Avnery reports in his autobiography, from an early age "I knew I would devote my life to politics, that compared to politics everything else was unimportant, wasteful. I was going to teach myself the things one must know to be effective in politics—history, military science, psychology, economics, social affairs."[25]

In other words, NF's lack of a sense of the impossible is reflected not in its use of extraordinary political strategies, but rather in its use of very ordinary ones. This is where Zichroni came in. Although he did not display much interest in Avnery's ideology—and as a conscientious objector he definitely did not share in NF's patriotic stance—he turned NF into a model party in a country lacking a parliamentary tradition, and he did so with the specific aim of demonstrating the lack of such a tradition. This goal underlay a large part of NF's activities as an anti-system party. Its grand vision was channeled into hundreds of legislative proposals, parliamentary queries, speeches, and press releases penned by Zichroni. He introduced modern methods into a dormant parliament, such as institutionalizing his own role as a professional parliamentary aide. Furthermore, he was extremely adept at utilizing the procedural tools available to small parties in parliamentary systems in order to forestall attempts to undermine NF's power, as well as to make an anti-system point.

To cite one example, immediately after the announcement of Uri Avnery's election to the Knesset in 1965, the house committee issued regulations which appeared to be designed to deny a one-member party the full status of a parliamentary faction. Had this succeeded, NF would have been deprived of important rights, such as the right to initiate no-confidence motions. Zichroni prepared a memo demonstrating the undemocratic nature of such procedural decisions, and Avnery was recognized as a faction. This was the beginning of an ongoing battle in which NF often faced off against the entire Knesset, and in which both sides sharpened their parliamentary tools to a fine edge. Thus somewhat paradoxically, the presence of an anti-system party in the Knesset strengthened, rather than weakened, Israeli parliamentarism, as the procedural battles it sparked gave rise to numerous procedural precedents, such as the regulation of the number of legislative proposals in proportion to party size. NF showed the way for small parties in the years to come to assert themselves despite their size. For example, it chose to abstain on many votes, as the Knesset codex grants extra time for members to explain the rationale for their abstention. Avnery, who made it a point to participate in all Knesset sessions, soon became the most visible member of the house.

A review of the many bills framed by Zichroni and placed on the table by Avnery and Cohen during those eight years reveals an amazing array of issues: NF fought corruption and economic protectionism, called for separation of religion and state, proposed long-term national planning, raised civil rights issues, demanded the abolition of discriminatory laws against Israeli Arabs, fought for freedom of the press, initiated policies encouraging the construction of rental housing, worker mobility, and the establishment of a central fire-fighting force, introduced diplomatic initiatives, and advanced the cause of underprivileged families, prisoners, pregnant women, reserve soldiers, war widows, gays, hospital patients, school children, drivers at intersections, sports fans, etc., etc. This prolific parliamentary record encouraged a number of Avnery's colleagues in the Knesset to mock him as a utopian tamed by his entry into the practical world. Indeed it seemed that way at times, such as when the party reversed a previous decision not to accept the government funding it was entitled to as a Knesset faction. Nevertheless, the use of routine parliamentary strategies did not alter the anti-system nature of the party, as it never ceased to cater to an imaginary, rather than a real, civil society.

This is not to say that Israel suffered from a shortage of underprivileged families, minorities plagued by discrimination, or women denied the right to an abortion by a paternalistic religious establishment. But NF had never made a serious effort to establish a firm political base within these groups. Its legislative initiatives pointed a finger at the evils of a corrupt state in a desire only to reform it. In this sense, its approach always remained Platonic; whereas Aristotle recognized the need for a balance between the state and the social groups that compose it, Plato sought political perfection. The distinction between the real and the imaginary social group the party professed to represent was not always clear. When NF proposed a bill obliging drivers to pick up soldier hitchhikers, for example, there was obviously a group that could benefit from it—soldiers thumbing for a ride. Nonetheless, the suggestion was not only merely symbolic, as no democratic society could be expected to enact a law requiring drivers to give anyone a ride, but actually had little to do with these potential beneficiaries. Like most initiatives taken by NF, it was offered on behalf of an abstract group, "the men and women soldiers of the IDF," and justified by the debt of honor Avnery owed, as he admitted upon presentation of the bill, to "comrades in the past, the present, and the future."[26]

Crick, Sartori, and others who have made us aware of the dangers posed to democracy by its "friends," would be hard put to find a better illustration than NF. It constituted a clear case of a party upholding the democratic ideal to such an extent that it threatened to undermine it. The most striking example was the stubborn presence of Uri Avnery in every single parliamentary session, in a potent demonstration of the negligence of those who were absent. The photograph of the bearded, lonely man sitting for long hours in an empty chamber listening to clearly boring speeches, while his colleagues refrained from fulfilling the duty for which they had been elected, became one of the most effective images ever created in Israeli journalism. Not only did it appear time and again in Avnery's own newspaper, where he informed his (mainly young) readership on a weekly basis of the faults he discovered in their representative assembly, but it was gradually captured by the mainstream media and became a major factor in the emergence of an anti-Knesset attitude.

The argument that membership in the Knesset involved more than mere presence in the plenum chamber could not compete with the message that the Knesset was a sick, rotten, and corrupt body, as Zichroni states explicitly in his book, *1 against 119*. It was a message reiterated time and again in NF rhetoric which, like the image itself, exposed the shortcomings of democracy by adhering to democratic procedure. Avnery, for example, sometimes prefaced his parliamentary speeches with a paraphrase of the customary words: "Mr. Chairman, Members of Knesset," beginning instead with "Mr. Chairman, empty Knesset." Similarly, he proposed a series of bills, spawned in Zichroni's inventive mind, that exposed the Knesset's flaws, such as the one that required the presence of a quorum of Knesset members in every session, justified by the need to restore the Knesset's lost dignity. Avnery claimed that as a Knesset member who had not missed a single session, he actually sympathized with those who did not attend, because sitting in the empty chamber engendered a terrible feeling of frustration, waste, and hollowness.

Another remarkable example of the dialectical process of using democratic means to expose the imperfections of democracy was a bill framed by Zichroni in February 1968 which called for the establishment of a House of Lords to accommodate the current leaders of the State of Israel. The country's entire senior leadership was defined as a bottleneck impeding the natural life-cycle of generation change that was barricading itself inside the institutions it had created. The bill, couched in all the formal phrasing demanded of legislative proposals in modern democracies, explained the reluctance of the leaders to step aside in terms of the inevitable void that would gape open in their lives, as they lacked any interest in the arts or sports, making partisan politics the only element of their personality. The Knesset members (whose average age at the time was 58) were depicted as elderly people who were gradually losing their physical energy and capacity to adapt to changing circumstances.

However amusing this proposal may appear, its timing was not incidental. A few months earlier, in May 1967, as a result of the strategic danger perceived on the eve of the Six Day War, a deep political crisis had erupted in Israel. Under severe public pressure, the ruling Labor Party was forced to form a national unity government and transfer the security portfolio held by Prime Minister and Labor leader Levy Eshkol to former chief of staff Moshe Dayan. Israel's victory in the Six Day War was largely attributed to Dayan, who became a mythological figure with unprecedented power. Although NF had not supported many of Dayan's policies, its House of Lords suggestion was a stage in the creation of a mythology that denigrated the country's elected leadership and political institutions while glorifying fifty-two-year-old Dayan as the champion of the imagined community of Israel's "youth." And although the democratic system proved itself quite viable in the face of the Dayan myth, and he himself turned out to be a rather tame political actor, it is hard not to concur with the warning voiced by a number of senior politicians at the time—clean-up operations of the kind conducted by NF may result not in a perfect democracy, but in a loss of democracy. For democracy, as most of us know, cannot survive the many challenges threatening it without true friends who are willing to accept its imperfections.

NF's perfectionism jeopardized not only democracy, but the party itself, which was badly damaged by the gap between its alleged purity and the need to survive in the political arena. This was felt especially when the rotation agreement was not honored in 1971. It is hard to say what motivated Shalom Cohen to refuse to yield his seat to Zichroni. It may have been some sort of rebellion on his part. As a Sephardic Jew, Cohen may have been influenced by the rise of the Israeli "Black Panthers," who gave voice to the distress of Sephardic Jews in the country, and have come to see his life in the shadow of Avnery in the same terms. Whatever Cohen's reason, newspaper headlines from 1971 reveal the embittered battle over the unfulfilled rotation agreement, turning NF into a party wallowing in the very political mud it had always pretended to eschew. The fact that it conducted itself like any other party is not surprising; it is one thing to attack the political system in the name of "fallen soldiers," but it is another thing entirely to sustain a political party. One way to avoid ugly political infighting is through adherence to procedure, but the Israeli political system has never been known for honoring procedure. The rotation agreement of 1969 was part and parcel of that political culture; it was a pragmatic arrangement designed to solve the problem of how to enable three people to occupy two seats in the Knesset. The absence of a formal rule providing for this sort of rotation made it easy for Cohen to refuse to yield his seat to Zichroni. The result was a split in the small party, with

Cohen pursuing a failed political career in association with the Black Panthers, while Avnery and Zichroni prepared for the next elections in 1973.

This time Avnery ran as the self-proclaimed leader of the Israeli peace camp. In an article published in *Ha'aretz* in 1970, he called on all the political organizations, movements, groups, and individuals who were opposed to the Israeli occupation of Arab territories in the Six Day War of 1967, and who supported the establishment of an independent Palestinian state, to join forces in founding a political party to be known as MERI (both an acronym of the Hebrew name "Israeli Radical Party" and a word meaning "rebellion"). Avnery again recycled the story of the wounded soldier in 1948, and spoke of a great spontaneous movement that would constitute the Israeli "peace camp" and change the face of the region. With Avnery as number one on the slate and Zichroni as number two, MERI did not win even one seat in the Knesset in the elections of 1973.

The elections were held shortly after the Yom Kippur War, which has been justifiably portrayed as an "earthquake" that rocked the nation. In October 1973, Egypt and Syria launched a surprise attack which enabled them to establish a stronghold in the occupied territories in the Sinai Peninsula and the Golan Heights, and to inflict thousands of casualties on Israeli soldiers, along with the total demoralization of the country. The only thing that appeared to be unaffected by the war were the patterns of political behavior. Zichroni spent long hours fighting off attempts by the ruling Labor Party to gain an electoral advantage by employing such stratagems as exploiting the opportunities they enjoyed as government officials for partisan propaganda. He claimed, for example, that the Prime Minister and the Minister of Defense were delivering campaign speeches to soldiers in military camps.

The brutal war, in which the army was caught off-guard, the political leadership was left helpless, and the grand strategy of holding on to the vast territories conquered in 1967 was proven to be an illusion, did not lead to the unification of the diverse political movements that comprised Avnery's virtual "peace camp." In the 1973 elections, MERI had to compete against two other peace parties, Moked, consisting mainly of ex-Communists, which won one seat in the Knesset, and the Civil Rights Movement, which won three seats. Although the latter party, headed by attorney Shulamit Aloni, was more adept than MERI in responding to the personal distress of many Israelis as a result of the Yom Kippur War, which may explain its relative success, the elections bore out what NF had demonstrated during its entire eight years in parliament—that the peace camp did not have a strong foothold in Israeli society. This is not to say that Israelis did not wish to live in peace, but that the civil society did not support its peace activists. The middle-class had grown enormously after the Six Day War, when the Israeli economy was flooded with cheap Arab labor, practically eliminating the Jewish working class. These egg merchants, cosmetics dealers, cinema owners, clerks, teachers, and the like wanted peace, but they also wanted to travel in the occupied territories, were afraid of Palestinian terrorism, and admired Moshe Dayan. Avnery wrote his article about the glorious peace camp waiting to be united at a time when a coalition between the civil circles and the right was gradually taking shape. The political alliance between the Liberal Party representing the civil circles and Menachem Begin's right-wing Herut party, which in 1973 was reconstituted as the Likud, now became the most powerful political factor in Israeli politics, combining as it did the fears of the civil society with the determination of the ultra-nationalists.

Even this fundamental socio-political change did not deter Avnery and other members of the peace camp from continuing to pursue perfectionist solutions to the Israeli–Palestinian conflict. Several hundred intelligent, well-meaning people would meet, debate, demonstrate, issue statements, found parties, and argue with each other in a manner more suitable to the "street aliens" of the 1950s and 1960s than to the political reality of the 1970s. While the Israeli public was being persuaded by right-wing politicians that an independent Palestinian state would constitute a security risk to the country, the left-wingers were fighting tooth and nail with one another over the intricate details of that imagined state. The Israeli peace camp in the 1970s had a compelling agenda, arguing that without peace a war between Israel and the Arab world would break out every few years; that the Soviet Union might intervene on the side of the Arabs in that war; that Israel would become more and more dependent on the United States; that its economy could not withstand a prolonged crisis in the region; that security could be achieved only in conditions of peace; and that peace required recognition of the legitimate right of the Palestinians to a state of their own within the pre-1967 borders.

The problem was that their program had no disciples, and rather than appealing to the public, the peace camp remained engulfed in its own terminological quagmires and marginal political activity. Zichroni understood this quite clearly. Since the days of his obstinate stand as a conscientious objector, he had matured in many ways. During the standoff in May 1967 that had preceded the Six Day War, with the State of Israel threatened by attack from Egypt, he wrote to Prime Minister Eshkol, admitting that under the new circumstances he saw no choice other than to serve in the army. He received a warm reply from the prime minister and was recruited as a military defense attorney, and later served as an army social worker. Although he continued to assist Avnery in his political ventures, most notably in establishing yet another peace party called Sheli, he now distanced himself more and more from political activity and began to focus on his legal career, where his primary skill and motivation as a champion of civil rights would come to bear.

Notes

1. *Ha'olam Ha'ze*, October 27, 1965, 16.

2. Don Peretz, *The Government and Politics of Israel* (Boulder, Colo.: Westview, 1983), 104.

3. Rael Jean Isaac, *Party and Politics in Israel: Three Visions of a Jewish State* (New York: Longman, 1981), 199.

4. Asher Arian, *Politics in Israel: The Second Generation* (Chatham, N.J.: Chatham House, 1989).

5. Otto Kirchheimer, "Germany: The Vanishing Opposition," in *Political Oppositions in Western Democracies*, ed. Robert A. Dahl (New Haven, Conn.: Yale University Press, 1966), 237.

6. Gordon Smith, "Party and Protest: The Two Faces of Opposition in Western Europe," in *Opposition in Western Europe*, ed. Eva Kolinsky (London: Croom Helm, 1987).

7. Giovanni Sartori, *Parties and Party Systems: A Framework for Analysis* (Cambridge: Cambridge University Press, 1976), 132–33.

8. Smith, "Party and Protest," 59.

9. Piero Ignazi, "The Silent Counter-Revolution: Hypotheses on the Emergence of Extreme Right-Wing Parties in Europe," *European Journal of Political Research* 22 (July 1992): 3.

10. Bernard Crick, *In Defence of Politics* (London: Weidenfeld and Nicolson, 1962).

11. Andreas Schedler, "Anti-Political Establishment Parties," *Party Politics 2* (July 1996): 293.

12. George L. Mosse, *Fallen Soldiers: Reshaping the Memory of the World Wars* (New York: Oxford University Press, 1990).

13. Thomas Hurka, *Perfectionism* (New York: Oxford University Press, 1993); George Sher, *Beyond Neutrality: Perfectionism and Politics* (Cambridge: Cambridge University Press, 1997).

14. John Rawls, *A Theory of Justice* (Oxford: Oxford University Press, 1973), 325.

15. Rawls, *A Theory of Justice*, 328.

16. Giovanni Sartori, *The Theory of Democracy Revisited* (Chatham, N.J.: Chatham House, 1987), 58.

17. Sartori, *Theory of Democracy Revisited*.

18. Sartori, *Theory of Democracy Revisited*, 59.

19. Sartori, *Theory of Democracy Revisited*, 72.

20. Uri Avnery, *Israel without Zionists: A Plea for Peace in the Middle East* (New York: Macmillan, 1968), 4.

21. Avnery, *Israel without Zionists*, 13.

22. Avnery, *Israel without Zionists*, 16.

23. *Ha'olam Ha'ze*, September 1, 1965.

24. *Ha'olam Ha'ze*, September 1, 1965.

25. Avnery, *Israel without Zionists*, 12–13.

26. Quoted in Amnon Zichroni, *1 against 119: Uri Avnery in the Knesset* (Tel Aviv: Daf Hadash, 1969).

CHAPTER SIX

Politics, Religion, and Civil Rights

In early 1974, Zichroni wrote to a friend in the United States:

> Giving some thought to expanding the business . . . want to open a
> branch office in the U.S. and be there three times a year. There is a
> large market for investments from Israel in the U.S., and the fact is that
> Americans often find it hard to get good legal advice. The office will of-
> fer them advice right on the spot.[1]

A sad mood can be detected between the lines of this simple letter. The
Yom Kippur War of 1973 had not ended in a resounding victory for either
side. The IDF now had to call up thousands of tired and reluctant reserves
to man the new army posts on the hostile cease-fire lines with Egypt and
Syria. The massive supplies airlifted from the U.S. to Israel during the war
resulted in increased political dependence. Secretary of State Henry
Kissinger was looking to achieve a separation of forces in the Middle East
while strengthening American influence in the area, and his hammerlock
on Israel was deeply resented. Protesters demonstrated against the failure
of the Labor Party leadership to foresee the surprise attack by Egypt and
Syria, and generals traded accusations over the failure of the IDF to maintain its traditional superiority. For their part, the leaders were busy preparing a defense for the commission of inquiry headed by Supreme Court Justice Shimon Agranat that was to investigate the events leading up to the
war and the conduct of the war itself.

Lacking a credible leadership, the country was in a mood of despair. Although the Labor Party, led by Golda Meir, was reelected in 1974, both
she and her defense minister, Moshe Dayan, were eventually forced to

resign. They were held largely responsible for the shortsighted policy that had enabled the surprise attack, despite the conclusions of the Agranat Commission which put the blame squarely on the shoulders of the military. Israel has still not recovered from the effects of the Yom Kippur War. When the father of the country, David Ben-Gurion, died that same year, with him died the belief that tiny little Israel could become "a light unto the nations." Israel lost not only its sense of security, but also the delusion that it could maintain norms of universal justice within the constraints of Middle Eastern politics. From that moment on, there has never again been a general consensus on any issue on the public agenda.

The Yom Kippur War reinforced messianic tendencies both on the right and on the left. This is a form of what is known as "political messianism,"[2] that is, the search for redemption outside the normal sphere of human activity. A quarter of a century of sovereign Jewish rule was insufficient to eradicate the messianic thinking that had characterized Jewish life in exile.[3] The period following the war saw the founding of Gush Emunim (literally: fraternity of the faithful), a religious-national movement that settled the occupied territories and whose rhetoric justified this action in terms of the divine promise of the Land of Israel to the Israelites in the Old Testament. The peace movements on the left, although claiming to represent a sober realism, developed a utopian notion of peace that sounded no less messianic. But messianic politics cannot solve concrete problems, nor does it encourage public consensus regarding the nature of their solution. Moreover, it diminishes civil values. In point of fact, the 1970s saw glorious triumphs for Israel: the Entebbe operation, in which Jews and Israelis held hostage by Palestinian terrorists in Uganda were rescued in a surprise military action, or the defeat of Moscow's legendary Z.S.K.A by Tel Aviv's Maccabi basketball team in the European Cup games, but these could not lift the general sense of frustration and helplessness pervading the country.

During this period, Zichroni was still accompanying Avnery along the winding paths by which political peace movements came and went. In 1977, he was active in establishing Sheli (the acronym of the Hebrew words for "peace and equality for Israel"), appearing eighth on the party slate and serving as a member of the party executive and chairman of the charter committee. These activities made him a familiar figure on the Israeli left. One of its leaders, Arie Eliav, described him in the following terms: "Zichroni was my greatest surprise in the Sheli executive. He is intelligent, perceptive and very easy to work with."[4] On the surface, Sheli seemed a fitting framework for Zichroni, with its program including a section on human and civil rights. It called for a written constitution, non-existent in Israel, that would define the limits of the government's power; the protection of individual freedom; the separation of powers; the separation of religion and state; national, ethnic, and gender equality; expansion of the Knesset's authority; the public financing of political parties so as to assure their autonomy; a smaller bureaucracy; the elimination of emergency laws; the abolition of the censorship of culture and art (carried out by a Ministry of the Interior committee that censored the theater and cinema); a prohibition on wiretapping; and so on. Nonetheless, Zichroni was not at ease within this framework, and shortly after the elections, in which Sheli won two seats in the Knesset, he proposed that it disband and join the Labor Party in order to further the cause of peace.

Zichroni's comrades on the left, who felt betrayed by this suggestion, dismissed it as evidence of his growing affinity for the establishment's "bear hug," but this explanation is unconvincing in light of his involvement in the 1970 and 1980s in activities that were decidedly "non-establishment." Instead, his inability to remain "one of the guys" seems to be more related to the political culture of the Israeli left. In the 15 years between 1965 and 1980 in which he was involved in one way or another in partisan activity, the Israeli peace camp failed to relate to the civil society. For years, Zichroni framed position papers, participated in meetings, and conducted negotiations on behalf of NF, MERI, and Sheli, to all of which some abstract concept of peace was invariably more meaningful than were the citizens of Israel. This is not to say that Zichroni was more "human" or "civil" than his left-wing colleagues. Rather, as a lawyer he had developed a sensitivity to the rights of the people who sought his help, while the political parties, even those with civil and human rights agendas in their platforms, never paid serious attention to the distress of individuals or social groups. For cultural and structural reasons, principally the lack of regional representatives in the Knesset, politicians were not motivated to consider the concerns of specific electorates, unless they could be used to garner short-lived political capital, particularly in response to media interest. Thus they would occasionally enter "an urgent legislative motion" in the matter of a hungry child interviewed the day before on the radio or the false arrest of some innocent citizen, but the many hours spent in party headquarters and coffee houses were devoted to what seemed to them more vital and pressing issues.

The lack of concern for the citizen was common to all parties on all sides of the political spectrum. The relative electoral success of Shulamit Aloni's Civil Rights Movement in 1974, which won three seats in the Knesset, and the stunning success of the Democratic Movement for Change (DMC) in 1977, which won fifteen, raised certain hopes. Yet even these parties soon realized the difficulty of pursuing their agendas when they either got mired down in the murky waters of coalition politics, as in the case of Dash, or became caught up in the endless conflicts and rifts within their own camp.

Although conflicts and rifts were not unique to the peace camp, they were particularly common there, largely as a result of its small electorate. When a group of good-intentioned, peace-loving people form a political party that has a chance of winning no more than two seats in the Knesset, conflict is to be expected. To demonstrate the dynamics involved, Sheli consisted of Moked headed by Meir Pa'il, the Independent Socialists led by Arie Eliav, MERI headed by Uri Avnery, the Black Panthers headed by Saadia Martziano, and the Independent Arabs led by Walid Tzadek. With five separate groups in the party, composing the slate of candidates to be presented to the voters required complex juggling. First, the order of the various factions had to be determined; it was decided that the Independent Socialists would come first, followed by Moked, MERI, the Black Panthers, and the Independent Arabs, in that order. It was then decided that each of the factions would arrange its candidates so that all number ones appeared first, all number twos second, and so on. The leaders of the groups were obviously the first on each list. The second in line for the various factions were Ruth Dayan (Moshe Dayan's ex-wife who was not involved in politics but was willing to lend her name to the party as a favor to her friend Arie Eliav) for the Independent Socialists, Ran Cohen for Moked, Amnon Zichroni for MERI, Michael Mimon for the Black Panthers, and prominent Jewish author A. B. Yehoshua, who appeared as number two for the Independent Arabs as a gesture of goodwill and coexistence.

With the slate finally readied, a picnic was organized in the Ben Shemen forest near Jerusalem to celebrate the "unity." But instead of enjoying the fresh air, the Sheli leaders found themselves holding an emergency meeting in under the trees, a meeting that was triggered by Moked's demand that Ran Cohen be allotted the sixth rather than seventh slot, despite the fact that they all knew that Sheli did not have the slightest chance of occupying any more than the two seats it ultimately won. After protracted negotiations, the political crisis was resolved when Ruth Dayan, who couldn't care less, agreed to switch places with Cohen. Zichroni's eighth slot remained unchanged, but his patience was wearing out.

Thus, toward the end of the third decade of his life, Zichroni began to devote less time to meetings with political activists under the trees and more to the protection of civil rights as an attorney in private practice. This was not a decision to abandon politics, but rather to play in a different court, that of civil society. The lawyer who takes on the political system on behalf of citizens whose concerns are not met (or not even considered) by the factions is no less of a political player than the party activist. Although Zichroni gradually gave up his involvement in the peace camp, he continued to play the game of politics, and to be concerned with the "allocation of values" in society by challenging the government in the High Court of Justice, defending the rights of prisoners, and serving as attorney for many citizens disenfranchised by the rabbinical courts. Starting in the late 1960s, much of his legal activity was devoted to preventing the domination of society by the state. Having studied at the feet of Stein and Avnery, he maintained this stance even after he had become one of the country's best-known lawyers.

When the Agranat Commission published its findings, Zichroni was traveling abroad. He expected a harsh response from the legal community. He felt it was wrong that while Chief of Staff David Elazar and Chief of the Southern Command Shmuel Gonen had been found guilty by the commission, the political leadership had not been held responsible. But Israel's legal community, notably the Bar Association, rarely raised its voice on public issues, and this was no exception. On his return to Israel, Zichroni printed an article in the ruling party's organ *Davar* in which he accused the Agranat Commission of being negligent in its application of legal protections. Although the findings of the public commission might involve serious criminal charges, he wrote, it had not guarded the rights of the people whose fate was in its hands. For instance, it had not issued an appropriate warning to Gonen that he might face criminal charges, an omission that would be out of place even in traffic court. Zichroni criticized the attempt by the commission, two of whose members were Supreme Court justices, to explain away the failure to issue letters of warning on the grounds that such letters were required only when the accused were not aware of the evidence brought before the tribunal. In a manner very unlike that of most lawyers and legal commentators, who tend to be exceedingly cautious in their criticism of judges, Zichroni called this argument "legal maneuvering,"[5] and warned that it was eroding the status of the court. He accused the commission of disregarding fundamental principles of justice, and concluded his article with a quotation from Franz Kafka's The Trial, which he would often use again in later years, regarding the impossible position of the defense in any trial in which it confronts a system that barely tolerates its existence.

The article reflected Zichroni's freedom from partisan thinking. Gonen, whose rights he defended, was a tough general who represented everything Zichroni condemned in political terms. Although a political motive might be found in that defense of Gonen indirectly implied an indictment of Minister of Defense Moshe Dayan, it would be more correct to see the article as the start of a trend in which Zichroni focused on civil rights, even those of a militaristic general. The Zichroni who defended Gonen was no longer a member of esoteric political leagues, but an attorney enjoying good relations with the political establishment, mainly as a result of his effective role as the "121st Knesset member." In fact, Zichroni had spoken with Minister of Justice Shimshon Shapira before his article appeared. Nevertheless, his new status, although it raised quite a few eyebrows among former political associates, did not detract from his independence of mind; he drew support neither from the government nor from the opposition, but from civil society. The more trustful the government became of him, the more he pursued his independent role as a bulwark against the hegemony of government over its citizens.

Over the years, Zichroni dealt with some very delicate matters, such as the defense of alleged spies, but he always remained in the public eye. He insisted that when there was no clear and present danger to justify secrecy, everything should be out in the open. In 1976, for example, he spoke out at a meeting of the Bar Association against a bill banning publication of the names of suspects before the filing of formal charges. Any ban on publication, he claimed, allowed the government a free hand. Only under ex-

traordinary circumstances should anything at all be banned from publication. He justified his stand in utilitarian terms. When the press is censored, information flows in the form of rumors that may be motivated by
people with malicious intent. Voicing his apprehension over allowing the
police to arrest a person without public oversight, he argued:

> It is hard to imagine what would happen if the police were exempt from
> public scrutiny. The possibility of arresting someone and interrogating
> him when he is humiliated, ripped from his normal environment and
> way of life, is obviously appealing to the police and more tempting than
> conducting long investigations that do not infringe on individual free-
> doms. Will policemen withstand such a temptation when they are free
> of the nagging press? That is hard for me to believe.[6]

Zichroni's office became the main recourse for people who needed protection from the authorities: those who had suffered police harassment;
the mentally ill who had been involuntarily committed; detainees who
had been the victims of police brutality; Bedouins claiming the right to
bear arms. Once, in the best nomadic tradition, a grateful Bedouin tribe
slaughtered a sheep in front of his law office, at that time located at 4
Ha-Gilbo'a Street, a tiny elegant boulevard in central Tel Aviv. In addition to his case work, Zichroni took part in forums such as the human
rights commission of the Bar Association, and often stated his opinion on
the rights of prisoners. In an article published in the *Prison Authority
Gazette*, for example, he claimed that prison is the true test of the protection of human rights, since these rights are not taken for granted there.
"The human rights of prisoners," he wrote, "and their treatment as equal
human beings, is our test as human beings, and the test of whether the society we live in is a humane and democratic one."[7]

No other subject enraged him more than religious coercion, one of the
most complex issues in Israeli life. Like many secular Israelis, Zichroni felt
that the State of Israel, conceived by its founders as a modern, secular democracy, was losing its raison d'être as a result of a series of political dealings that had led to the imposition of religious restraints on all citizens.
The proportional electoral system, the large number of political parties,
and the failure of any one faction to gain a majority of the popular vote
afforded the religious parties enormous power, disproportional to their
electoral strength. They were eager to join any coalition that would cater

to their demands, including some that could not be tolerated in a democratic society.

Particularly intolerable was the exemption from military service of students in religious seminaries (yeshivas). During the War of Independence, Ben-Gurion, in his capacity as Minister of Defense, was presented with a demand from religious leaders to exempt a few hundred such students, whose religious studies were perceived as contributing to the survival of the Jewish people in another sense, especially in light of the destruction of the yeshivas in Europe during the Holocaust. Ben-Gurion agreed. The arrangement remained in effect, however, even when the number of students exempt from military duty reached the tens of thousands. Its continued enforcement was a prerequisite of all coalition agreements, and the issue eventually became a major bone of contention, pitting those who fulfilled their civic duties against those who did not. Religious pressure also resulted in maintaining the "status quo agreement" signed between Ben-Gurion and religious leaders before the establishment of the state, stipulating, among other things, that public transportation would not operate in most parts of the country on the Sabbath. Rather than living in a free sovereign state distinct from the Jewish ghetto of the past, Zichroni and his generation felt they were living in a setting that lacked most of the features of such a state, i.e., separation of religion and state, protection of individual rights, and an absence of discrimination on the basis of race, nationality, gender, or religion. The infringement of individual rights and discriminatory policies stemmed from the control of the religious parties over government ministries like the Ministry of the Interior, where religious rather than civil criteria were invoked in regard to such matters as the issuing of marriage licenses. As Jewish religious law bans intermarriage, there were many personal tragedies when certain young couples were denied marriage licenses, or when newcomers from Ethiopia or Russia, for instance, were not registered as Jews because their affiliation with Judaism did not correspond to Orthodox criteria.

Israelis had become accustomed to life in the shadow of coalition agreements. Although the opposition they engendered was often fierce, it always remained fruitless. Discourse over the "status quo," in particular, was characterized by ignorance of the meaning of the term. Now and then certain issues, such as the opening of a swimming pool in Jerusalem, sparked demonstrations, protests, or even acts of violence, but on the whole relations between religion and the state were established in accordance with the relative power of the contending forces in the Knesset at any given point in time. Thus despite the overall secularization of Israeli society, the law books were filled with restraints on the free will of the citizens. The Orthodox minority, constituting less than 20 percent of the population, controlled the life of an entire country from birth to death. The registration of newborn babies, the issuing of marriage licenses, and the burials of all Israelis were controlled by religious laws dating back thousands of years.[8]

However much they grumbled about religious coercion, secular Israelis came to perceive any attempt to oppose it as futile. This attitude was the result of simple fatigue, of the persuasive skill of politicians who insisted that the situation was immutable, and of the fact that those who suffered most were minority groups. Until the arrival of large numbers of immigrants from the former Soviet Union in the 1990s, many of whom were non-Jews or harbored strong political opposition to religious coercion, on the whole the people afflicted most by religious proscriptions had no political power. Several cases came to public attention: a navy officer married to a Presbyterian woman whose children could not be registered as Jews because Jewish law determines a child's religion by the mother; a jurist named Cohen who insisted on marrying a divorcee despite the prohibition against the marriage of a "cohen," a member of the ancient sect of Jewish priests, to a divorced woman; or the case of a family forced to reinter their Christian mother outside the fence of a Jewish cemetery. But most military officers were not married to Presbyterians, most judges named Cohen did not marry divorcees, and most of the deceased were buried inside the cemetery walls as long as their relatives were willing to go along with a religious ceremony.[9]

Given the proportional voting system, whereby seats in the Knesset are allocated in proportion to the distribution of the popular vote, the minority unwillingly affected by religious legislation had no one to turn to. Israelis vote for political parties, not for representatives of geographical regions. The chances of the political system taking up the cause of the individual are therefore very low. This is the role of the civil rights lawyer.

From early on, Zichroni handled the cases of the victims of religious coercion. His stand on the matter was unmistakable. It was the only issue that made him lose his legendary aura of serenity. Even if there were no religious coercion in Israel, he wrote, it would be necessary to fight against the very existence of religious parties. As he saw it, religious politics contradicted the principle of the separation of religion and state, a principle cherished by the enlightened portions of humanity. He called the religious parties "an incurable disease in the body politic; they endanger the future of Israel, undermining its healthy organs and poisoning its tissues."[10] After 1967, when religious politics began to be associated with settling the territories in the West Bank and the Gaza Strip that were occupied in the Six Day War, he accused religious leaders of opposing both democracy and peace: they suppressed the rights of Palestinian Arabs, prevented reconciliation between Jewish and Arab youth, and perpetuated the occupation. From birth to death, he thundered in numerous speeches and articles, the modern Israeli is subject to a religion that is a product of the dark ghetto of the Middle Ages in which persecutions and torture stripped people of their livelihood. He considered the maintaining of a lifestyle that harked back to the ghetto an obstacle both to the participation in modern society's pursuit of happiness and to the achievement of equal status for women, as religion had never recognized such equality. Religion, in his opinion, adopted an arrogant attitude toward "the other," and was opposed in principle to majority rule and to the notion of democratic decision making.

Zichroni's harshest criticism was reserved for politicians who latched onto religion as a way of gaining power. He considered the marriage laws enacted by the Knesset to be evidence of sheer racism. These laws, he wrote, contravened the Universal Declaration of Human Rights that proclaimed that every adult should be allowed to choose a marriage partner without restrictions of race, nationality, or religion. According to Zichroni, a true religion did not need a ministry of religious affairs of the kind that existed in Israel, and citizenship should not be linked to religious identity.

Zichroni put this claim to the legal test in the Tamarin case of 1970, one of the most important cases in the history of Israeli jurisprudence. The definition of citizenship is recognized as one of the thorniest issues in a modern state. The classical world developed a republican notion of the citizen virtuously serving the city-state largely as a result of the institution of slavery, which freed the citizens to perform their civil duties. In the modern world, citizenship is associated with elements that go beyond membership in the political community, such as ethnic origin, religion, class, and nationality. The modern state is therefore termed a "nation-state," because it does not relate solely to its citizens per se, but includes a national component as well. An international symposium on citizenship has demonstrated how strong is the need of the modern state to coexist with forces such as nationalism that define citizenship in exclusionist terms. Yet few modern democracies have failed to spell out the various criteria of citizenship as dismally as Israel. Although it may not be easy to become a citizen of France, Canada, or the United States, for example, Orthodox control of the Ministry of the Interior in Israel created situations that were unheard of even in countries clearly meeting the definition of nation-states.

The Law of Return of 1950 granted citizenship to every Jew who immigrated to Israel. This immediately became a source of bitter controversy over the question "Who is a Jew?" as Jewish law applies the strict definition of a Jew as someone who is born to a Jewish mother or who has undergone conversion according to religious dictates, leaving the children of a Jewish father and non-Jewish mother with no status in the Jewish state. In 1970, Dr. George Tamarin, a psychologist at Tel Aviv University, tried to combat this form of state control over personal status. That same year, the Supreme Court rendered a decision that the children of Benjamin Shalit, a Jewish naval officer who was married to a non-Jewish woman, were to be registered as Jews, and recommended that the designation of "nationality" be eliminated entirely from the Israeli identity card. What followed was a coalition crisis, instigated by the religious parties, from which they emerged victorious. The Knesset passed a law stipulating that only children born to Jewish mothers would be registered as Jews. On April 18, 1970, Tamarin, enraged by the outcome, wrote to the Minister of the Interior asking to change the designation of "nationality" on his identity card from "Jewish" to "Israeli." Since a change of registration required public notice, he filed a petition with the district court requesting that the court affirm that he had appeared before it and alleged in good faith his commitment to the Israeli nationality, which, he claimed, was defined by one's subjective sense of belonging to an ethnic group.

In the petition to expunge his Jewish nationality, which was prepared by Zichroni, Tamarin argued that it had been determined by an immigration officer upon his arrival from Yugoslavia in 1949, and that he should have been registered as "Jewish and Croatian," as nationality cannot be exclusive. At that time, he claimed, the Israeli nation did not yet exist, but over the years he had developed a sense of belonging to and identification with the nation, while his feelings toward his native Croatia had diminished. To support his argument, Tamarin offered quotations from modern philosophers that stressed subjective, rather than objective, criteria in determining nationality, and defined the Knesset law, which forced upon individuals a nationality based on data relating to their mother, as categorically racist.[11]

Despite the district attorney's plea that Tamarin's request not be considered on the grounds that the court was not an arena for academic debate, Judge Yitzhak Shilo decided to rule on the matter. He understood all too well the nature of the challenge he had accepted. Here was a citizen of the state demanding to be exempt from the social contract because of recent legislation that redefined its fundamental principles in a way he could not condone. The judge did not take issue with Tamarin's claim (supported by the Supreme Court decision in the Shalit case) that a democratic state cannot force on an individual an affiliation which is open to ideological disagreement. Had Tamarin argued that basic disagreement with the government's policies had led him to identify fully with the Croatian nation, he said, he would have granted him permission to change his registration to "Croatian." However, no Israeli nation existed as distinct from a Jewish nation, and none ever had, not even in biblical times, when King Solomon's kingdom was divided between Israel and Judea.[12]

The judge did not deny the oppressive nature of laws that imposed on an individual an unwanted affiliation which far exceeded the social contract in the Hobbesian sense, i.e., the agreement by which citizens are obligated to the sovereign in order to assure their safety. He even agreed that national affiliation ought to be determined by individual choice. However, he admitted, separation between the Israeli state and the Jewish nation seemed an impossibility to him by virtue of his "living amongst [his] people." In other words, he was part of a national consensus that did not allow a redefinition of the social contract. His verdict was upheld by the Supreme Court, which was also part of the same national consensus.

In the appeal Zichroni submitted to the Supreme Court on behalf of his client, he argued that the decision of whether an Israeli nation does or does not exist cannot be made by a judge on the basis of his "living amongst his people." In an extremely lengthy document, the attorney attempted futilely to establish a concept of Israeli citizenship that was not based on national-religious affiliation, calling on the court to rid the concept of citizenship from Hegelian connotations. Whether or not a nation exists and what its nature is cannot be determined by consensus, he claimed. It involved scientific and ideological questions to which a variety of answers were possible, and the opinion of the judge was irrelevant. The law did not include a list of recognized or unrecognized nationalities, and it was neither the duty of a judge nor that of a registry clerk to determine such matters. The fact that the judge abided by the opinion of the majority or the Minister of the Interior did not justify his verdict. What would he have decided if someone had asked to be registered as a Basque? Would he have refused merely because Spain's dictator Franco did not recognize the Basque nation? Would he have relied on his personal opinion here as well?

Zichroni sought to demonstrate that no nationality exists beyond the subjective feeling of those who belong to it, and that the national collective group is nothing but a baseless abstraction that had come to be accepted because of Hegel's irrational and dangerous philosophy based on the notion of *volkgeist*, or national spirit, assuming the existence of a national entity as distinct from the individuals composing it. It is not by chance, he claimed, that no similar term exists in English or French. The fathers of Zionism, who had come from Eastern Europe, were influenced by Russian mysticism, and as speakers of Yiddish, a language closer to German than to English or French, understood the term "nation" in its mystical rather than civil sense. The district court had operated under the same misapprehension, mistakenly assuming the possibility of objective criteria for the existence of a nation, beyond the feelings of individual citizens. Zichroni distinguished between nationality and citizenship, and stated that while he did not insist on imposing this distinction on everyone, Tamarin should be entitled to stand by his own convictions.

Zichroni added that the definitions of "nation" that might have been appropriate in the nineteenth century had become obsolete in the twentieth, when new nationalities emerged as a result of decolonization and the great waves of migration throughout the world. He offered an example drawn from the World Cup soccer games that had taken place in Mexico that year:

Here, the name of Pelé, the soccer player, appears, along with the notation that he is a Brazilian. The parents of that same dark-skinned Pelé, who belonged to some African country or tribe (and it is doubtful if he himself knows which) arrived in Brazil as immigrants between the sixteenth and nineteenth centuries. What common historical past can he have with his teammates when one of them may be the son of German immigrants who arrived thirty years ago, another the descendent of a Portuguese count, and a third the grandson of a Jewish immigrant from Poland?

Just as Pelé's identification as a Brazilian depended on his citizenship, not his origin, so Zichroni asked the court to free Jewish Israelis from their identification by criteria derived from the world of religious orthodoxy. Religious legislation, he showed, could create absurd situations. Consider Hanan Frank, a young man born in Holland to a Jewish father and non-Jewish mother. Although his family had suffered persecution as Jews, and he himself had lost both legs during his military service in Israel, he was rejected by the legislature of the country with which he had chosen to share his fate. On the other hand, a Japanese living in Kyoto, who continues to reside there and is considered Japanese by his government and probably in his own eyes as well, could undergo Orthodox conversion to Judaism and would then become a member of the Jewish nation. Zichroni claimed that whether or not that Japanese person converted, once he decided to live in Israel and identified himself with Israeli society, he should be considered an Israeli.

These views were not shared by the Supreme Court. Judge Shimon Agranat, who wrote the decision, agreed that individuals should be allowed to determine their national affiliation by personal judgment rather than having it imposed by the collective. However, he added that this held true only in regard to nations that could be proven to exist by objective criteria. He quoted a large number of studies indicating that most Israelis felt a sense of Jewish identity, and claimed that the request by Tamarin and several others to replace their ethnic identification as Jews with a new Israeli affiliation was merely a separatist trend that could not be justified by the principle of self-determination. Were this to be allowed, Agranat wrote, it would lead to the political and social disintegration of the entire Jewish nation.[13] Thus, in order to maintain the integrity of the Jewish nation, Israel's Supreme Court endorsed a situation whereby the state was not defined in accordance with civil criteria, but in relation to Jewish nationalism.

Another case in which Zichroni was involved concerned the conversion of Helene Seidman. It was typical of the three-tier manner in which religious affairs are handled in Israel: open political contention over the question "Who is a Jew"; behind-the-scenes political battles within the religious establishment; and the framing of a compromise that creates the illusion of a solution while actually making the problem more complicated. In 1970, Helene Seidman, a non-Jew who lived on a kibbutz in southern Israel, was converted to Judaism by a Reform Rabbi. The Reform Movement, which attempts to adapt the Jewish religion to modern circumstances, is prominent in the United States but not recognized by religious authorities in Israel. Consequently, her conversion was not validated by the Ministry of the Interior, controlled by the National Religious Party. As this was the first test of the new version of the Law of Return that had been enacted after the Shalit case, she applied to the High Court of Justice, triggering a political crisis. Shlomo Goren, the chief military rabbi, acting either in the service of the National Religious Party (which was looking for a way to remain in the government despite the crisis) or in an attempt to maintain the status of cultural hero he had gained by blowing the shofar at the liberation of the Western Wall in 1967, summoned two other military rabbis and they converted Seidman again, this time according to Orthodox practice. The conversion was confirmed by Rabbi Ovadia Yosef, the chief Sephardic rabbi of the district of Tel Aviv. ("Sephardic," literally meaning "Spanish," refers to the religious tradition that originated in Spain in the Middle Ages and is common among Jews of Middle Eastern and North African origin. Its religious precepts are less strict than those of the Ashkenazi—literally "German"—tradition characteristic of Jews from Central and Eastern Europe.)

Judging by press accounts from that time, many secular Israelis were pleased with this compromise, as it allowed them to believe that even Orthodox Judaism had the means to adapt to modern circumstances. Moreover, both Goren and Yosef were quite adept at operating in the spotlight, and the radio and press reports they initiated referred enthusiastically to the conversion that had saved the country from yet another government crisis. The fact that a rabbi in military uniform was engaged in a religious ritual and involved in what was obviously a political affair did not seem to bother the public, who were delighted to learn that Helene Seidman had declared her willingness to live the life of a "Kosher Jew" and abide by the laws of the Torah. The press, always happy to print juicy gossip, reported that Rabbi Goren had sent Mrs. Seidman a pair of candlesticks so that she could light the Sabbath candles for the first time in her new life as a real Jew. The exultant nation was also given the good news that Seidman had been invited to the office of the Ministry of Interior in the town of Ashkelon, near her kibbutz, where, after office hours, she would receive a new identity card in which her religion was noted as Jewish. Although she discovered that in order to be registered in her new Jewish name, Rivka, she would have to pay the token fee of three Israeli liras, this little detail did not spark a new crisis, and she withdrew her petition to the High Court of Justice.[14]

Zichroni, still operating within the framework of NF at the time, was not pleased by the turn of events. On behalf of NF's MK Shalom Cohen, he petitioned the Chief Rabbinical Court of Appeals to overturn the Orthodox conversion performed by the chief military rabbi. Zichroni was less swayed than the public at large by the national-religious feelings that swept the country after the triumph in the Six Day War of 1967, which many saw as proof of the coming of the Messiah, an interpretation reinforced by Rabbi Goren when he blew the shofar at the Western Wall. Moreover, he had little liking for a military rabbi whom he felt embodied a dangerous combination of religion, militarism, and nationalism. Zichroni and his NF colleagues objected to the conversion because it constituted a victory for those who did not recognize Reform Judaism and demonstrated that only Orthodox conversions were valid. For them, Helene Seidman's conversion was not a compromise but a political act that preempted any future Reform conversions.

Naturally, the petition that Zichroni submitted to the Rabbinical Court of Appeals did not object to the easing of conversion procedures in Israel, but argued that these procedures should be applied equally to everybody. Traditionally, conversion entails considerable difficulty, and Zichroni claimed that Seidman's conversion, motivated by the specific political circumstances, discriminated against others whose cases had not received such publicity. If a summary conversion of the type performed by Goren was recognized, so should those performed by Reform rabbis.[15] The rabbinical court rejected the appeal on technical grounds, claiming that its authority was limited to hearing appeals of decisions by rabbinical district courts, whereas this case had been considered by a private court. Zichroni tried again, responding that the court's authority was not limited exclusively to district courts, and that private court decisions could not be appealed anywhere else, but the rabbis, who had never dreamt they would have to deal with a character like Zichroni, remained unmoved, and the Helene Seidman affair came to an end.

While serving as parliamentary aide, Zichroni framed numerous legislative proposals that sought to restrict the rabbinate's authority over matters such as conversion, but they were never adopted by the Knesset. In fact, because of coalition politics, the Israeli parliament actually relinquished its control over the personal status of its citizens. In 1971, Zichroni drafted a bill that would allow civil marriage. Among other things, it was intended to prevent the traditional discrimination of women in rabbinical courts in cases of divorce. According to the bill, anyone who chose to do so could be married in a religious ceremony, but there would also be the option of civil procedures in regard to property agreements between couples. In notes he wrote during his work on the bill, which was never passed into law, Zichroni stated that it would enable Israel to become a pluralistic, secular, modern state. How far that vision was from reality is demonstrated by a macabre case in which he was involved a decade later.

In December 1982, a woman named Theresa Angelowich died and was buried in a cemetery in the town of Rishon Le Zion, south of Tel Aviv. A week after the funeral, two representatives of the Chevra Kadisha, the Orthodox burial society which had a monopoly over all interments in Israel, appeared in the widower's home and demanded that he remove his wife's body from the cemetery as they had received information that she was not Jewish. They further demanded that he also exhume the body of his daughter, who had been buried in the cemetery fourteen years earlier. In shock, the elderly gentlemen appealed to the Chief Sephardic Rabbi of Rishon Le Zion, Yosef Azran, and was offered a "compromise": the two bodies could be transferred to an isolated section in the cemetery near the toilets. He refused. Several weeks later, he received a letter from Chevra Kadisha reiterating its demands and explaining that it was operating in accordance with a verdict handed down by the country's chief rabbis.

Angelowich's daughter, Adina Harpaz, turned to Zichroni, who submitted a petition to the High Court of Justice claiming that the demand to remove the bodies contradicted fundamental civil and human principles. Moreover, it was a violation of the criminal law forbidding the dishonoring of the dead, which was a religious prohibition as well. Exhuming a body constituted "a barbarian act that is unacceptable in any civilized human society, and is even very rare in uncivilized societies."[16] Once a person had been buried, the universal human requirement to honor the dead must be given priority. The petition referred back to the Shalit case of 1968, arguing that in respect to burial, the determination of who is a Jew should be made by the norm accepted by the majority of the people rather than by Orthodox law. A person who had lived as a Jew and was buried as a Jew should not be subjected to investigation, and the matter should be closed. Even if there were doubts about Theresa Angelowich's religion, it should be recognized that she had lived as a Jew in her country of origin, Romania, where she and her family had been persecuted by the Nazis during the Holocaust, and had continued to live as a Jew in every respect since her arrival in Israel in 1964. Although she was not registered as a Jew, her children were, and her case was not exceptional, as there was a large Jewish population in Israel that maintained a secular lifestyle and did not accept religious authority, yet identified itself as Jewish. If the position of Chevra Kadisha was accepted, the petition added, then citizens who did not belong to a specific religious sect would be disenfranchised.

While the case was being considered by the court, the body of Theresa Angelowich was removed from her grave in the dead of night. As a result of the public outcry that ensued, and after the intervention of the chief justice of the Supreme Court, it was reinterred in its original grave. Chevra Kadisha now submitted its own petition to the High Court of Justice, but its request to be allowed to exhume the body a second time was rejected.[17]

Notes

1. Letter to David, February 6, 1974.
2. See J. L. Talmon, *Political Messianism: The Romantic Phase* (New York: Praeger, 1960).
3. See Michael Keren, *The Pen and the Sword: Israeli Intellectuals and the Making of the Nation-State* (Boulder, Colo.: Westview, 1989).
4. Quoted in Amnon Abramowitz, "Amnon Zichroni Ba'derech Le'ei Sham" [Amnon Zichroni on the way to somewhere], *Hotam*, June 27, 1980.

5. Amnon Zichroni, "Ha'va'ada Lo Hikpida Al Ekronot Mishpat Besisi'im" [The commission did not consider basic legal principles], *Davar*, June 14, 1974.

6. *Hedei Din* 13, January 1976.

7. Amnon Zichroni, "Ezra'h Lamrot Shlilat Heruto" [Citizen despite his imprisonment], *Biton Sherut Bate'i Ha'sohar.*

8. See Izhak Englard, "Law and Religion in Israel," *The American Journal of Comparative Law* 35 (1987): 185–208.

9. See Frances Radai, "Religion, Multiculturalism and Equality: The Israeli Case," *Israel Yearbook on Human Rights* 25 (1995): 193–241.

10. Amnon Zichroni, "Equal, Less Equal, Not Equal at All. . . ." *Al Awdah* (May 4, 1986), 24.

11. Tel-Aviv–Jaffa District Court, 907/70.

12. Tel-Aviv–Jaffa District Court, 907/70.

13. Supreme Court in its Role as a Court for Civil Appeals, 630/70.

14. Report by Avraham Rotem in *Maariv*, June 19, 1970.

15. The Chief Rabbinical Court in Jerusalem, request no. 788/1970.

16. Petition prepared in Zichroni's office in 1983.

17. Chevra Kadisha v. Director General of the Health Ministry, Supreme Court 637/85.

CHAPTER SEVEN

Freedom of Speech and Association

Novelist Yizhar Smilansky, better known by his pen name S. Yizhar, was a member-in-good-standing of the "War of Independence Generation," the group of Israeli writers whose literary works in the 1940s and 1950s expressed the stirring and awe-inspiring experience of the war and the state-building effort that followed it. Born in 1916 to one of the first families of Jewish farmers in Palestine, Yizhar became a national icon, particularly prized by David Ben-Gurion, who considered him the model of a true Israeli writer committed to the national cause. Yet Yizhar never allowed his fascination with the Zionist endeavor in Palestine to lull his social consciousness. He produced some of the most thought-provoking works on the War of Independence, most notably two short stories, "The Prisoner," published in November 1948, and "Hirbet Hiz'ah" (the name of a fictitious Arab village), in May 1949. "The Prisoner" describes the predicament of a soldier guarding an Arab prisoner despite his urge to release him, and "Hirbet Hiz'ah" tells the story of the forced evacuation of an Arab village by Israeli soldiers from the perspective of a narrator who is reminded by the scene of the past deportations of Jews.

The publication of these stories in the midst of the War of Independence incurred a fair amount of criticism in the young state of Israel,[1] but Yizhar managed to steer clear of the political discourse, refusing to subject his literary talent to ideological debate. When asked whether his stories were motivated by political protest, he insisted on their artistic integrity, claiming: "Picasso's 'Guernica' is a protest, but it is also a work of art. Otherwise, as soon as the political context had changed, it would have become an advertisement, a placard, a poster. If 'The Prisoner' is nothing but a protest against the mistreatment of Palestinian villagers during the War of Independence, it should be consigned to oblivion."[2] Thus, at a time when efforts were being made to harness literature to national goals, Yizhar managed to maintain his artistic autonomy. Three decades later this was all but impossible.

In the elections of May 1977, the Labor movement's dominance of Israeli politics came to an end with the victory of the right-wing Likud party. The Likud had its base in the civil circles, and led a coalition of middle-class parties, notably the DMC, composed of technocrats who opposed the partisan political culture and called for a modern, technological state. In principle, then, its assumption of power might have been expected to encourage a civil society free of the demands of a socialist state seeking cultural hegemony. This, however, did not happen, because, as the Likud leadership rightly sensed, most of the country's writers had their ideological roots in the socialist movement and were suspicious of the new regime. Rather than "letting a hundred flowers blossom," the political changeover of 1977 gave rise to a polarized, politicized discourse that left little room for any sort of public sphere devoid of political orientation. Politicization of the public discourse was characteristic of the left and right alike, both of which infringed upon the principle of freedom of speech as perceived by modern political thought.

Freedom of speech refers to the right of individuals and groups to express themselves freely as long as they do not violate the rights of others. John Stuart Mill believed that the individual possesses an "inward domain of consciousness" that ought to be preserved by society, if only for utilitarian reasons.[3] According to Mill, a society in which freedom of thought and expression is not maintained has no chance to flourish. The classical role model for the fight for freedom of speech is Socrates, the valiant individual holding onto his inner truth, facing off against a government holding the bowl of hemlock. This model has become less applicable with the emergence of modern democracies where, alongside legislation ensuring the freedoms of speech, press, and association, such as the American Constitution, there is a mass media controlled by huge conglomerates that can hardly be compared to Socrates. Moreover, these new societies cast doubt on the existence of an autonomous domain of consciousness. As Herbert Marcuse has noted, while the illusion of such a domain exists in the media, for example in the form of TV advertisements which appear to appeal to the individual viewer, the human consciousness is increasingly controlled by the mighty economic and political forces behind those advertisements.[4]

Yizhar's "Hirbet Hiz'ah" was a victim of these developments. On February 7, 1978, Israel Television scheduled the broadcast of a dramatization of the story. By the Likud and its religious coalition partners, this was perceived—probably not without justification—as an attempt by certain people at the national television station to embarrass the new government. Consequently, two government sympathizers in the Israeli Broadcasting Authority appealed to the Minister of Education, a member of the National Religious Party, to forbid the airing of the drama. The broadcast was put off, and all hell broke loose. Politicians, journalists, lawyers, and others joined forces in a battle for freedom of speech that was waged partly in the courts and partly in the mass media in the form of crusades in support of democracy. While the terminology employed resembled that of Socrates and John Stuart Mill, the discourse had little to do with their notions. Rather, it turned into an emotional uproar involving moving declarations by almost every politician, intellectual, and commentator in the country. At the center of the commotion was a last-minute appeal to the Supreme Court to overrule the Minister of Education's decision. It was submitted by Zichroni and his colleagues, who broke innumerable traffic laws in their rush to get from Tel Aviv to Jerusalem before the scheduled airing of the teleplay. As often happens, the affair ended in a whimper: Israel Television broadcast the drama a few weeks later, and Jordan Television taped it and used it as part of an anti-Israeli propaganda campaign. The lessons of the incident, however, are worth noting. On the surface, it had all the makings of a classical struggle for freedom of speech, with the champions of artistic freedom on one side and the government on the other, but in the public sphere of 1978, artistic expression was the last thing on anybody's mind.

Yizhar's work became a ploy in a political skirmish that actually jeopardized artistic autonomy. The story of the young soldier tormented by the evils he observed, thus exposing the tragedy, complexity, and ambivalence of war, was no longer treated as a thought-provoking work of art, but as current affairs. There was no difference between those who banned the play because of its political overtones and those who produced it in the first place in order to embarrass their political opponents. Like Jordan Television, for whom Yizhar's dilemma was purely a propaganda device, the Israeli discourse politicized it and made it into a weapon in its street fights. The lifting of the hegemony of the socialist state thus did little to contribute to individual freedom. On the contrary, Ben-Gurion's appeal to writers to lend a hand in the state-building effort did not prevent the creation of "Hirbet Hiz'ah," whereas the crusade of 1978 invaded the autonomous domain which had made it possible.

Although in this case Zichroni was a team player, he fought many of his tougher battles for freedom of speech and association as a lone warrior. Indeed, one important case is known as "the Zichroni Decision."

After the "Hirbet Hiz'ah" affair, the Likud appointed its loyalists to the Broadcasting Authority, hoping for them to counterbalance what it considered to be the "leftist mafia" that controlled the media. Particularly disturbing to the right was the fact that PLO activists from the occupied territories were appearing on Israel Television (which at that time had only one channel). In April 1982, the Likud-dominated Executive Committee of the Broadcasting Authority passed a resolution banning interviews with public figures who identified with the PLO. As a result of a petition submitted to the High Court of Justice by Attorney Avigdor Feldman of Zichroni's office, the resolution was amended to allow, under certain conditions, the expression of opinions by these people as long as they were not interviewed directly. Their words could only be paraphrased by a reporter or announcer. This arrangement, however, satisfied neither the petitioners nor the court. The petition claimed that the prohibition violated the citizens' basic right to full disclosure from a public institution with a monopoly over information. The right to free information, it was argued, related not only to its content, but also to its being conveyed directly by its original source. Filtering it violated the principle of fair reporting. The broadcast of any item of information should be considered in light of the specific circumstances, and not be banned a priori. Moreover, there was no mechanism for determining who was a "public figure" and who identified with the PLO.

The court's decision was rendered by Justice Dov Levin, who surveyed at length the Israeli precedents concerning the principle of freedom of speech and described the difficulty of maintaining this freedom when the state was engaged in an ongoing war against terrorist organizations. Israel's war with the PLO, he wrote, was over the very survival of the country and its right to exist as an independent Jewish state. Precisely for this reason, it was crucial that the public should not be prevented from receiving information about the PLO and its programs and intentions. The judge believed the public should be familiar, for instance, with the Palestinian Covenant, and detailed its various clauses in order to demonstrate that the organization was a threat to the security of Israel and rejected its very existence. This seemed to him reason enough to prevent the PLO from using the one Israeli television channel as a propaganda device, as the law recognizes the right of any state to maintain its security and freedom against external and internal enemies. "Indeed, civil rights . . . are dear and important to a freedom-loving state. Generally, it is imperative to maintain them meticulously and without discrimination. However, a state should beware of blindly adhering, through its institutions, to those important principles and marching behind this flag of progress toward an abyss, while these rights are exploited to destroy its security and international status."[5] It did not really matter to Levin whether the people being interviewed were accredited PLO officials or public figures who identified with the PLO. He did, however, accept the petition on the grounds that it was impossible to clearly define identification with the PLO. The two other judges, Yehuda Cohen and Gabriel Bach, joined in the decision, but Bach supported it not only on the basis of this technicality. He stated that the public interest would be jeopardized if certain people's opinions were expressed freely while others were only heard through the mediation of a reporter or announcer. This would not allow for balanced and fair discourse. It was not only in the interest of the speakers to express their opinions directly, but it was also in the interest of the public, which had to be in possession of the optimal tools to enable it to form an opinion on controversial issues presented in the media. The decision of the Broadcasting Authority seemed to him too strong a means for achieving the legitimate aim of preventing Israel television from becoming a forum for PLO propaganda. The ban would prohibit the presentation of important issues that had nothing to do with state security, and would unjustifiably detract from the public interest, which was to receive comprehensive and reliable information in the best and most direct way possible.

But Zichroni's toughest battle was still to come. It concerned the right of a political party with a Palestinian nationalist agenda to run for election. In 1984, after prolonged debates between Jewish and Arab citizens, the Progressive List for Peace (PLP) was founded as an alternative to existing Arab parties, most of which were affiliated either with Labor or with the Communists. It was headed by Arab attorney Muhammad Mi'ari, who had previously been involved in issues designed to advance the conditions and aspirations of Israeli Arabs, mainly on the municipal level. He was joined by former general-turned-peace-activist Mati Peled and Uri Avnery. The following points were included in their platform:

1. Securing equal civil and national rights for Jewish and Palestinian citizens of the State of Israel within the June 4, 1967 borders. Conducting a tireless struggle against national discrimination and racism of all kinds, and the securing of this equality of rights in a democratic constitution to be legislated in the State of Israel. The constitution will provide full equality between all the citizens of Israel—Jews and Arabs, Ashkenazi and Sephardi, men and women, secular and religious.

2. Mutual recognition of the rights of both nations—the Jewish–Israeli and the Arab–Palestinian—for national self-determination. The implementation of this principle requires the withdrawal of Israel from all the territories occupied in the 1967 war, including East Jerusalem, and abolition of the occupation and all manifestations of it. These territories will be returned to their legitimate owners, the Palestinian Arab nation, for the establishment of an independent state therein, side by side with Israel. The two states will maintain peaceful relations and good neighborliness.

3. Mutual recognition between the State of Israel and the Palestinian state to be established The withdrawal of Israeli forces from the occupied territories and the peace agreement will be the product of negotiations between the government of Israel and the sole legitimate representative of the Palestinian nation, which is the Palestine Liberation Organization.[6]

The platform also called for the immediate, unconditional withdrawal of Israeli forces from Lebanon (which they had entered in 1982 in an attempt to crush PLO strongholds and enthrone Israel's Maronite Christian allies), emphasized the importance of dialogue and cooperation between Jews and Arabs, and called upon all parties in the elections to conduct a fair campaign. Yet, before they could begin their fair campaign, Mi'ari and his colleagues had to fight a pitched battle to prevent the nationalist party that called for coexistence between Jews and Arabs in Israel, and between Israel and a future Palestinian state, from being outlawed on the grounds that it was subversive.

The perception of Palestinian nationalism as subversive was firmly rooted in Israel. Since the establishment of the state, various means had been used to curb the rise of nationalist organizations within the Arab population. In one prominent case in 1960, the Arab Socialist List was outlawed and prevented by a Supreme Court decision from running for election. This was a group of Arab intellectuals who had split off from the Communist Party in the wake of the rift in the Arab world of the 1950s between the communists and the nationalists who followed Egypt's president Gamal Abdul Nasser. Better known as "Al-Ard" (Arabic for "the land") after the name of the newspaper it published, the party advocated equal rights for Arabs, the abolition of military rule imposed since the War of Independence, and a halt to the confiscation of Arab lands.[7]

When military rule was revoked in the mid-1960s, the Arab citizens of Israel began to play a more significant role in the parliamentary and municipal systems. The Arab vote was divided between the Communist parties and those affiliated in one way or another with the ruling Labor Party. In 1972, a committee of Arab local government leaders was established, and concerned itself mainly with municipal issues. However, after Earth Day in 1976, when violence erupted in protest against the confiscation of Arab land by the Israeli government, it became clear that political activity among Israel's Arab citizens was not going to be limited to local issues (which were serious enough, as there was very little investment in Arab villages and towns). Various steps were taken, largely by the General Security Service, to curb Arab politics. At the same time, however, the occupation of the West Bank and Gaza Strip in 1967 was gradually inspiriting Palestinian nationalism in Israel's Arab population. In 1980, attempts on the lives of Arab mayors in West Bank towns by a Jewish underground of West Bank settlers triggered violent demonstrations by Israeli Arabs, resulting in the implementation of emergency measures. These included an order restricting Mi'ari's movements. Thus, in 1984, when this lawyer from Haifa, a former Al-Ard activist and member of the Committee to Restore the Lands, put forth a new political program framed in collaboration with Jewish peace activists, the authorities were understandably concerned.[8]

It was only natural for Mi'ari to turn to Zichroni for legal assistance. Zichroni was infuriated by the treatment of Israel's Arab citizens. In an article in the East Jerusalem newspaper *Al Awdah*, to which few Israelis contributed, he labeled this situation "the original sin."[9] During the first years of the state, he roared, there was discrimination against the Arab citizens in the form of laws applicable only to them. Arab land was confiscated without compensation, and the areas in which they lived were declared closed. They were forbidden to enter or leave without written permission from a military officer. Even the change in their legal status in the 1960s, and the decline in the implementation of discriminatory measures, had not eliminated the inequities. He claimed that as the Law of Return did not apply to Arab residents of Israel, they were discriminated against in respect to the acquisition of Israeli citizenship, and suffered further discrimination on the administrative level, especially as regarded the procurement of land. Most of the land was owned by the Land Administration, which would not lease it to Arabs. Despite the burgeoning population in Arab villages, no new Arab settlements were constructed and the existing villages were not included in regional development plans. Arab building projects presented for approval were pushed to the back of the drawer in the Ministry of the Interior. As building permits were not issued to Arabs, they resorted to illegal construction on agricultural land in order to ease their housing crisis. Demolition orders were issued by the hundreds and thousands, while the authorities generally turned a blind eye to illegal construction by Jews.

Zichroni was enraged by the fact that although Arabs constituted seventeen percent of the population of Israel in the mid 1980s, they were treated as if they hardly existed at all. He claimed that in the entire country, there was not one Arab in a top government position, and that the only time anyone paid attention to them was immediately before elections when their votes were needed. He believed that it was official policy that turned Arabs into laborers, as they were blocked from entry into jobs in the government, the security establishment, and the like. "Several thousand Arab laborers spend long hours traveling to and from work, and those who do not return daily to their villages live in inhuman conditions. The increase in unemployment has hit the Arab sector and Arab workers hardest. As they do not enjoy the protection of Labor unions, they are the first victims of fluctuations in the slave market. We must take a warning from this discrimination and fight against it."[10]

This was not an easy fight, because the effort to improve the administrative status and economic conditions of the Arabs had to contend with
the fear of PLP, whose nationalist orientation was perceived as a threat to
state security. On June 1, 1984, shortly after announcement of the establishment of PLP, its leaders received a letter from the Ministry of Defense
legal adviser, Moshe Kochanowski, informing them that Minister of Defense Moshe Arens would be invoking the authority granted him by the
Emergency Laws to declare the party "an illegal association."[11] The letter
made it clear that the defense minister had learned from an informer who
had participated in a meeting of the group in April that its call for coexistence between Arabs and Jews was nothing but lip service, and that the
party's true aims were extremist and dangerous. Its platform, the informer
had apparently reported, referred to the 1967 borders of a future Palestinian state as merely a tactical move, whereas in actuality, it did not recognize the right of Israel to exist. It was Arens's intention to outlaw PLP on
the basis of his knowledge that its members had, in the past, expressed the
view that the Arab citizens of Israel were an integral part of the Palestinian nation, and had supported that nation's right to self-determination
and to establish an independent state on the "homeland," that is, not side
by side with Israel but instead of it. Some of the Arabs in the party, the
letter went on to say, regarded its foundation as a service to the Palestinian nation and its right to a state headed by the PLO. The inclusion of
Jewish members on the slate, such as Peled and Avnery, was seen as a
cover that would enable the party to seat in the Knesset the agents of nationalist Arab organizations which considered the PLO, a terrorist organization, the exclusive representative of the Palestinians. By means of this
tactic, it was claimed, the Arab members sought to create a national Palestinian infrastructure that would, in the long run, bring together most of
the extreme political entities in the Israeli Arab population that rejected
the very existence of the state.

Zichroni protested vigorously against the banning of PLP. He wrote
to the Minister of Defense declaring that the very idea of preventing
Israeli citizens from running for election was outrageous, especially in
light of PLP's program, which pointed the way to the liberation of Israel from the cycle of war and provided for peace and security. The ban
was particularly appalling as it was based on mandatory laws enacted by
the British to thwart the Jewish struggle for an independent state. He

could not imagine, he wrote, what had led the Minister of Defense to make such a decision, and claimed that the informer on whose report the decision was based must have been a little dense, as he had missed the point entirely. In none of the discussions held in anticipation of the announcement of the party's founding had there been any hint of an objection to the existence of the State of Israel or to its right to exist within the June 4, 1967 borders. Moreover, the demand for a return to those borders was often voiced publicly by other political parties as well, including NF, Moked, Sheli, and the communist Hadash. The suggestion that the boundaries of Israel should be determined in negotiations rather than by Israel alone could in no way serve as evidence that the party did not recognize Israel's right to exist, as the informer apparently understood it to mean, and no one had proposed any "tactical" wording to conceal subversive intents. Zichroni proclaimed that the argument that the Arab members of PLP viewed their Jewish colleagues as a mere cover to hide their true motives "lowers the discussion to a level that dishonors everybody involved in it. It assumes that the slick Arabs have found themselves a few brainless Jews who, unawares, serve as a cover for their sinister plots. Must my clients respond to this kind of argumentation, or should they rather reject it as clear evidence of shameless racism?"[12]

Zichroni objected to a political body being declared an illegal association without any actual evidence, and expressed his amazement that only now, when it was running in national elections, had the decision been taken to ban the party, although the group had been active on the municipal level for several years. He found it insulting to his clients, distinguished public figures, whose views the minister had first heard of from an informer. Their political positions, he stated, were no secret, and there was no need to ferret them out in this way. The party members were involved in public life in a variety of spheres, had a high political consciousness, were devoted to the public they represented, had strong convictions about the discriminatory policy toward the Arab population, and identified themselves as members of the Palestinian nation who lived in the State of Israel as law-abiding citizens. Their main feature, and that of their Jewish colleagues, was their dedication to public affairs on the basis of their convictions, rooted in the belief that the future well-being of Israel depended on its capacity to devise a blueprint for peaceful coexistence. None of the members, he stressed, had ever operated surreptitiously. Everything they did was open to public scrutiny, and they should therefore be judged by their deeds. All members of the party were opposed to violence and the use of terror by either side. They did not regard the founding of the party as a service to the Palestinian nation at large, and, like most countries in the world, they considered the PLO the sole representative of the Palestinian people outside Israel, a position that had been adopted by even former Israeli ministers of defense. On the other hand, they did not regard the PLO as the representative of the Palestinian population in Israel, but rather acknowledged their status as citizens of the state and accepted its existence without reservation. The party was devoid of any elements that opposed the existence of Israel. Indeed, by running for election, its members were demonstrating their faith in the democratic process in the country.

On June 8, Minister of Defense Arens met with the PLP leadership, accompanied by Zichroni. As a result of this meeting, the minister reversed his decision to declare the party "an illegal association," apparently realizing, with the help of his advisers, the legal and political complexities of such an act. Arens's change of heart might also be attributed to the civic conscience he developed during the many years he lived in the United States. But whatever the reason, it is interesting to examine the protocol of the meeting in Arens's office.[13] Despite the ultimate reversal of the decision, the protocol brings to light some of the elements that impede civilized democratic discourse between Jews and Arabs in Israel. It reveals how politicians engage in power games rather than in serious consideration of the issue at hand, the patronizing attitude of officials toward the Arab community, and the fact that some jurists see themselves as guardians of Zionist values rather than as public servants representing all citizens.

According to the protocol, the meeting began with the declaration by ex-general Mati Peled that "we are here under protest," a remark that elicited the expected response from the minister that the guests were invited to leave if they did not wish to be there. Instead of explaining PLP's position so as to enable Arens to reverse his decision on the basis of fact, Peled uttered declamatory pronouncements about the treatment of the Arab minority in Israel:

Dr. M. Peled: . . . we protest the very readiness to outlaw the party, and the way in which the Security Service treats the Arab population.

Minister of Defense M. Arens: I would suggest that instead of launching an attack on the Government of Israel, you present your position.

Dr. M. Peled: Not the Government of Israel, the heads of the Security Services.

Minister of Defense M. Arens: Don't interrupt me!

The minister himself repeatedly interrupted the speakers with questions indicating a lack of trust in the motives of the country's Arab citizens, who had been depicted as hostile and subversive by his informants.

> Minister of Defense M. Arens: I would ask you to be brief. We want to end before the start of the Sabbath!
>
> Atty. Muhammad Mi'ari: . . . the Arab population . . . demands equal rights as citizens of the State of Israel. We feel that thus far equality has not been established, and there are reasons and excuses for this. We are of the opinion that notwithstanding the reasons and excuses, equality of rights must be ensured.
>
> Minister of Defense M. Arens: Is there an equality of duties?
>
> Atty. M. Mi'ari: Of course, duties too, and in all areas.
>
> Minister of Defense M. Arens: Including military service?

Arab citizens have never been drafted into the military in Israel. This policy, adopted by all governments, stems from the dilemma posed by the service of Arabs in an army that is fighting Arabs, a problem for all the parties involved. Placing the burden for that policy on Mi'ari's shoulders in order to gain a momentary rhetorical victory indicates a lack of seriousness. When Dr. Rashid Salem, who accompanied Mi'ari and Peled, tried to explain the difficulty, he was answered with the counter-argument often offered at this point in the discourse, that the Druzes (an Arabic-speaking sect whose historical conditions are totally different from those of the Palestinian Arabs) do serve in the Israeli army and thus demonstrate their loyalty to the state. This diverted the discussion to the question of the loyalty of the Israeli Arabs, forcing Mi'ari and his colleagues to reiterate their allegiance to Israel, while Zichroni attempted to draw the meeting back to the subject for which it had been called, claiming that the fact that Arabs did not serve in the army did not constitute the violation of any law. He also tried to avert the crisis that threatened to erupt when several PLP members left the room to speak with journalists:

Minister of Defense M. Arens: I am told that some people here went out to report on the meeting. This is unacceptable to me, and if it is true, there is no reason to continue our discussion.

Dr. M. Peled: This is a public event, it is of interest to the public. We are entitled to report to the public the things we say here. They are no secret, they are no different from what we say every day.

Minister of Defense M. Arens: If you want to turn this into a demonstration—be my guest. But I will not be a party to it.

Atty. A. Zichroni: We can get the people back. It was only the result of a misunderstanding, not an intention to turn the meeting into a demonstration.

Minister of Defense M. Arens: There is no symmetry here. You wouldn't have acted differently if I had gone out to report to the press. It is dishonest, impolite, and inappropriate.

Atty. A. Zichroni: I wouldn't say impolite. Inappropriate.

With this crisis behind them, it was time for one of the minister's aides, Ran Yagnes, to "cross-examine" Mi'ari. He wanted to hear about Mi'ari's meetings with PLO officials and the content of their discussions, an apparent attempt to demonstrate that the PLO had determined the party slate. Peled protested the fact that this question was addressed to the Arab members when Jews were also meeting with the PLO. A new crisis ensued, during which Mi'ari stated that Israel's Arab citizens were not represented by the PLO but by their own government. At this point, both lawyers, Kochanowski and Zichroni, realized that the reason for which the meeting had been convened had been satisfied, as Mi'ari's declaration removed the pretext for outlawing the party. The discussion, however, was not over yet. Yagnes and Yehudit Karp of the Attorney General's office did not intend to miss the opportunity to question Mi'ari's adherence to the Zionist ideal:

R. Yagnes: Are you familiar with the Declaration of Independence?

M. Mi'ari: Yes.

R. Yagnes: Do you identify with what it says?

M. Mi'ari: Would that the Declaration of Independence, from the point of view of equality, the norms of equality in it, were implemented.

Atty. A. Zichroni: He is ready to propose as his first bill in the Knesset that the Declaration of Independence be adopted as a constitution.

Atty. Y. Karp: Including the Law of Return?

This last remark, hinting at Mi'ari's understandable objection to the Law of Return, which lies at the heart of the definition of Israel as a Jewish state by granting Jewish immigrants automatic citizenship, was indicative of the lack of sensitivity with which the Arab minority was treated. PLP could not be expected to accept the whole of the Zionist agenda in order to qualify for participation in the elections. But this was apparently just what some people wanted it to do, given that the Central Elections Committee decided to disallow the party on the basis of information it received from the military according to which "there are indeed subversive elements and intentions in the party, and central people on the slate operate in a way indicating identification with enemies of the state."[14] The decision of the committee, which, although chaired by a Supreme Court justice, was composed of representatives of political parties, was reached by majority vote, and included the conviction that "the party advocates principles that endanger the integrity and existence of the State of Israel and its unique status as a Jewish state . . . as recognized in the Declaration of Independence and the Law of Return."[15]

In other words, the fact that the Arab lawyer refused to accept the Law of Return and believed that Israel was not only a Jewish state but must also care for its Arab minority, was perceived as a subversive element. This might have been reasonable later during the Gulf War of 1991, when PLP supported Saddam Hussein and the party's Jewish members severed their connections with Mi'ari, but it was hard to justify the position of the Central Elections Committee in 1984. In point of fact, the Supreme Court overturned the decision and the party was allowed to stand for election.[16]

The court had to consider a major constitutional issue: whether a democracy had the right to ban the political activity of forces perceived as threatening the existence of the state or challenging democracy itself. The decision was particularly difficult because it involved not only PLP, but also a racist party called Kach, led by Rabbi Meir Kahane, which wished to run for election as well. Without question, the appearance of Kach on the scene posed a greater challenge to Israeli democracy than PLP ever did. Nonetheless, the precedent set in the Al-Ard case of 1960 held that a party could be banned only if it represented a physical threat, not an ideological one. Although Kach defied the most fundamental norms in the Declaration of Independence, particularly those calling for the equal rights of minorities, it could not be readily defined as threatening the physical existence of the state. On the other hand, the need of the court to render a decision regarding the two parties may have made it politically easier to approve both. It declared that they both had the right to participate in the elections, since extreme caution must be exercised in banning any party. In the words of Justice Meir Shamgar, who wrote the decision: "The fundamental freedoms, including the freedom of speech and the freedom of belief and equal opportunity to run for public office, all these are basic assets of our system of government and consequently of our legal system. . . . They entail arguing and finding ways to win over even those [who hold] unconventional views and opinions. Prohibitions and limitations are merely an extreme instrument that can serve only as a last resort. The primary standpoint is that freedom of speech truly comes to bear when it is granted to those whose opinions are seen as wrong or even dangerous."[17]

Zichroni was pleased with the verdict, which was upheld four years later when another attempt was made—this time by means of legislation—to prevent PLP from participating in the 1988 elections. Yet Zichroni's rationale for sanctioning the party was different. For him, it was not just a matter of freedom of speech and association. As always, he adopted an autonomous stand, arguing that PLP's participation in the elections made a genuine contribution to Israeli democracy, not despite its views and opinions but because of them. He considered it a blessing that an Arab nationalist party with a platform that clearly and unequivocally recognized the right of Israel to exist in peace and security had appeared on the Israeli political scene. Zichroni claimed that the party should be welcomed for Israel's own patriotic motives, as it encouraged Arab nationalists to play the game within the political arena. As he saw it, PLP represented a possible way out of the cycle of war, and a chance for Jews and Arabs to live in peace, security, and prosperity. He considered it a grave mistake to ban the party and thus delegitimize the 700,000 Arabs living in Israel. PLP, he concluded, opened a channel of political expression for that large population within the most cherished democratic process in Israel— elections to the Knesset.[18]

Notes

1. Gila Ramras-Rauch, *The Arab in Israeli Literature* (Bloomington: Indiana University Press, 1989).

2. Esther Fuchs, *Encounters with Israeli Authors* (Marblehead, Mass.: Micah, 1982), 22-23.

3. John Stuart Mill, *On Liberty* (Indianapolis: Bobbs-Merrill, 1956), 16.

4. Herbert Marcuse, *One-Dimensional Man* (Boston: Beacon, 1964).

5. Amnon Zichroni v. The Broadcasting Authority's Executive Board, High Court of Justice, 243/82.

6. "Hareshima Ha'mitkademet Le'shalom: Hoda'at Ha'yessod" [PLP: the founding announcement], May 30, 1984.

7. See Fauzi Al-Asmar, *Li'hiot Arvi Be'israel* [Being an Arab in Israel] (Jerusalem: Dr. Israel Scha'hak Publication, 1975).

8. See Ian Lustick, *Arabs in the Jewish State: Israel's Control of a National Minority* (Austin: University of Texas Press, 1980).

9. Amnon Zichroni, "Equal, Less Equal, Not Equal At All. . . ." *Al Awdah*, May 4, 1986, 25.

10. Zichroni, "Equal," *Al Awdah*, May 4, 1986, 25.

11. Moshe Kochanowski to PLP, letter, June 1, 1984.

12. Amnon Zichroni to Moshe Arens, letter, June 3, 1984.

13. "Pegisha Im Netzigei Ha'reshima Ha'mitkademet Le'shalom" [Meeting with PLP's representatives]. Minister of Defense's office, Tel-Aviv, June 8, 1984.

14. Gabriel Bach to Uri Avnery, letter, June 18, 1984.

15. Back to Avnery, letter, June 18, 1984.

16. See Claude Klein, "The Defense of the State and the Democratic Regime in the Supreme Court," *Israel Law Review* 20 (1985): 397–417.

17. Neiman and Others v. Chairman of the Central Elections Committee to the 11th Knesset (1985) 39 (III). Verdicts 225.

18. Based on a memo prepared in Zichroni's office towards the meeting of the court.

CHAPTER EIGHT

In the Occupied Territories

The history of Jewish settlement in the Land of Israel can be divided into three periods: the purchase of land and founding of towns and villages; the establishment of an internationally recognized sovereign Jewish state and the quest for peace with its neighbors; and the disarray that began in 1967. When the West Bank and Gaza Strip were occupied in the Six Day War, no thought was given to the fate of these territories. Subsequently, both the left and the right salvaged notions from the watery grave of defunct ideologies for use in their endless debates of the issue. Israel's strategic position after 1967 may thus be described as a compromise between opposing parties representing the past while ignoring the new geopolitical conditions in the region. The Labor government in power in 1967 regarded the occupied territories as a bargaining chip in future peace negotiations, which meant that as far as the fate of this area was concerned, it decided not to decide. Minister of Defense Moshe Dayan, emerging as a hero from the Six Day War until his downfall in 1973, opened up the Israeli economy to the flood of cheap Arab labor from the territories. At the same time, the religious messianic interpretation of Israel's victory became a potent ideological force that offered a persuasive alternative to the state of uncertainty. Moreover, it served as justification for settlement of the territories, first in opposition to government policy, then sanctioned in part by the Labor government, and eventually in line with official policy after the Likud won the elections in 1977.

The rise of the Likud to power, and the declaration of its leader, Menachem Begin, that thousands of settlements would blossom in the occupied territories, did not diminish the strategic confusion over those territories. In contrast to the earlier stages of Jewish settlement in Palestine and the establishment of a recognized sovereign state, Israel had little international support after 1967. Even the right-wing Likud government did not have the power to annex the territories, however much it would have wished to do so. As a result, in a situation familiar from the history of other developing societies, the political leadership sent mixed messages to the military in charge of administering the occupation. Thus for many years, the fate of the territories was left in the hands of military commanders who had to make complex decisions that affected the lives of millions of people, and to Supreme Court judges charged with preventing the violation of international conventions. It is no wonder that the opponents of the occupation directed the brunt of their criticism at the two institutions that had stepped into the vacuum created by the policy of political indecision: the military which did so involuntarily, and the court which did so by explicit rulings. And so, while the political and public discourse was preoccupied with futile debates over the fate of the territories—futile both because a consensus could not be reached within Israeli society and because that fate did not depend on the outcome of ideological debate but on complex regional and international dynamics— military commanders had to make life and death decisions, and judges had to consider the legality of those decisions.

The military and the Supreme Court were therefore the only institutions attempting to cope with the impossible situation whereby, for decades, one nation directed the affairs of another without any clear policy. It was all too easy to blame both these entities for their roles in the occupation, but the attitude of university professors who accused the court of legitimizing the occupation did not much differ from that of settlers who accused it of restricting their settlement efforts. Neither of them took into account the daunting task of the military and legal systems. The decisions they had to make were formidable not only because of the lack of clear guidance from above, but also because the general public preferred to ignore what was going on across the Green Line (the pre-1967 border).

This was a clear case of escapism. Until the uprising in the occupied territories in the second half of the 1980s (the *intifada*), and even afterwards to some extent, Israel's civil life continued as if there were no occupation: merchants bought and sold, teachers taught, clerks worked at their desks, musicians played music, and teenagers were drafted into the army. In the meantime, the occupation was effecting enormous changes in Israel. Jews, who had always been the victims, were now beginning to feel like the victimizers; former refugees found themselves responsible for turning other people into refugees; and a nation of pioneers that had sought since the turn of the century to create a working class now realized it contained an intolerable number of contractors and exploiters of cheap labor.

From time to time, violent events in the occupied territories came to public attention, but for the most part, Israeli society ignored what was happening there, lulled by the politicians' rhetoric that the violence was only temporary until peace came and the fate of the territories was determined in peace agreements ratified by international bodies. Israelis were able to come to terms with many of the paradoxes imposed by their contradictory status as a democracy employing non-democratic means a few miles away across the Green Line. For years, the familiar cliché was that the occupation was "enlightened" and that it actually improved the economic conditions of the Palestinian Arabs. Indeed, the intifada came as a surprise to many people who failed to understand why people whose economic condition had improved so much were seeking independence. Another popular cliché referred to the "integrity of arms," i.e., the assumption that the Israeli army did not use its weapons unless absolutely necessary for purposes of defense. It took many years for the Israeli public to realize how unrealistic that expression is, as even the best intentions cannot guarantee that weapons directed at a hostile population will be used purely with "integrity."[1]

Israelis also failed to grasp that democracy cannot prevail under such circumstances. The rule of law is particularly vulnerable. Once the laws of a state are not applied equally throughout the territory it controls, they become meaningless. The implementation of two separate legal and normative systems on either sides of the Green Line did not bode well for adherence to the law within Israel itself. Zichroni was one of the foremost figures striving to make Israelis aware of this problem. He repeatedly argued that although the country had neither the will nor the power to annex the territories, the situation jeopardized the rule of law within the Green Line. No matter how liberal the occupation was meant to be, he contended, a clash with the population under occupation was inevitable. It was a vicious circle. The military authorities responsible for maintaining order in occupied territories encounter resistance which they have to suppress, and the suppression in turn generates stronger resistance and extremism. Ultimately, the occupation ceases to be liberal and the norms within the occupying nation change: "The liberal of yesterday has become a suppressor today and is a liberal no more. The moral deterioration of the nation is a contagious disease we all suffer from and it is difficult to resist."[2]

To Zichroni's mind, the dual system of laws, one for Jews and another for Arabs, would lead to apartheid:

> The policies carried out by the Israelis in the Occupied Territories cannot be kept a separate entity so that the Israeli is an occupier in the territories but remains a liberal at home. In the Occupied Territories, as under every occupation, the occupier enjoys special powers; the ruling dimensions of legislation, judgment and implementation are concentrated all in one hand, and this is sufficient to alienate the occupier and the rule of law."[3]

Challenges to the rule of law under continuing occupation were often noted by jurists who monitored its application in the occupied territories. Felicia Langer, Leah Tzemel, Avigdor Feldman, Amnon Zichroni, and a handful of others tried hard to bring the dangers of a dual system to public attention. In a discussion of this issue held at Attorney's House in Tel Aviv in 1988, attorney Shlomo Cohen, who had organized the event, claimed that it was not a political matter but a legal and normative one. Lawyers could not accept a situation of illegal arrests and trials conducted behind closed doors, as occurred in the occupied territories. He also bemoaned the sad fact that only thirty lawyers, most of them young, had shown up for the discussion. The press noted that none of the "top drawer" members of the profession had attended.[4]

Indeed, protecting the rights of Palestinian Arabs in the occupied territories was not a popular undertaking. Only a tiny group of lawyers took on the job, and they became the object of criticism, not only from right-wingers expressing nationalist sentiments, but also from left-wingers who believed that the defense of Palestinian Arabs in the territories legitimized the occupation. A left-wing journal called *Hotam*, for instance, maintained that Arabs in the occupied territories should not endeavor to appeal to the High Court of Justice, and cited a sociological study demonstrating that the Court had rejected numerous petitions relating to houses that had been sealed up, land and property that had been confiscated, expulsions, restrictions on an individual's movement, and the like.[5] Several academics pointed out that in the long run, the Supreme Court's decision to hear petitions submitted by inhabitants of the occupied territories, despite the fact they had not been annexed to Israel and therefore came under the authority of international conventions, had a negative effect. In reviewing a series of rulings, Ronen Shamir claims that a number of highly publicized liberal decisions actually enabled the implementation of anti-liberal policies concerning the confiscation of land, freedom of the press, and so on, that received less publicity.[6]

On the other hand, in a study of a strike by Palestinian lawyers called in the 1980s for these very reasons, George Bisharat shows that the question of legitimacy was considerably more complicated. He argues that the participation of lawyers in military tribunals in the occupied territories, even when enlightened legal norms were not maintained, was functional in reducing the degree of oppression.[7] Legal action could not make the occupation go away, but it did help individuals. The fact that people whose houses were slated to be blown up could appeal the decision, for example, gave the petitioners time to remove their belongings, which may have been a trivial concern for those who opposed the occupation in principle, but not for the individuals involved. The task of defending Palestinians in the occupied territories was not treated lightly by the lawyers who undertook it. Some were overwhelmed by frustration with the difficulties. Indeed, Felicia Langer left the country in despair. At the Attorney's House discussion, Avigdor Feldman lost his temper and appealed to the members of the bar who served as military judges during their reserve duty to refuse the assignment, calling the system of justice in the occupied territories "a parody."[8] But the small group of lawyers who worked in the territories was unwilling to sacrifice this minimal check, provided by the legal system, on the arbitrary decisions of local commanders or civil administration officials.

Zichroni repeatedly made his opinions known: the concentration of excessive authority in the hands of military governors violated the principle of separation of powers; military tribunals generally ruled in favor of the military government; and the fact that Jewish settlers in the West Bank came under Israeli law while the Arabs did not was inconsistent with accepted legal precepts. One of the first cases he undertook involved an attempt to constrain the power of the military commander in the West Bank.

In October 1972, a group of seven left-wing Israelis demonstrated in the West Bank city of Hebron, handing out fliers against the occupation. They were arrested and brought before a local military tribunal for violating an ordinance issued by the IDF commander of the West Bank in 1967 against incitement and propaganda. The charges included publishing a document of political significance without the permission of the local military commander, and attempting to influence public opinion in a manner that endangered public order. Freed on bail and taken back across the border into Israel, a military policeman handed them a subpoena that ordered them to appear before the military court in Hebron on a certain date. This procedure was in accordance with paragraph 4a of the mandatory emergency laws, renewed annually by the government, which states that a person suspected of an offense in an area controlled by the military is to be handed over by the police or the military police to stand trial before a military tribunal in that area.

In December, Zichroni submitted a petition to the High Court of Justice against the Attorney General and the Chief of Police demanding that they refrain from using the authority granted them in the emergency laws. The petition, heard by three Supreme Court justices, sought to establish the precedent that trial by an Israeli military tribunal in Hebron was the same as extradition to a foreign land. Zichroni argued that international law did not afford an occupying country property rights over the occupied territory. As the West Bank had previously been controlled by the Hashemite Kingdom of Jordan, which was not currently in a position to exercise its authority there, Israel was required by international law to set up a judicial system. These circumstances, however, did not empower it as an independent source of authority. Therefore, in order for someone to be brought before a military tribunal in Hebron, he or she must be extradited. Since the seven demonstrators were accused of political offenses, especially in light of the charge that they had distributed material that was political in nature, they should benefit from the law forbidding the extradition of individuals accused of political crimes to a foreign country. Moreover, both Israeli and international law contained provisions for freedom of speech and the right to disseminate political views. Handing out fliers was protected by these provisions. In addition, whereas the Geneva Convention grants an occupying force authority over the local population, the seven Israelis did not belong to that population. International law makes no reference to the population of the occupying country itself, and the charges against the defendants involved acts that were not crimes within the borders of Israel.

In his response, Justice Joel Sussman, presiding over the High Court panel and known for his strict adherence to procedure, corrected the typing mistakes in the petition and concerned himself at great length with the French version of the Hague Convention cited by Zichroni. Having done that, he then denied the right of Israeli citizens to demonstrate in the occupied territories, thereby allowing a political act which is a fundamental right in Israel—the demonstration—to be defined as an act of "incitement and propaganda" as understood by some local military commander in Hebron. According to the court's ruling, the transfer of the seven Israelis to Hebron was legal because the emergency laws took precedence over other laws: "Even if you argue that the transfer of a person to a court in the administered territory constitutes extradition—and we do not think this is so—the law of extradition is overridden by an emergency regulation, which is a special legislative act and more recent than [the law]." [9] The ruling also stated that according to the law, extradition is defined as the "sending of a person who is in Israel to another state," and although the Kingdom of Jordan was "another state," it could not exercise its sovereignty in the administered territories (the court consistently referred to the territories as "administered" rather than "occupied"), so that Israel had de facto sovereignty. As for the claim that the defendants were accused of political crimes, the court held that in accordance with the Hague Convention, the country administering an area is obliged to maintain civil and public order, and this may include the right of the military government to limit, or even prohibit, political activity in that area and sanction those who violate the prohibition.

When the Supreme Court decided to exercise its authority as a High Court of Justice to oversee the rulings of military tribunals in the occupied territories, Zichroni fully supported the decision. As he saw it, the court's intervention was a means of controlling the agents of the state who operated across the Green Line, and ensuring that they did not abuse the law or turn it into an arbitrary instrument of power. As critical as he was of the Supreme Court's readiness to accept security reasons as justification for certain actions taken by the military government, such as the confiscation of land, he did not consider the court's decision to be a legitimization of the occupation. Accordingly, he worked within the parameters it set.

One noteworthy case that demonstrates this approach occurred in 1979, when a Palestinian named Azat Dowikat and sixteen others, represented by the attorneys Zichroni, Feldman, and Elias Houri, appealed to the High Court of Justice against the Government of Israel over confiscation of their land for a Jewish settlement called Elon Moreh. A year earlier, the court had approved the establishment of two settlements in the Beth-El area on the grounds that their construction was necessary for security reasons. This time, however, an entirely different matter was involved, as it was argued that the land belonged to the settlers for religious–historical reasons. As Zichroni put it, "in this petition, the real antagonists in the struggle for land met for the first time…the Jewish settlers and the local Arab inhabitants."[10] Although the land owned by the petitioners was properly registered in Nablus, they had received a confiscation order signed by the West Bank military commander, Binyamin Ben-Eliezer, issued on the grounds that the land was needed for security purposes. The order was delivered to the landowners only three days before the bulldozers were to arrive, which smelled like an obvious attempt to deny them sufficient time for the High Court of Justice to intervene. Nevertheless, the petition was filed and the court heard the case.

IDF Chief of Staff Raphael Eitan responded by confirming Ben-Eliezer's claim of the military importance of the area. He elaborated on the role of civilian settlements in the defense of Jewish life in Palestine since the early days of modern Jewish immigration, particularly during the War of Independence, and argued that the failure to reinforce civilian settlements in the occupied territories immediately after 1967 (when Labor was in power) was partly responsible for the fiasco of the Yom Kippur War of 1973.

The High Court, composed of five judges presided over by Justice Moshe Landau, remarked that the chief of staff sounded fully convinced of the validity of his theory on the basis of his professional experience. However, the court had before it an opposing opinion, held by none other than Minister of Defense Ezer Weizman, along with two generals, Mati Peled and Haim Bar-Lev, who submitted an affidavit claiming that the security of the State of Israel could be ensured without the establishment of Elon Moreh. Even more interesting was a counter-affidavit submitted by the settlers, who were granted the right to be heard on the matter. They made it clear that the entire debate over security was utterly irrelevant, at least in their eyes. For them, resettling the site of ancient Elon Moreh, which appears in the book of Genesis, was a divine commandment, dictated, not by reasons of security or physical needs, but by "the power of purpose, and the power of the return of [the people of] Israel to its land." They saw Elon Moreh as part of the Land of Israel not because of its geographic and strategic location, but because it was the site on which God promised the land to Abraham. Although conceding that for them the issue of security was beside the point, they added that the settlement of the people of Israel in the Land of Israel was the most genuine, fundamental, and effective way to provide security.

As Zichroni later suggested, the settlers' counter-affidavit constituted an admission on their part of "what was already known to all beyond the courtroom walls—that the settlers, together with the majority of the Israeli public and its leaders, conceived of the occupation not as a temporary military phenomenon but rather as a permanent, national, territorial realization, and that the security reasons are nothing other than the paying of lip service before the courts."[11]

Justice Landau expressed his appreciation of the deep religious conviction evidenced by the settlers' affidavit, but maintained in his decision that Israel was not a lawless country in which religious commandments prevailed over the law. He did not consider the confiscation of Arab land without proven military purpose to be legitimate in terms of international law, and was therefore disallowing construction of Elon Moreh.[12] Unfortunately, this was a short-lived victory for Zichroni's clients. Although at this time the settlement could not be built on the site, the court's ruling taught the settlers to adopt a more sophisticated approach in the years to come. Landau stated explicitly in his decision that private land could be confiscated for the purpose of establishing a civilian stronghold if it were proven that it was mandated by military considerations. However, he set certain constraints on the approval of settlements: that the chief of staff bring the matter before the civilian authorities; that the civilian settlement be confined to specific areas and remain there only for as long as the military conditions that had led to its establishment continued to prevail; and that when negotiations over the fate of the occupied territories were conducted, the future of the settlement would be determined in accordance with their outcome. Although the Elon Moreh decision did not prevent future governments from settling the West Bank, it represented two important achievements: an unwillingness to justify the settlements on any grounds other than security, that is, the Supreme Court did not accept the religious claim over the whole of the Land of Israel; and the principle of the reversibility of the settlements, i.e., the statement that in a future peace agreement, their dismantling would not be unthinkable.[13]

Another case in which Zichroni was involved was the defense of Raymonda Tawil, a Palestinian journalist.[14] The Acre-born mother of five, who headed a Palestinian women's organization in Nablus, had been active since 1969 in organizing demonstrations and strikes to protest the torturing of prisoners, the demolition of houses, and the expulsion of political activists from the occupied territories. She was a familiar figure among left-wing Israelis, who demonstrated side by side with her on various occasions, such as when the crops of the Palestinian village of Akraba were sprayed with poison in 1973. In November 1974, she was arrested by the military authorities, and subsequently moved to Ramallah. There she became a well-known face to foreign consuls and journalists, who regarded her as an unofficial spokeswoman for the PLO in the West Bank.

In May 1976, Raymonda Tawil organized a series of actions in response to a march by Gush Emunim to Jericho in the West Bank, and in June 1976 she participated in the funeral of a detainee who had died in an Israeli military prison and also called for a strike to protest the arrest of students at Bir Zeit College. A month later she was summoned to the office of the military governor in Ramallah and ordered to cease her activities. When she refused, she was placed under house arrest. This was the first implementation of the power granted by paragraph 86 of the Security Act issued in the territories, which also allowed for appeal before a special commission. Zichroni stepped in, working pro bono because he considered his appearance before the commission a matter of "public interest."[15] The representatives of the military government argued that the women's group headed by Tawil was a subversive organization involved in extremist acts of protest, and that when she had been summoned to receive a warning, she had worn on her lapel the emblem of the PLO, an organization at war with Israel.

Zichroni painted a different picture of the organization as an apolitical group engaged in charity work. He claimed that some of the subversive activities attributed to his client were associated with her tasks as a journalist, and the fact that she demonstrated together with Israelis indicated her desire for peaceful coexistence between Arabs and Jews, rather than subversive intentions. He ridiculed the matter of the emblem, which he showed to be produced by an American organization, with many Jewish members, which advocated the right of the Palestinians to self-determination. Had Tawil actually committed any crimes, he argued, she could be brought to trial, but the expression of opinions that are unacceptable to the military authorities can not serve as justification for administrative measures such as detention and house arrest. Zichroni quoted from government directives stating that these steps can be taken only in the case of incitement which is directly related to acts of terrorism. If she had violated the censorship regulations, for instance, she could be tried for it, but placing her under house arrest without trial imposed unwarranted restrictions on her journalistic freedom and her efforts on behalf of women's rights. Although Zichroni did not deny his client's political opinions, he claimed they were insufficient cause for a restraining order. Raymonda Tawil, he argued, was a woman fighting for Palestinian rights, much like many Israelis, and there was no call to harass those who advocated peace on either side of the Green Line. He also added a few choice words regarding the effectiveness of house arrest, which did not prevent her from giving interviews to the foreign press.[16]

In letters to the minister of defense and the regional commander, Brigadier General David Hago'el, Zichroni stressed the peremptoriness of their actions in the occupied territories. He called the house arrest "an arbitrary execution of ruling power,"[17] and argued that the clause on which it was based was not intended to serve the whim of some military commander: "It is unthinkable that the taking away of all of a person's fundamental human rights be executed in such an arbitrary manner and without explanation."[18] He added that nobody had told Tawil what she was accused of or why she was being punished. Disconnecting a journalist from the outside world, he declared, was an unprecedented act unjustifiable by any law or regulation. In reference to the fact that the authorities had disconnected her telephone, Zichroni wondered whether there was a law which applied to the occupied territories that allowed military governors to take over the telephone services or to disconnect a telephone line as a form of sanction. Since the telephone was registered in the name of Tawil's husband Dowd, a banker, Zichroni also wrote to the director of the post office (in charge of the telephone service) in Ramallah demanding that it be reconnected immediately as the military commander was not empowered to instruct him to disconnect telephone lines.

This point is more significant than it may appear at first glance. The question of the authority to disconnect a telephone in an area under occupation may seem marginal, but it is not. It touches on the very issue of whether Israel, which controlled the territories as the result of a war it never wanted, would hold onto them as a bargaining chip, administering military rule in the meantime, or would take over the region and unleash the full power of its elaborate bureaucracy. In Israel, like elsewhere, bureaucrats have taken over all aspects of life, subjecting the state and the individual alike to contingencies that constrain their effective functioning. In the wake of technological development, the fictional nightmare imagined by Franz Kafka, in which the individual is victimized by the power of the bureaucracy, has become a routine condition of modern life. Although felt more sharply under occupation, the condition is not unique to it. We would be hard put to count the number of bureaucrats—tax collectors, electric company clerks, water board members, switchboard operators, military officers, land assessors, tourist guides, road construction contractors, and so on—who turned a state of occupation into a nightmarish world in which one society virtually controlled the life of another. The functionaries operating in the occupied territories could, of course, be considered the agents of an oppressive state, but this is too simplistic. The Israeli bureaucracy has proven itself to be as much an enemy of the state as of the individual. To judge by Zichroni's letters, in 1976 he still believed that the occupation could be conducted in accordance with international law. Ultimately, however, his attempts to combat human rights violations in the courts were thwarted, not by the power of the state, but by bureaucratic exigencies such as a disconnected telephone.

In 1978, Raymonda Tawil was again detained. Detention without trial would later become common practice in the territories, but in 1978 it still shocked Zichroni and the colleagues in his law practice who protested this violation of the rule of law. Tawil, they declared, had not been told the reason for her detention, had never been suspected of endangering national security, and had always acted within the law. It was simply wrong to devise all sorts of questionable regulations in order to detain someone who could not be prosecuted under the law for a specific crime. In a letter to Minister of Defense Ezer Weizman, Zichroni stated that he had had no intention of interfering in Tawil's interrogation as long as it was conducted properly. However, after visiting her in prison, he now saw fit to ask the minister to intervene to ameliorate her conditions. He explained that a new interrogator had joined the team. This man, who went by the name of "Abu Jamil" (General Security Service agents customarily gave themselves Arab nicknames), had shifted the interrogation in a new direction. He threatened the detainee with physical harm, called her a "whore," "an animal," and similar obscenities, warned her that he would throw her into a cell with prostitutes, and more. Such treatment was abhorrent and could not be condoned.[19] Taking advantage of his good relations with the press to put pressure on the minister, Zichroni demanded that the interrogation be conducted fairly and that the woman not be made an object of abuse because of her gender. He revealed that Tawil was being held in solitary confinement and was not allowed to have books, and claimed this was an attempt to break her spirit so that she would admit to crimes she did not commit.[20] Ten days later, Zvi Kahane, another lawyer in Zichroni's office, sent a second letter to the minister of defense charging that Tawil had been beaten and was subjected to verbal abuse, spitting, and threats. Although the law permitted the security services to detain people without specifying the reasons, this power should not be exercised at will.[21] The pressure paid off, and Raymonda Tawil was released. Many others, however, were not, and they spent months in prison without benefit of trial.

Zichroni often voiced his objection to detentions which, in contrast to arrests to which the rules of habeas corpus apply, are decided upon too quickly and violate basic human rights, such as the right to know why and for how long a person is being detained. He was particularly concerned by the detention of journalists, which he saw as a gross violation of the freedom of speech. He argued that freedom of speech should not be restricted to certain regions, but must be ensured across the Green Line as well. Although not all the constitutional principles effective in Israel, such as the right to vote and be elected to the Knesset, could be expected to apply to the occupied territories as they were not and should not be annexed, the right to freedom of speech did not stem from the status of citizenship but from a person's natural right to free expression, and therefore could not be denied the inhabitant of an occupied zone. Even if the freedom of the press, for instance, were not ensured on the same level as it was within

Israel because of the differing circumstances, certain universal principles must be upheld; publication should be prohibited only when a clear and present danger could be demonstrated, as American courts had determined. Zichroni complained that this principle had not been internalized by the authorities in the West Bank and Gaza Strip, and that even the Arab press in East Jerusalem, which had been annexed to Israel, suffered from unwarranted restrictions. Censorship regulations that were hardly ever applied in Israel were enforced in East Jerusalem, several newspapers had been shut down, and others were banned in the West Bank and Gaza Strip. Well aware that the Israeli public displayed little interest in the issue of the freedom of the Arab press, Zichroni argued that the existing state of affairs could lead to the gradual imposing of similar restrictions on the Israeli press, especially in light of the lack of a constitution to guarantee the right to information of Israeli citizens.[22]

The steps taken to constrain the flow of information in the occupied territories and East Jerusalem included the detention of Radwan Abu-I'ash, head of the Palestinian Press Association, the revoking of existing newspaper licenses and refusal to grant new ones (required by British mandatory laws that remained on the books), and the imposition of military censorship, which, although it was also in effect within Israel, was used here for political purposes, according to Zichroni. He charged the military censors with abusing their power by censoring political items, and claimed that military censorship was employed as a tool to influence political trends in the occupied territories. In lectures on the subject, he demonstrated the counter-productiveness of this tactic: the use of the censor's authority to silence supporters of the PLO in the territories only strengthened the power of the extremist Palestinian organizations that took a much more radical stand toward Israel. One interesting example of the abuse of military censorship that he offered was the rejection of a feature in an East Jerusalem newspaper which contained a sharp denunciation of a murder committed by Palestinian terrorists. Zichroni claimed that the article was censored as part of the policy to paint a one-dimensional picture of the PLO as a terrorist organization, while promoting pro-Jordanian newspapers like *Al-Nahar*.

The thin line between military censorship and political control over the population under occupation, as well as the different positions regarding freedom of speech, is revealed by the correspondence between

Zichroni and the authorities concerning the decision by Minister of Defense Yitzhak Rabin to ban the East Jerusalem weekly *Al Awdah* in the West Bank and Gaza Strip. Rabin's justification for his directive was its "hostile nature and its extremist and inciting content."[23] In July 1985, Zichroni, representing the newspaper, wrote a letter to Efraim Sneh, the head of the civilian administration of the West Bank (established in 1981 in subordination to the military commander), claiming that the ban prevented the weekly from reaching its main body of readers, thereby causing it severe economic hardship. He depicted the paper, which appeared both in Arabic and in English, as being affiliated with the most moderate elements in the Palestinian community. The editorials clearly and unequivocally advocated peace and coexistence based on the mutual recognition of Israel and an independent Palestinian state. It openly supported peace talks between Israel and the Palestinians, as well as all forms of political dialogue between the peace groups on both sides. Zichroni noted the paradoxical situation in which a wide variety of Palestinian newspapers with a range of political outlooks were available at the time in the territories, including one that was openly affiliated with the extremists. This made it hard to understand why *Al Awdah* was to be banned, unless, of course, it was its moderation that was feared. As it was in Israel's interest to strengthen the moderates rather than the extremists, he asked for Sneh's personal intervention as a last resort before filing a petition with the High Court of Justice.[24]

The matter was handed over to the state prosecutor. In March 1986, Zichroni was informed by Renato Yarak of the prosecutor's office that investigation of his complaint had found that the weekly had violated censorship regulations. In reference to the question of whether the same regulations should apply in Israel and the occupied territories or whether there should be stricter criteria in the territories, Yarak explained that in this case, the newspaper had contravened the rules that applied to all Israeli newspapers (based on the1945 British emergency laws). He gave several examples of items that were published without first being submitted to the censor, as required by law, including a photograph of someone throwing an explosive device, a picture of hooligans beating an Arab who was tied up in a manner reminiscent of images of World War II, and a poem about the greed of the Jews in Palestine in which the poet claimed that the Jews stole Arab money and would make off with everything on the face of the earth until the time came when those "wolf-men" got their due. Yarak also noted that numerous pictures of PLO leader Yasser Arafat had appeared in the same issue. Another issue of the paper that was similarly not submitted to the censor contained support of the PLO's armed struggle, and dubbed anyone who did not join in it a traitor or coward.

Several political cartoons were also cited by Yarak as violating the Prevention of Terror Ordinance. One showed Israel and King Hussein of Jordan forcing a Palestinian to sign a document calling for a joint Jordanian–Palestinian delegation to negotiate the fate of Palestine (in contrast to Palestinian nationalist sentiments), and another depicted Prime Minister Peres as an armed soldier with a steel fist confronting a bound Palestinian who was being beaten by a snake with the face of the king of Jordan. Also included in the list of offenses was a picture in the colors of the PLO flag (which it was illegal to fly at the time) showing hands raising a flag in support of the "legitimate rights of the Palestinians." Yarak asked for Zichroni's response before the final decision regarding the sale of the weekly in the occupied territories.

Zichroni's response is interesting because it reflects just how thin the line between security threats and legitimate political expression is, and how difficult it is to conduct a discourse over freedom of the press within the political context of a national liberation struggle. Zichroni expressed his surprise at the reference to political cartoons as a violation of the censorship laws. "Are cartoons that deal with political contacts in the region, that condemn the pressure applied by the King of Jordan and the limitations on the political activity of the Palestinians under a condition of occupation a form of criticism to be suppressed?"[25] he asked. Moreover, Arafat's picture appeared frequently in newspapers all over the world, and thus could not be considered illegitimate in any publication.

As for the way the Arab was tied up, Zichroni claimed this was not reminiscent of World War II, but a symbol of any occupation. It was not the fault of the newspaper if it was associated with something else in somebody's mind. Furthermore, Zichroni had not noticed an explosive device in the hand of any figure in the weekly, and saw what Yarak apparently considered an anti-Semitic poem as something else entirely. In any case, poems must be treated differently from standard political commentary, he contended, adding that in this case the poem referred to the confiscation of land, which had been defined as robbery not only by

Palestinians but also by a former Israeli supreme court justice. There was no cause to prohibit the victims from making a political statement of this kind. Finally, he referred to the use of the colors of the PLO flag, claiming that although indeed red, green, and black had been chosen by the PLO, they had earlier been adopted by the entire Arab nation and appeared in the flags of nearly all Arab countries. He was dealing here with a 1980 law, to which we will return in the following chapter, that outlawed public acts expressing identification with or sympathy for a terrorist organization, including the raising of the PLO flag. Zichroni argued that the emergence of a Palestinian national consciousness and the symbols associated with it preceded the founding of the PLO, and that the colors and accompanying text could be found in all the Arab newspapers in East Jerusalem and the occupied territories. He concluded by assuring Yarak that if and when permission was granted for the weekly to be sold in the territories, his clients would be willing to adapt to the new regulations, readership, and circumstances.

Notes

1. Felicia Langer, *With My Own Eyes: Israel and the Occupied Territories 1967–1973* (London: Ithaca, 1975).

2. Amnon Zichroni, "Politics and Human Rights," *Israel and Palestine* (October 1987), 23.

3. Zichroni, "Politics and Human Rights," 23–24.

4. Reported in *Ha'aretz*, August 24, 1988.

5. Oded Lifshitz, "Al Telrch Le'Bagatz, Ya Muhamad!" [Don't go to the High Court of Justice, Muhamad], *Hotam*, July 31, 1987, 8.

6. Ronen Shamir, "'Landmark Cases' and the Reproduction of Legitimacy: The Case of Israel's High Court of Justice," *Law and Society Review* 24 (1990): 781–805.

7. George E. Bisharat, "Courting Justice? Legitimation in Lawyering Under Israeli Occupation," *Law and Social Inquiry* 20 (1995): 349–405.

8. Reported in *Ha'aretz*, August 24, 1988.

9. High Court of Justice 507/72, Arie Arnon v. Attorney General

10. Zichroni, "Politics and Human Rights," 24.

11. Zichroni, "Politics and Human Rights," 24.

12. High Court of Justice 390/79, Azat Muhamad Mustafa Dowikat v. State of Israel.

13. See Ian Lustick, "Israel and the West Bank After Elon Moreh: The Mechanism of De Facto Annexation," *The Middle East Journal* 35 (1981): 557–77.

14. See Raimonda Tawil, *My Home, my Prison* (New York: Holt, Rinehart and Winston, 1979).

15. Letter to Raimonda, March 8, 1977.

16. "Notes based on memory," memo found in Zichroni's archive.

17. Amnon Zichroni to Brigadier-General Hago'el, letter, August 24, 1976.

18. Zichroni to Hago'el, letter, August 24, 1976.

19. Amnon Zichroni to the Minister of Defense, letter, April 4, 1978.

20. *Ma'ariv*, March 27, 1978.

21. Zvi Kahane to the Minister of Defense, letter, April 16, 1978.

22. Amnon Zichroni, "Palestinian Political and Human Rights," Geneva, Fourth UN International NGO Meeting on the Question of Palestine, September 1987, 7–9.

23. Yitzhak Rabin to MK Abed Al'wahab Darawshe, letter, February 1986.

24. Amnon Zichroni to Efraim Sneh, letter, July 15, 1985.

25. Amnon Zichroni to Renato Yarak, letter, May 30, 1986.

CHAPTER NINE

Civil Disobedience

∾

In 1986 an amendment to the Prevention of Terror Ordinance of 1948 was passed in the Knesset, banning contacts between Israelis and officials of the PLO. The amendment, ratified by a vote of 47 to 25, imposed a sentence of imprisonment up to three years on any Israeli citizen or resident conducting an unauthorized meeting with a senior official of an organization defined by the government as a terrorist organization, or with a representative of such an organization. Three types of meetings were excluded from this penalty: (1) support given to a relative who happens to be a member in such an organization; (2) meetings at an international press conference, provided that representatives of the international media are present; and (3) scientific symposia, so long as they do not involve political discussions.[1]

The amendment was the product of a unique political development—the formation of a national unity government in 1984. Israel was in deep crisis in the early 1980s, its army engaged in a controversial war in Lebanon, the economy suffering from a large deficit in the balance of payments and three-digit inflation, and deep social strife. A deadlock in elections held in July 1984, with neither of the two major parties—Labor and Likud—able to form a viable coalition, led to an agreement to cobble together a national unity government, with the prime minister's position rotating between Labor's leader Shimon Peres and the Likud's Yitzhak Shamir. Peres served as prime minister during 1984–1986 and Shamir during 1986–1988.

The two parties could hardly agree on anything, especially in foreign and security affairs, and, since the cabinet was composed of an equal number of ministers from the rival political blocs, neither could get its way. This resulted in nuanced, often contorted, wheeling and dealing. One result was that in order to gain the Likud's support for an anti-racism law restricting the activities of Rabbi Meir Kahane, who was elected to the Knesset on a racist ticket and caused enormous damage to Israel's foreign relations, Prime Minister Peres agreed to support the Likud's demand for the highly controversial amendment to the Prevention of Terror Ordinance.

The passing of the amendment constituted a victory for the right-wing Likud. Its members were long outraged by meetings held since the late 1960s between Israelis of the left and PLO officials. After many unsuccessful attempts to discourage such encounters, the government now had the legal means to ban contacts perceived to hinder Israel's position in the Middle East conflict. Labor, for its part, could support the legislation, however reluctantly, because contact with the PLO was widely resented by the public. Participants in such talks, although often prominent, were viewed by many as politically marginal, and their civil rights, therefore, were not a major concern of the major political parties. Moreover, since the amendment was part of a compromise that allowed the passing of anti-racist legislation, voting for it could be presented as a liberal act, despite its serious civil rights implications.

While Israel had a questionable civil rights record regarding its Arab citizens and the Arab residents of the territories occupied in the Six Day War of 1967, this amendment was the first major ban on the freedom of speech and association of Jewish citizens of the state. It also marked an emboldened use of the law as a political means. However unpopular the handful of individuals were who conducted talks with the PLO, their activities had been recognized as motivated by a legitimate political position, and were now classified as a criminal offense. This was necessitated by the perception, articulated by the Likud's MK Dan Meridor, that the war against the PLO "is not just a war conducted by the air force, intelligence and the army; it is above all an ideological war of total de-legitimation."[2]

As a tool in the "war of total de-legitimation," however, the amendment ultimately failed. It transformed the talks from marginal political events into publicized cases of civil disobedience that elicited growing support. Zichroni, who had been active in the talks from the start, now played a major role in defining them as acts of civil disobedience. This role was by no means a simple matter for him. Nowhere has the legal profession come to terms with the question of its right to participate in acts involving a breach of the law, and Zichroni, despite his demonstratively pacifist background, was no exception. In the Israeli context, however, certain conditions—the absence of a written constitution, severe security stress, and the formula of compromise dictated by the national unity government—not only called for the participation of lawyers in civil disobedience but may have made their involvement crucial to the preservation of the rule of law. This argument requires some elaboration.

Civil disobedience has been defined by Christian Bay as "any act or process of public defiance of a law or policy enforced by established government authorities, insofar as the action is premeditated, understood by the actor(s) to be illegal or of contested illegality, carried out and persisted in for limited public ends and by way of carefully chosen and limited means."[3] This definition stresses the caution demanded by such an actor, who is charged with the difficult task of challenging a law deemed immoral without shaking the foundations of the rule of law. This dual task—challenging the law and maintaining respect for the rule of law at the same time—has led legal and political thinkers to lay down stringent conditions for civil disobedience. Philosopher John Rawls, for example, restricted it to instances in which serious infringements on the principles of justice occur, and demanded that it be used only after normal appeals to the political majority have been made in good faith and failed. Concerned with the breakdown of respect for the law if too many instances of civil disobedience occur, Rawls noted the need to coordinate among them and to make sure that any action taken be "properly designed to make an effective appeal to the wider community."[4]

In light of this caution, why accommodate civil disobedience at all? The answer is that the need to do so in modern democracies stems from the realization that the law is not identical with morality.[5] Free and thoughtful individuals, concerned with the immoral nature of a law, may thus risk punishment in order to challenge a law deemed unjust, an activity viewed positively by many democratic thinkers. "What kind of person can we admire," historian Howard Zinn has asked. Can we ask young people of the next generation to emulate . . . the strict follower of law, or the dissident who struggles, sometimes within, sometimes outside, sometimes against the law, but always for justice? What life is best living, the life of the proper, obedient, dutiful follower of law and order, or the life of the independent thinker, the rebel?"[6]

This argument, however, cannot be easily applied to lawyers. The question of lawyers' involvement in such acts has been raised whenever their services were sought during lawbreaking events staged by the civil rights movement, the woman's rights movement, protesters against the Vietnam war, demonstrators against nuclear tests, participants in "operation rescue," and others. With the rise in the U.S. of civil rights and anti-war struggles during the 1960s, in which laws were challenged in large-scale illegal demonstrations and sit-ins and the tearing up of draft cards, legal scholars began to give serious consideration to the question of lawyers' involvement in such acts, whether they participated in them personally or counselled those who did so.

Commentators on the subject have mostly insisted that lawyers refrain from civil disobedience, as such involvement would be professionally, legally, and morally wrong. This position was stated by Dean Lindsey Cowan of the Georgia Law School, who argued unequivocally that the lawyer's professional obligation is to counsel obedience. "The client's obligations to his conscience are not a matter within the lawyer's professional concern,"[7] he wrote. Cowan objected to lawyers' involvement in any violation of the law, demanded that they advise against it if they conclude that a law is valid, even if unjust or immoral, and notify the authorities if they have reason to believe that a violation will occur. With this, as citizens lawyers have a greater obligation than lay persons to rectify allegedly unjust or immoral laws within the existing legal structure.

Another observer, Judith McMorrow, based her objection to lawyers' involvement in civil disobedience on the relation of the lawyer to the law:

> Lawyers work with, under, and around the law as their professional livelihood. Lawyers are called "officers of the court," "officers of the law" and "ministers" and swear allegiance to support and defend the Constitution of the United States. Even the title "lawyer" reinforces the relationship between the person and the law. The very nature of law binds the lawyers to the content of the law.[8]

McMorrow acknowledged that the obligation to uphold the law and at the same time strive to make it just poses a dilemma to the lawyer who may feel morally compelled to engage in acts of civil disobedience. Since one cannot be at the same time an agent of the law and a violator of the law, the lawyer who is so compelled by conscience is all but advised to resign from the bar: "By becoming a member of the legal profession the lawyer takes on special responsibilities, which require the lawyer to make certain personal and professional sacrifices."[9]

Lawyers on the other side of the fence justified their or their colleagues' involvement in civil disobedience along the lines of Henry David Thoreau's reference to a higher law that applies to lawyers as much as to other citizens. Thoreau claimed that under certain conditions civil disobedience can become a citizen's duty. In his famous essay on civil disobedience, he justified his refusal to pay taxes to the State of Massachusetts by the immoral conduct it tolerated in the matters of slavery, the Mexican war, and the treatment of Indians. In Thoreau's thinking, the government must be just. Majority rule by itself, he pointed out, is not identical with justice. Right and wrong are not the products of decisions by majorities but of human conscience, which should be given greater weight than the law. This implies that lawyers, as others, may at times cultivate a respect for what is morally right as much as for the law.[10]

Thoreau's argument, however, could not be easily applied to the Israeli scene. However unjust the conduct of his government seemed to him during the night he spent in jail for refusal to pay taxes, Thoreau never doubted the presence of a solid constitutional structure in his country that accommodated most, although not all, of his moral convictions, and a judicial system with the available legal and cognitive means to reach a reasonable decision on whether his act could be defended by the rule of absolute necessity. Moreover, he could present his objection to the law in terms of natural law, a doctrine sanctioned by both religious and secular thought in his country which lays down a universal moral code to which legislatures are expected to yield.

Israel, by contrast, had no written constitution. Moreover, it lacked a tradition of judicial review or a political culture that perceived legal challenges of the kind posed by Thoreau as building blocks of democracy. Israel also had no jury system, and the lawbreakers, rather than having their "day in court", could expect to be brought before a short-tempered judge committed to the letter of the law. The small group of leftist mavericks who sought channels of communication with the PLO when that organization was still openly committed to the destruction of the State of Israel could not count on sympathy from the public, however persuasive its arguments in favor of maintaining contact with the enemy. Public opinion was impatient when state security was perceived to be at risk and meeting with terrorists was viewed as endangering state security. Moreover, Israel lacked a sanctioned set of norms to serve as a shield against the instability caused by acts of lawbreaking by a minority of individuals.

Even when a disobedient minority in Israel operated in the name of well-defined moral convictions, as in cases of civil disobedience during the Lebanon war of 1982, it had difficulties basing its argumentation on natural law. Israeli courts often paid tribute to natural law but the belief in universal moral principles stemming from reason was alien to Jewish tradition, which recognizes a higher law attributed to God, but assigns its interpretation to rabbinical authority rather than to individual reason. To the extent that arguments based on natural law were used in the Israeli discourse on civil disobedience, they were raised either as a means to mobilize world public opinion, or as evidence by those objecting to state laws for contradicting the laws of the Torah.[11]

Additionally, the Israeli political scene of the 1980s was marked by deep ideological strife as a result of conflicting opinions on the necessity of the war in Lebanon. Thus, the common model of civil disobedience according to which an individual or small group commits a cautious act of lawbreaking with the hope of drawing the attention of the majority to a higher law, which ought to (and has a good chance to) guide legislation in the future, did not apply. There was no existing consensus, within parameters defined by law, that could be readily challenged, because although the political system maintained a degree of stability through pragmatic arrangements, such as the national unity government, there was no single normative system but rather two such systems: To a Likud member, someone who communicated with the PLO was simply a traitor.

During the Lebanon War, for example, MK Yedidia Be'eri of the Likud demanded that General (Res.) Mati Peled, who held an anti-war press conference in London together with PLO official Issam Sartawi, be prosecuted in accordance with Clause 99 of the penal code, which imposes a sentence of life imprisonment or death for aid to the enemy during war. This put Zichroni, who was Peled's attorney, in a different position from, say, an anti-abortion demonstrator trespassing on the private property of an abortion clinic in the U.S., both because of the severe punishment that could be meted out to his client, and because Peled's beliefs did not conflict with state law (in fact, the attorney general decided they did not) but did conflict with a higher law upheld by his opponents with no less conviction.

The 1986 amendment could not even be regarded as the imposition of one set of moral norms over another set; it was the outgrowth of a compromise between politicians. The persons who held talks with the PLO, and continued to do so after 1986, never intended civil disobedience, and certainly did not have martyrdom in mind. They were citizens of a democracy whose government, for complex political reasons, had turned their political activity into a criminal offense. They had no constitution to turn to, and, in light of an entrenched ideological divide, had no option to presenting their case as a moral challenge to a mainstream legal system. The defense of their continued activity, therefore, required careful planning and the mobilization of support from legal professionals. Israel's legal profession, however, had hardly ever taken a stand on political issues. The Bar Association, for example, had always been conscious of the material advantages of aloofness in a highly politicized society, while judges preferred to cling to legal formalism rather than to step into the murky water of politics, especially the politics of occupation after 1967.[12] Although this situation did not change dramatically in 1986, the amendment did prompt a small but significant number of lawyers, law faculty, and legal commentators to become involved with the issue. Although most of them had little sympathy for talks with the PLO, and even less for civil disobedience, they supported the right to hold such talks when the issue came up in courtrooms, Knesset committees, and the press.

Before describing Zichroni's struggle against the 1986 amendment banning the talks, some historical background on the talks is in order. The organizational structure of the Palestinian struggle against Israel emerged in the 1960s in the form of various guerrilla organizations—Fatah, the Popular Front for the Liberation of Palestine, the Democratic Front, and several others. They were headed largely by students and intellectuals who, from the mid-1960s, held sporadic talks with Israeli students, mainly in European universities. In 1969 Yasser Arafat, leader of the Fatah, gained control over the Palestinian Liberation Organization, established in Cairo in 1964, and turned it into an umbrella organization over the various guerrilla groups and a major vehicle of Palestinian nationalism. This prompted Israeli peace activists to engage in talks with PLO officials. Various meetings were held in Moscow and elsewhere between Israeli Communist groups and their Palestinian counterparts. A meeting between Israeli Communists headed by Benjamin Gonen and Yasser Arafat was held in Berlin in 1973. An organization that was particularly involved in these talks was Matzpen (Hebrew for "compass"), a group of students who split off from the Israeli Communist party in 1962 and pursued an ideology combining anti-Zionist, new-left and bohemian views. Some of the Matzpen group went into "permanent exile" in Europe, where they reached out to Palestinian guerrilla groups whom they perceived as sharing their revolutionary outlook.

The minutes of a meeting between Moshe Machover, one of Matzpen's founders, and Sa'id Hamami, the PLO's representative in London, published by Matzpen in November 1975, shed light on such talks in their early stages.[13] The agenda consisted of a joint search for a common socialist front that would act against reactionary, imperialistic elements in the Middle East, both Jewish and Arab. The meeting was marked by an initial agreement between the extreme leftist Israeli and the representative of the Palestinian guerrilla organization over the final aim: the establishment of a secular democratic state in Palestine in which socialist fraternity and tolerance would prevail. This agreement made for a smooth discussion, but toward the end Machover raised the delicate question of whether the two discussants represented anyone besides themselves. Replying, Hamami stressed that he was an official representative of the PLO, and although this body was no bureaucratic organization exerting strict control over its members he could not express his recognition of Israel as a national entity without the substantial support of his colleagues. Hamami admitted that his views did not constitute official PLO policy, but believed that most members of Fatah and of the Democratic Front agreed with him, as did PLO chairman Arafat.

Hamami was assassinated in January 1978 by an unidentified assailant whom he apparently knew and had let into his London office. The talks, however, did not stop. They were continued on the PLO side mainly by Issam Sartawi, a high-ranking PLO official who had first approached Israeli peace activists in Paris in 1976 through Henri Curiel, an Egyptian Jew. Sartawi, who was later to be assassinated himself (April 1983), held extensive talks with many leaders of the Israeli peace camp—Uri Avnery, Mati Peled, Ya'acov Arnon, Lova Eliav, Zvi Lam, Simha Flappen, Amnon Zichroni, and others. Up until 1977, when the Likud came to power, the content of these talks was conveyed in detail to Prime Minister Yitzhak Rabin, Foreign Minister Yigal Allon, and other government officials, mainly by Peled, the ex-general-turned-peace-activist, who had a close personal relationship with Rabin.

An important organizational framework for the talks was the Israel Council for Israeli-Palestinian Peace founded by Zichroni in 1976. The line pursued by the council in the talks was reflected in its manifesto, which affirmed that the land on which Israel and the Palestinians live is a homeland for both peoples and that the only path to peace is through coexistence between two sovereign states, each with its distinct national identity. The manifesto called for the establishment of a Palestinian Arab state alongside the State of Israel following a process of negotiations between the Israeli government and the PLO (recognized by Israel only in 1993). The manifesto also defined the future border between the two states as the pre-1967 lines, except for changes agreed upon by the parties after settling of the problem of Jerusalem.

From the start, the talks with the PLO evoked governmental attempts at suppression. The Israelis involved in them were always under the threat of prosecution in accordance with clauses 111–114 of the Israeli criminal code pertaining to the transmission of information to enemy organizations and contact with foreign agents. In 1960, as a result of the conviction of Middle East scholar Aharon Cohen, a member of the left-wing Mapam Party, for political contacts with a Soviet official, the Supreme Court demanded of the legislature to amend the criminal code so as to exclude contacts with foreign agents which involve no harm to, and no intention to harm, state security.[14] With the greater proliferation of political talks with the PLO in the mid-1970s, the Israeli right grew alarmed, yet could do little about it. The matter was raised in the Knesset several times during Yitzhak Rabin's first term as prime minister (1974–1977), but his ministers of justice pointed out that although the government objected to meetings with the PLO, these were not illegal so long as they could not be proven to harm state security.

The founding of the Council for Israeli-Palestinian Peace in 1976 was intended to provide a legal shelter for the meetings. Shortly thereafter, the council's loyalty to the Zionist cause was questioned in a newspaper article, prompting a libel suit brought by attorney Avigdor Feldman of Zichroni's office. The suit was won, providing the council with a degree of legitimacy. In 1977, the Likud, under the leadership of Menachem Begin, came to power, with the clear intent, inter alia, of banning contacts with the PLO. It initiated an amendment to the Prevention of Terror Ordinance, passed in the Knesset in 1980, which outlawed public acts expressing identification with or sympathy for a terrorist organization, e.g., raising flags, displaying signs, or singing anthems.[15] The amendment was used mainly to prosecute Arabs in the occupied territories supporting the PLO but it also constituted a problem for the Council for Israeli-Palestinian Peace. A placard showing both the Israeli and the PLO flags exhibited at a public meeting held by the council was confiscated by police. T-shirts with the same symbol worn by demonstrators led to their detention. Following a plea by Zichroni, and intervention by the Israel Civil Rights Association, the Attorney General's Office issued a clarification that while the public display of such symbols might be an offense under certain circumstances, those circumstances must be determined before an arrest is made.

Another measure intended to de-legitimize contacts with the PLO was an order issued in April 1982 by the supervisory council of the Israel Broadcasting Authority prohibiting interviews on radio and television with Palestinian leaders in the occupied territories who were affiliated with the PLO. As discussed before, a plea to the Supreme Court filed by Feldman, arguing that the order denied the access of citizen Amnon Zichroni to uncensored information, was won on a technicality: the difficulty in determining what "affiliation with the PLO" is.

The participants in the talks understood, however, that such limited victories were short-lived, especially in light of public outrage over meetings held by Israelis and PLO officials during the Lebanon War of 1982, which was intended to crush the PLO. Shortly after Yitzhak Shamir, a hard-liner who replaced Begin as prime minister in 1983, came to power, the Arab–Israeli attorney Mohammed Mi'ari was arrested after meetings with PLO leaders in Geneva, and journalist Ibrahim Kara'een, editor of the East Jerusalem Palestinian weekly, *Al Awdah* was detained on the basis of the 1980 amendment to the Prevention of Terror Ordinance.

Zichroni, who served as attorney for both men, realized the potential harassment that he and his associates faced by a government that viewed them as traitors. He therefore sought international sponsorship for the talks and found it in the United Nations: the Council for Israeli-Palestinian Peace registered as a nongovernmental organization (NGO), its members meeting with PLO representatives within the flexible context of NGO activities affiliated with and protected by the UN. Zichroni participated in a variety of meetings within this framework. In 1982 he testified before the International People's Tribunal convened in Tokyo to investigate the Israeli invasion of Lebanon, his testimony constituting one of the strongest expressions by an Israeli against the war:

> I am an Israeli lawyer active in civil rights issues and committed to a just Israeli Palestinian peace. I am a member of the Israeli Council for Israeli–Palestinian Peace, a Zionist organization formed in 1976, which supports the principle of an Israeli–Palestinian peace based on coexistence between two sovereign states, each with its distinct national identity. Cardinal to this is the establishment of a state for the Arab Palestinian people, which will exercise its right of self-determination in the political framework of its choice alongside of the state of Israel. The border between these two states should correspond to that existing prior to the war of June 4, 1967.[16]

Based on his experience in talks with PLO officials, Zichroni stated, that organization was willing to accede to a just peace based on the above principles and was willing to recognize the State of Israel. Therefore, he held, the responsibility for continuing the conflict lay with the present Israeli government, which maintained a policy of occupation and annexation. The invasion of Lebanon was directly related to that policy, he charged. "This is a concept of endless war with the Palestinians, of destroying their organizations—mainly the PLO—and of annexing the West Bank and Gaza Strip."[17] Zichroni made a clear distinction between the Israeli government and the people, blaming the government led by Prime Minister Menachem Begin and Defense Minister Ariel Sharon for crimes against humanity as defined by international law. He enumerated five such crimes: military acts against the civilian population and the bombing and shelling of peaceful cities and villages; the use of cluster, phosphorous, fragmentation, and other bombs; the bombing of hospitals and clinics protected by the Red Cross or Red Crescent; the cutting off of food, water, energy, and essential medical supplies from the civilian population; and the refusal to grant prisoner-of-war status to Palestinian fighters. He explained his harsh stand against his government by his concern over the success of the government's propaganda in persuading Israelis that there was a danger to their national existence in the Middle East, and that they had no choice but the road of endless war with the Palestinians. Not surprisingly, Zichroni was commended by the investigating jury for his courage to appear before it in an atmosphere of harassment at home that forced him to keep in his office chemical spray as a deterrent against potential attackers.

In 1984 Zichroni took part in the first international conference of nongovernmental organizations devoted to the Palestinian question, which took place in the Palais des Nations in Geneva. The ninety-four NGOs in the conference included the PLO headed by Labib Terezi, the permanent observer of the organizaion in the UN, and the Israel Council for Israeli-Palestinian Peace. The conference, discussing various ways to promote the rights of the Palestinian people, endorsed a proposal to convene an international peace conference on the Middle East under the auspices of the UN. It also formed an interim coordinating committee on Palestine, with Zichroni as a member of its standing council. The event was the first of a series of conferences that were held in Geneva, Vienna, and in the UN General Assembly Hall during the latter 1980s in which dozens of Israelis and Palestinians met, shook hands, held political talks and formulated detailed resolutions. In each of these conferences, Zichroni spoke soberly and at length about the situation in the occupied territories, conditions for building support for a Palestinian state in Israeli public opinion, or the emerging role of NGOs. He also prepared various legal documents, reminiscent of his time as parliamentary assistant to MK Uri Avneri, to serve as drafts of an Israeli–Palestinian peace treaty. Here is an example:

> *Peace Agreement*
> *Made and signed this ___ day of ___*
> *By and between*
> *The Palestine Liberation Organization*
> *(hereafter the PLO)*
> *   of the first part*
> *and*

The Government of the State of Israel
(hereafter "Israel")
    of the second part
and
the Arab States
    of the third part
and
the United States of America
    as guarantor
and
the Union of the Soviet Socialist Republics
    as guarantor

The small chance that such documents would be signed by the partners to the Middle East conflict sparked some mockery in the press. Journalist Hannah Kalderon, who often covered Zichroni's contacts with the PLO in the 1980s, vividly described the surreal international milieu of the talks. Leaving Tel Aviv in the morning, she would find herself standing in line at the reception desk of some European hotel in the afternoon surrounded by characters she recognized as the world's most notorious terrorists, unsure whether she might be assassinated by them or by the Mossad agents trailing them. She described with irony how she quickly discovered the good life associated with the activities devoted to solving the problems of the displaced and impoverished refugees of the Middle East: how she was flown business class by the UN; dined in luxurious European restaurants with Israeli peace activists, PLO terrorists, and well-intentioned international figures such as Austrian Chancellor Bruno Kreisky; and how Zichroni stood out in his focused single-mindedness and sobriety amidst all the posturing— conferring secretly with Soviet representatives, giving legal advice to PLO activists, receiving mysterious phone calls from China, or disappearing for a few days in some Eastern Bloc country. Kalderon, stressing Zichroni's seriousness of approach, pointed out that while the encounters with the PLO began to assume an aspect of "bon ton" for Israeli leftists excited about the opportunity to meet with their government's most notorious enemies, Zichroni by contrast would spend long hours in the plenum, delivering his carefully prepared lectures in a monotonous voice.

A meeting that attracted considerable attention was the NGO meeting on the question of Palestine that took place in Geneva in September 1985, attended by two hundred Israelis and PLO officials. The Israeli NGOs represented there included the Council for Israeli-Palestinian Peace, the Rakah Communist Party, the Association of Democratic Women, and the Organization for the Defense of Arab Lands, while the PLO delegation included high-ranking officials such as Labib Terezi, Shafik al-Hut and Zuhir al-Wazir. Representatives of NGOs from the US, East and West Europe, Asia and Africa were also present. Mati Peled lectured on the dangers of a nuclear Middle East, Shafik al-Hut called for the return by Israel to its pre-1967 borders, and Zichroni demanded more explicit commitments by the PLO regarding their recognition of the State of Israel. One of the statements made in the conference called upon Israel's Prime Minister Shimon Peres not to lend a hand to the legislative initiative being debated at the time for a law banning meetings between Israelis and the PLO. Peres, however, more concerned with the need to satisfy his uneasy Likud partners in the national unity government than with a group of marginal leftists meeting with the country's enemies in Geneva, was unmoved. The controversial amendment banning the talks came into effect on August 6,1986.

Zichroni chose to express his anger over the amendment in an article in the East Jerusalem weekly *Al Awdah*. Politically speaking, he wrote, this legislation has nothing to do with the prevention of terror. It is rather a law for the prevention of peace. Legally speaking, it stands in contempt of the fundamental principles of criminal law. The legislature, he claimed, does not have as its concern the prevention of terror but of political activity. The supporters of the law, who have their own political viewpoint regarding Israel's relations with the Arab world, cannot, however, impose their ideology on others by the use of criminal sanctions without shaking the very foundations of a free and democratic state, within which differing political views are allowed to exist. He added:

> The question now is, can we continue to legitimately classify ourselves as belonging to the free world if we limit the right of the individual to simply associate with another only on the condition that such meetings will not be 'tainted' by a political nature deemed as undesirable to the state. And if it is prohibited for the individual to establish such contact, why not prohibit the existence of such parties completely?[18]

On November 5, 1986, two months after the ratification of the amendment, amid heightened security measures and harassment by demonstrators, a delegation of 21 members of leftist organizations boarded a plane at Ben-Gurion Airport bound for Rumania for meetings with representatives of the PLO. The head of the delegation, Latif Dori of the Mapam Party, who several months earlier had founded the Committee for Israeli-Palestinian Dialogue, explained that the rationale for the trip stemmed from the amendment: "After the law was passed, such a meeting became more important and significant in order to prove that in spite of it, dialogue should continue."[19] Dori was unsuccessful in his effort to mobilize a larger delegation, as some participants cancelled following a warning issued by the attorney general and condemnations by political leaders and the press. He was more successful, however, in attracting world attention to the move. Returning three days later, the delegation encountered more than a hundred journalists and television crews from all over the world, at which time Dori displayed an order summoning him and three other members of the delegation to a police investigation.

Zichroni, who accompanied the delegation, insisted that no law had been violated. In Rumania, and in all subsequent meetings with the PLO in Geneva, Vienna, New York, and elsewhere, he pinned a sign on his jacket reading: "Palestinians, please do not approach me" and instructed delegates on how to behave without drastically breaching the law so as to allow its challenge in court. According to his account of the event in Rumania, "until 6:00 p.m. when the session was due to start, the Israeli delegates sat on one side while the Palestinians sat on the other and the Rumanians sat in the middle. Later, divided by roses, the two sides talked by addressing the Rumanians and not the other side to the dialogue."[20] These and many other barbed statements issued by those who took up disobedience in the years to come helped underscore the paradoxes inherent in the law and mobilized support for the struggle against it.

While such support was not forthcoming from the public at large, which was outraged by, or at the very least contemptuous of the sight of Israelis shaking hands with the enemy, it did come from a handful of legal scholars. They did so not as political activists impelled by moral rage. Professor Emeritus S. Z. Feller of the Hebrew University, for example, a respected criminal law scholar, was anything but a moralist. In an interview given in 1989, he stressed that his involvement in the struggle against the amendment was based solely on "dry analysis in light of the principles of the criminal code."[21] This, of course, was exactly where his contribution became invaluable. An effective civil disobedience campaign could not rely on devoted activists only; it required the support of persons who were not lawbreakers yet could back up those who were by exposing the shortcomings of the law. Feller and colleagues of his in the Israeli law schools, the Israel Civil Rights Association, media organizations and Jewish groups abroad mostly objected to contacts with the PLO as well as to civil disobedience, but they equipped Zichroni and Feldman with the weapons necessary in the public struggle against the amendment.

The opinions of legal scholars about the amendment were by no means unanimous. Even the Israel Civil Rights Association was divided over how to respond to the amendment when it was first debated in the Knesset Judiciary Committee. However, the minimum its members could agree on—that restrictions imposed on society by law must relate specifically to activities endangering state security, and that the task of the state was to combat terrorism, not persons who are neither terrorists nor participants in terrorist acts[22]—was an important starting point in the effort to prevent punishing people for holding political meetings.

In an article that became the main legal frame of reference in the struggle against the amendment,[23] Feller claimed that the amendment contradicted the principles of penal law as understood in free societies, e.g., that punishable behavior must be purposeful and intentional. He showed in detail that the amendment was inappropriate either as part of the Prevention of Terror Ordinance or as a specification of a new offense in its own right. Citing many examples (an Israeli doctor encountering a PLO official during an operation abroad, a garage owner approached by a customer who happens to be a supporter of an organization considered an enemy of Israel, etc.), Feller demonstrated that the endless exceptions to the offense specified in the amendment testified to its absurdity. While making clear that he did not approve of meetings with the PLO, and admitting that he personally would not shake the hand of a PLO official, he expressed doubt that the definition of such acts as criminal could effectively de-legitimize them and warned of the dangers this posed to democracy. Once an individual is forbidden to establish political contacts, the door is open to such measures as the banning of political parties advocating contacts with the PLO, or the banning of political parties altogether.

Many participants in the discourse argued along the same lines, claiming that they disagreed with the participants in the talks but would defend their right to hold dissident views. When the amendment was first discussed in public, Professor of Law Mordechai Kremnizer wrote that the very thought of shaking hands with the assassins of children evoked feelings of resentment and disgust in him, but banning such contacts infringed upon the cherished value of freedom of speech, as there could be no freedom of speech without the freedom to choose one's partners in dialogue.[24] Such statements, published by legal scholars in the press, were countered by the argument that freedom of speech and association was secondary to considerations of state security and that in light of the breach of the 1986 law, state control should actually be tightened. This prompted the lawyers preparing to challenge the amendment in the courts to solicit additional support in the form of scholarly opinions from Israel and abroad defining the 1986 amendment and more restrictive amendments that occasionally came on the agenda as serious violations of international law. One respondent was Professor Donna Arzt of Syracuse University's College of Law who warned in an article that a proposal debated in the Knesset Judiciary Committee in 1989 to limit the transfer of funds to organizations believed to serve as a shield for terror would lump Israel together with the Soviet Union and South Africa, "two countries widely known for their manipulative uses of law and the legal system to repress civil liberties and civil rights."[25]

In June 1988, Latif Dori and three other participants in the talks in Rumania were brought before the Magistrates Court in the City of Ramla and charged with violating the Prevention of Terror Ordinance and clause 499 of the criminal code (plotting to perpetrate an offense). Zichroni and Feldman were the four men's attorneys. The court in Ramla did not turn out to be a conducive location for far-reaching constitutional arguments. All attempts by the two attorneys to introduce such issues in their interrogation of witnesses ended in the disqualification of their questions by Judge Abraham Beizer, who refused to make his crowded courtroom available as a venue for the country's constitutional and political battles. The defendants were sentenced to six months in prison and one year suspended, along with a monetary fine.

The general line of defense became publicly known, however, when Zichroni's interrogation of an intelligence officer, summoned as a witness by the state prosecutor, was published in the press. Zichroni induced the witness to acknowledge that the PLO was the largest organization representing the Palestinians, that some of its members advocated political struggle in addition to armed struggle, that there were PLO members who showed flexibility and moderation in their views, and that the contacts between Israelis and the PLO constituted a factor that helped reinforce this moderation. The interrogation was clearly aimed at presenting the PLO as an organization that could not be defined merely as terrorist, as well as identifying the meeting in Rumania as a peace conference. It was also an opportunity to reveal to a hostile public that some of the talks with the PLO in the past had been actively encouraged by the government, and that participants in them had been asked to perform "certain tasks with relevance to Israeli intelligence."[26]

In appeals submitted to the District Court and eventually to the Supreme Court, Zichroni and Feldman presented a series of well-reasoned arguments that gave rise to some of the most important deliberations in Israeli judicial history. Their main contention was that a law limiting freedoms must be interpreted in the narrowest way possible, and that its interpretation must account for the basic constitutional principles prevailing in democratic states, such as the freedom of speech and assembly. Although Israel has no written constitution, they contended that the norm of peace between Israel and its Arab neighbors was sanctioned in the Declaration of Independence. For the first time in the history of Israeli legislation, they claimed, the Knesset had passed a law which clearly violated fundamental constitutional principles, for no legitimate reason.[27]

The long, detailed verdict by District Court Judge Hadassa Ben-Ito, while expressing discontent with the defense attorneys for their claim that the PLO was not simply a terrorist organization, and disapproval of demonstrative acts of civil disobedience such as the trip to Rumania, left no question as to the judge's positive attitude toward the defendants. She all but explicitly expressed admiration for persons who were in no way criminals but who held "a firm political view, who show personal involvement in public life, and are willing to risk a criminal offense in order to make their opinions known," calling them "people who have proven their desire for peace."[28] Moreover, she did not conceal her view of the amendment, which she held should not have been legislated in the first place. She agreed with Feller and others that the law infringed upon civil liberties, although not in a way, she wrote, that endangered democracy. Since the law had been legislated as part of a bitter ideological struggle, bypassing the legislature by a court decision would constitute a political statement. Once the legislature makes its point explicitly, she concluded, the court is not allowed to distort its original intent, even if the law is deemed undesirable and may impair individual liberties and civil rights.

In light of the problems acknowledged in the verdict of applying constitutional principles in a district court, the two attorneys filed an appeal to the Supreme Court in which they requested "a greater effort at interpretation."[29] Even if the legislature made its intent clear, they argued, the Supreme Court ought to consider the possibility of banning a law that contradicts "the constitutional spirit and soul of the legal system."[30] The Supreme Court, lacking the powers of judicial review, could not accept this plea, but its rejection left no doubt as to where its members stood. While recognizing the Knesset's right to evaluate basic liberties in light of the public interest, the court viewed the 1986 amendment as infringing in a very real sense upon the freedoms of speech and of political activity recognized in any democratic society.[31] While the court did not overturn the conviction, it abolished the punishment imposed on the violators of the law, since by the time of its convening, in June 1993, the amendment was no longer in effect.

Long before then, meetings with the PLO had become commonplace and included even government officials. Not only did such talks gain momentum after 1986 in a climate of reconciliation caused by the ending of the cold war, but in 1991 the Shamir government took part in the Madrid Conference, which launched negotiations between Israel and a Palestinian delegation reporting to PLO headquarters in Tunisia. Paradoxically, members of the Palestinian delegation, who were residents of the occupied territories, were subject to prosecution in accordance with the Prevention of Terror Ordinance. In spite of such absurdities, it took a change of government for the amendment to be withdrawn. On January 18, 1993, eight months before the dramatic handshake between Prime Minister Rabin and PLO Chairman Arafat, the Knesset voted to revoke it.

Notes

1. Official Law Publications 1191, August 13, 1986.
2. Knesset Record 39, August 5, 1986, 4048.

3. Christian Bay, "Civil Disobedience: The Inner and Outer Limits," in *Dissent and the State*, ed. C. E. S. Franks (Toronto: Oxford University Press, 1989), 42.

4. John Rawls, *A Theory of Justice* (Oxford: Oxford University Press, 1973), 376.

5. H. L. A. Hart, "Positivism and the Separation of Law and Morals," *Harvard Law Review* 71 (February 1958): 593–629.

6. Howard Zinn, "Law, Justice and Disobedience," *Notre Dame Journal of Law, Ethics and Public Policy* 5 (1991): 920.

7. Lindsey Cowan, "The Lawyer's Role in Civil Disobedience," *North Carolina Law Review* 47 (1968–69): 593.

8. Judith A. McMorrow, "Civil Disobedience and the Lawyer's Obligation to the Law," *Washington and Lee Law Review* 48 (Winter 1991): 139.

9. McMorrow, "Civil Disobedience," 141.

10. Henry D. Thoreau, "Civil Disobedience," in *Civil Disobedience: Theory and Practice*, ed. Hugo Adam Bedau (Indianapolis: Pegasus, 1969).

11. See Louis Rene Beres, "Civil Disobedience, Jewish Law and the Middle East Peace Process," *Outpost* (April 1996): 7.

12. George E. Bisharat, "Courting Justice? Legitimation in Lawyering under Israeli Occupation," *Law and Social Inquiry* 20 (Spring 1995): 349–405; Martin Edelman, *Courts, Politics and Culture in Israel* (Charlottesville: University Press of Virginia, 1994); Pnina Lahav, *Judgment in Jerusalem: Chief Justice Simon Agranat and the Zionist Century* (Berkeley: University of California Press, 1997).

13. "Doch Male Al Si'hat Ish Matzpen Im Natzig Ashaf Be'london" [Full report on the conversation between a Matzpen member and PLO's representative in London], (Tel Aviv: Matzpen Publications, November 1975).

14. P.D.16: 23/62.

15. Official Law Publications 980, August 5, 1980.

16. Amnon Zichroni, "An Israeli Jew Opposed to the War," *The Israeli Invasion of Lebanon, 1982* (Tokyo: Sanyusha, 1983), 14.

17. Zichroni, "Israeli Jew," *The Israeli Invasion of Lebanon, 1982*, 15.

18. Amnon Zichroni, "Politically Motivated Ban on Meetings with PLO Officials," *Al Awdah* (October 26, 1986), 18.

19. Latif Dori, "Interview with Dori,"*Al Awdah* 73 (November 16, 1986), 6.

20. Dori, "Interview with Zichroni," *Al Awdah* 73 (November 16, 1986), 4.

21. S. Z. Feller, "Ideologia She'hithapssa Le'mishpat" [An ideology masquerading as law], interview with S. Z. Feller, *Halishka* 6 (April 1989): 24.

22. Yehoshua Shoffman (excerpts from the memo), *Zechu'yot Ha'ezrah* 15 (March 1987): 3–8.

23. S. Z. Feller, "Ha'hok Sh'emevaze Et Diney Ha'onshin" [The law that scorns the criminal code], *Davar* (August 8, 1986), 17.

24. Mordechai Kremnizer, "Mi Shenoge'a Be'ashaf" [Whoever touches the PLO], *Koteret Rashit* (September 19, 1985), 48–49.

25. Donna E. Arzt, "Prevention of Terrorism in Israeli, Soviet and South African Legislation: More than a Striking Resemblance?" July 16, 1989, Zichroni archive.

26. *Al Awdah*, July 13, 1987, 15.

27. District Court appeal 1938/88 July 14, 1988.

28. District Court 1238/88–1311/88, p. 27.

29. Supreme Court appeal 621/88.

30. Supreme Court appeal 621/88.

31. Supreme Court 621/88, June 21, 1993.

CHAPTER TEN

Law and Security

As Israel has never enjoyed a true era of peace, the toughest dilemma facing democracy in the country is how to adhere to the rule of law under conditions of a continuous threat to security. Unless one of the two extremes is adopted—either completely forgoing the rule of law or totally ignoring security considerations—constant preoccupation with the friction between law and security is inevitable. Over the years, two main doctrines have emerged. The first subordinates security considerations to the law. As stated by Supreme Court Justice Aharon Barak, "Security is not only the army, it is also democracy. Our strength lies in our moral force and in our adherence to democratic principles, even more so when we are surrounded by great danger."[1] The second doctrine defines Israel as a "self-defending democracy"[2] and considers the value of national security and continued existence of the state to be a superconstitutional premise against which legislation is weighed and which every authority is bound to respect and enhance. Treading the thin ice of law versus security has never been a smooth process, and it has generated numerous fierce conflicts. In several of these Zichroni played a major role, not because he embraced either doctrine fanatically, but because he tried to find the golden mean between them.

One of the greatest challenges to the rule of law in Israel occurred in the mid-1980s and is known as the "300 Bus Affair."[3] On April 12, 1984, at 6:30 in the evening, four Arab terrorists hijacked bus number 300 en route from Tel Aviv to the southern town of Ashkelon. Roadblocks were set up, and soldiers managed to shoot out the tires of the crowded bus, bringing it to a halt in the Gaza Strip, less than eight kilometers from the Egyptian border. The bus was surrounded by large numbers of police, army, and General Security Service (GSS) personnel, including GSS head Avraham Shalom and his deputy Reuven Hazak. At dawn, army commandos stormed the bus, killing two terrorists and freeing the hostages. Among the passengers, one young woman was killed and several were wounded.

The two remaining terrorists were overpowered and stunned in order to prevent them from setting off their explosives. When they were taken off the bus, Brigadier General Yitzhak Mordechai, commander of the Paratroop and Infantry Forces, questioned them briefly and pistol-whipped them in order to find out whether there were any more terrorists in the crowd and whether they had booby-trapped the bus. They were then turned over to the GSS for interrogation, but on the orders of Avraham Shalom, were killed on the way to the hospital.[4] A 7 a.m. radio news bulletin reported that two terrorists had been killed and two captured, but this was corrected later in the day by an army spokesman who stated that all four terrorists had lost their lives in the rescue operation. His announcement raised doubts in the minds of reporters and photographers who had rushed to the scene and, in the confusion, had managed to take pictures of two terrorists being escorted alive from the bus. One showed a terrorist accompanied by Brigadier General Mordechai. This opened the door to a flood of demands for an explanation issued by the Israeli and foreign press.

One of the reporters on the scene was Anat Saragosi of *Ha'olam Ha'ze*, who had shot a dark fuzzy picture which the weekly intended to print in its April 16 issue. However, the photograph was banned by the military censor, as was a clearer picture taken by a photographer for the daily *Hadashot*. Representing *Ha'olam Ha'ze*, Zichroni appealed to the censor on the grounds that his order had nothing to do with state security or any other national interest protected by military censorship. If a terrorist had been murdered after surrendering his weapons and being taken into custody, he wrote, it was not the responsibility of the censor to suppress this information. The public was entitled to any news that did not unequivocally endanger state security. Furthermore, if the censor was right in claiming that no live terrorists could be discerned in the picture, then there was certainly no reason to disallow it. He noted the "Zichroni Decision," in which the Supreme Court had established the norm that the public's right to information had the status of a constitutional right parallel to other human rights, and argued that it was inconceivable that censorship be used to suppress information that might reveal the inappropriate behavior of a state institution.[5] Zichroni's threat to appeal to the High Court of Justice induced the censor to reverse his decision, and anyway the photograph was so dark and blurry that it could not be expected to make much of an impression. In fact, it was largely the picture in *Hadashot*, printed in defiance of the censor, that brought the matter to public attention.

Minister of Defense Moshe Arens appointed a commission of inquiry composed of Major General (Ret.) Me'ir Zore'a and a GSS official, included at the insistence of Shalom, to discover just what had happened that night. This was the start of a cover-up in which the GSS pointed the finger at Brigadier General Mordechai as being responsible for the death of the terrorists. The testimony of the GSS witnesses who appeared before the commission was carefully coordinated in nightly meetings attended by Shalom, his deputy Hazak, the GSS representative on the commission, and the organization's legal advisers. Mordechai, unaware that he was being set up, admitted to hitting the terrorists, whereas Shalom denied he had given orders to execute them. The commission's secret report of May 20, 1984, concluded that the two terrorists had died of fractured skulls, and that crimes had been committed. As a result, a criminal investigation was ordered by Attorney General Yitzhak Zamir on June 4, and eventually it was recommended that Mordechai be charged with assault and that five GSS men and three policemen be subject to a disciplinary hearing for improper conduct.

Zichroni was concerned that the Zore'a Commission would be used as a tool to conceal rather than expose the truth. On April 19, the day the commission was constituted, he wrote to the attorney general requesting that an Ashkelon magistrate's court judge be assigned to investigate the matter, as provided by criminal law. He claimed that news items, photographs, and eyewitness accounts raised the suspicion that two of the terrorists had been killed after being captured, so that a criminal investigation was called for. He also wrote to the chief of staff, reminding him of the obligation of all authorities to report the death of a prisoner to the police. To the best of his knowledge, he stated, the chief of staff had not submitted such a report despite the possibility that one or two of the terrorists had died while in military custody.[6] There were both strengths and weaknesses in this letter. The main strength lay in its reference to a specific law that required officials to take certain action even if it caused them embarrassment. Whatever anxieties the chief of staff or other officials might have had about the consequences of disclosing the death, the law required it to be duly reported to the police. This, however, was also where the main weakness of the letter lay. Strict reliance on the law gave an advantage to public officials, who were skilled in using the letter of the law in order to circumvent it, and this is exactly what happened in the 300 Bus Affair.

When the public was informed of the Zore'a report, most of whose conclusions remained secret, *Ha'olam Ha'ze* cast doubt on the integrity of the board. As in the Porush affair two decades earlier, it published seventy-one questions addressed to the country's decision makers and hinting at their complicity in concealing a crime. One of the questions asked the attorney general why he did not respond to a letter from Zichroni relating that the family of one of the terrorists had seen a bullet hole in his forehead and not signs of beating. In that unanswered letter, Zichroni demanded that the attorney general open a criminal investigation rather than leaving the matter to the commission.[7] Although Zamir did eventually order a criminal investigation, the politicians proved themselves to be more effective. Mordechai was court-martialed in August and acquitted, as were the GSS agents who were brought up before an internal disciplinary board presided over by a district court judge (the charges against the policemen were later dropped). Throughout all these procedures, the GSS continued to maintain its cover-up. At a certain stage, however, the duplicity began to spawn unease within GSS ranks, and Deputy Director Reuven Hazak brought it to the attention of Prime Minister Peres. The "300 Bus Affair" now became the "GSS Affair." Although Peres did not act on the information he received, word of the cover-up reached Attorney General Zamir, who ordered a police investigation despite the considerable pressure on him not to do so. He was cautioned that an investigation could jeopardize national security by revealing carefully guarded information about the operational tactics of the GSS. But Zamir did not knuckle under, and the resulting inquiry not only shook the GSS, but also had two additional consequences. First, on June 1, the government accepted the attorney general's resignation, submitted nine months earlier but never approved. Secondly, a deal was hammered out at the end of June whereby GSS head Shalom resigned in return for the promise of pardons from Israeli president

Haim Herzog for him and the others involved in the killings and the cover-up. Neither the security-minded president (a former intelligence officer) nor the new attorney general (a relatively unknown district court judge) objected to this deal, whose legal validity was later challenged in the Supreme Court by Zichroni and other lawyers, law professors, and civil rights activists—to no avail.

Zichroni contended with the law–security dilemma in many other cases that may have been less dramatic but were no less difficult. Professor Marcus Klingberg, who during World War II had served in the Red Army, was employed for years as chairman of the Department of Preventive Medicine at Tel Aviv University and deputy director of the Nes Ziona Biological Institute, known to work closely with the Ministry of Defense. In 1983, he vanished, with disinformation leaked to the press concerning the circumstances of his disappearance. One item appearing in November 1983 reported that he was in a hospital in Switzerland, while another reporter "learned" that he was undergoing an operation on his leg somewhere "abroad," although his colleagues were unable to provide information on where abroad. Two years later there were speculations in the press that he was in a mental institution in Europe following a nervous breakdown, and one story even referred to a mysterious woman who had lured him out of the country and taken him to the Soviet Union against his will. Only a decade later did the Supreme Court allow public disclosure of the fact that Klingberg had been arrested and convicted in Israel for passing military secrets on biological warfare to the Soviet Union.

In 1986, Intelligence Major Yosef Amit was secretly arrested in Haifa, investigated by the serious crimes unit, and imprisoned without notification. Only three months later did inaccurate news items appear in the local media, based in part on foreign press reports, claiming that an Israeli officer had been accused of spying for Syria.

At the end of the same year, Mordechai Vanunu, a former employee of the Atomic Energy Research Center in Dimona, rumored to be the main source of Israel's nuclear arsenal, sold information and pictures of the reactor to the *Sunday Times* of London. Subsequently, he was enticed by a woman called "Cindy," who appears to have been a Mossad agent, to accompany her to Rome where he was kidnapped and brought back to Israel on an Israeli cargo ship flying a foreign flag. There he was detained under a heavy cloak of secrecy. Following extensive pressure by the *Sunday*

Times, which demanded a writ of habeas corpus, along with the influence of incensed world public opinion, it was announced two months later that Vanunu would be tried behind closed doors.

In 1994, Robert Fisk, a correspondent for the British *Independent* in Beirut, reported that a Lebanese man who had been held in Ashkelon prison was alleged to have seen Klingberg and Vanunu there. The man claimed that they shared a cell with a third—unknown—prisoner also accused of espionage. This was the first indication of the arrest of Colonel Shimon Levinson, who had worked in the security department of the prime minister's office and had established contact with Soviet intelligence agents during a trip to Thailand. He was sentenced to twelve years in prison. His trial, which dragged on for two years, was conducted in total secrecy, with nothing whatsoever leaked to the media, not even in the form of disinformation.

Zichroni was involved in one way or another in all four cases. He represented Amit in his appeal before the Supreme Court, served as Vanunu's attorney after his arrest, was involved in an international prisoner exchange which included Klingberg, and represented Levinson. His involvement in these and similar cases—such as his defense of a Cypriot journalist named Pascalis Pantiotis who was arrested for spying in 1978, and his defense of a Russian immigrant named Shabtai Kalmanowich who in 1988 was sentenced to nine years in prison for espionage—obviously arouses a great deal of curiosity which has yet to be fully satisfied due to the incomplete nature of the information available. Nevertheless, all these cases were particularly significant from the point of view of civil rights.

The arrest of people charged with internal security crimes creates a thorny conflict between the need to maintain secrecy and the right to a fair trial in a democratic society, and Zichroni found himself at the center of this problem and the controversies it generated. The notion of habeas corpus, which ensures that a person accused of a crime is brought before a judge within a reasonable period of time, is a cherished principle in all democracies, and is one of the primary distinctions between a democracy and a police state. The citizens of a democracy are not expected to disappear in the middle of the night with no clue as to their fate. George Kennan, who served as the American ambassador to Moscow at the beginning of the Cold War, paints the horrifying picture of a state whose citizens live in constant fear and uncertainty.[8] When a car loaded with secret agents screeches to a halt in front of a tall apartment building in a totalitarian state, all the tenants freeze in terror since it is never clear who "they" are going to take away this time. People vanishing into secret dungeons and remote prison camps, or being executed following a summary trial or no trial at all, was a familiar phenomenon in police states such as the Soviet Union, Nazi Germany, Maoist China, Greece under the colonels, Argentina under the generals, Pinochet's Chile, Pol Pot's Cambodia, Mobutu's Congo, and many others. Democracies, on the other hand, are distinguished by the procedures that prevent undue uncertainty over a citizen's fate, even when emergency laws are in force. Individuals in democratic societies are sometimes victimized by Kafkaesque institutions where they are subjected to arbitrariness disguised as officialdom, but one can still expect to find some degree of a relationship between crime and punishment that makes it possible to assess one's future within a given range of possibilities. Moreover, anyone accused of a crime appears before a court that is independent from the executive branch. In order to ensure independence and due process, legal procedures are public, affording partial if not full transparency in respect to what goes on in the interrogation room and the courthouse.

There is no principle more important than public trials for preserving democracy, and no principle more prone to violation when internal security is involved. As a rule, security services operate covertly to carry out their duty of protecting citizens from the subversive activities of spies and traitors, and they therefore have trouble coping with the principle of public trials. In this respect at least, there is little difference between the secret services of the U.S., Great Britain, Canada, South Africa, or Israel. When a spy ring is uncovered and a number of its members are arrested, the security services are understandably reluctant to favor a writ of *habeas corpus* that might send a warning to those confederates who are still at large. Moreover, in trials involving internal security matters, every effort is made to prevent public exposure of the tactics employed by the secret services. In the 1980s, when quite a few democracies were threatened by international terrorism, laws were enacted to prevent the disclosure of national secrets in the courts, among them the Internal Security Law in South Africa,[9] the Law Protecting the Secret Services in Australia,[10] and the Official Secrets Act in Great Britain.[11] Although Britain's House of Lords confirmed the principle of public trials on the eve of World War I, it still imposed restrictions on reporting from the courthouse when official secrets were at stake.

All democracies operate here in a twilight zone between normative principles and security constraints. It is easy to take an extreme position that dismisses one or the other of these concerns, but as Justice Moshe Landau stated in 1987 when he headed an investigation into the 300 Bus Affair, perfectionist positions should be replaced by the recognition that democratic life is conducted in the gray area between ideological poles.[12] In every democracy the world over, security considerations have led to deviations from the principle of public trials; the problem is to maintain the proper balance between the conflicting needs of security and transparency. This is where the role of the civil rights attorney becomes crucial. The greater the guilt of a spy or traitor, the more heinous the betrayal of the country is perceived to be, the more important the role of the lawyers. It is they who mediate between the accused and the services detaining them, negotiate the conditions under which they are held, press for the implementation of habeas corpus, and see to it that due process is followed. This is not an easy job, as it entails two major problems. First, since legal procedures in such cases are conducted behind closed doors, defense lawyers do not enjoy the support they might otherwise expect from the press and other legal watchdogs. In some sense, secrecy may be an advantage to a person charged with espionage because it averts the lynching frenzy that such trials might generate. On the other hand, however, the defense attorney must stand alone in contending with the security services and their monopoly over most of the relevant information. Furthermore, since a great deal of confidential information is naturally involved in these trials, defense lawyers must be granted clearance by the same security services they are battling, perhaps resulting not only in the loss of their credibility in the eyes of their clients, but also, in the long run, in the accusation that they are "in league" with the defense establishment.

In his defense of individuals charged with espionage and treason, Zichroni sought to cope with the first problem by using his remarkable skills of communication. Although he was blocked from disclosing secrets, he adopted a strategy of constant visibility in the world and Israeli press, not actually revealing anything, but keeping the affair in the headlines. In early November 1986, when the press discovered that Vanunu was in Israel and that he had been permitted a defense lawyer of his own choosing, it had its hands out to catch any crumb of information that could be gleaned from that lawyer. Zichroni quickly rose to the occasion. On November 10, he declared in *Al Ha'mishmar* that a writ of habeas corpus had been issued after considerable pressure, and that the trial would be held behind closed doors. Asked for his impression was of the "Atom Spy," he took the opportunity to inject into the public consciousness the idea that would become his main defense strategy in the trial: Vanunu was a rational man motivated by the desire to bring out into the open an issue that warranted public discourse; his motives in revealing Israel's atomic secrets to the *Sunday Times* were ideological rather than financial.[13] He took advantage of an interview in *Ha'aretz* concerning the security clearance he had been granted allowing him to represent Vanunu, to give his client a human image. Refusing to reveal where he was being kept, Zichroni said only that he was in a "certain" prison, adding that when he visited him there, Vanunu complained that he was being stripped of his human dignity and being publicly lynched in the media.[14] Zichroni developed this idea further in *Ma'ariv*, where he reported that when Vanunu had heard about his negative image in the Israeli media, he had responded by saying that they were turning him into a monster for no good reason.[15]

All these interviews may have been part of a strategy to combat what appeared to be disinformation in the press. Newspapers items like the following may have been planted by Vanunu's captors:

> "Mordechai Vanunu was brought to Israel for interrogation in order to find out whether he had given the secrets of the Dimona nuclear reactor to Soviet agents; otherwise we could have shot him in the street abroad"—*Newsday* quoted an Israeli official yesterday. The newspaper adds that Israel is concerned over the possibility that the pictures of the reactor that were not published will reach Soviet hands.[16]

Zichroni protested that while he respected the court's gag order on the Vanunu affair, "government elements do not do likewise."[17] Indeed, his frequent press appearances often seemed like a public relations fist-fight with those same "government elements." He claimed that Vanunu was a very open-minded person of higher than average intelligence and spoke of the books he brought his client, especially ideological and political literature such as Uri Avnery's *My Friend, My Enemy* about his talks with

PLO officials, and Zichroni's own book *1 Against 119* about the attorney's Knesset activities. Since this was virtually all the information he could reveal about the Vanunu affair, the press, reluctant to give up on this juicy story, focused on the lawyer himself:

> Zichroni, 51, born in Tel Aviv, became famous in the early 1950s when he refused to be drafted into the IDF. Many were surprised; while still a student at Ge'ula high school, he handed out Irgun fliers. He was court-martialed and sentenced to 7 months in prison. Zichroni launched a hunger strike, causing considerable stir.[18]

During the Vanunu affair, the press was filled with colorful descriptions of the attorney who "is skilled in combining his left-wing attitudes with the pleasantries of the bourgeoisie, and loves the good life: good food, first-class whisky, an American car. He has a pot belly and a perennial cigar. He has connections with ministers, MK's, and senior officials, and now also with the organization that is holding Vanunu."[19] Zichroni's relations with the GSS would be hinted at from this time forward, and he began to be hounded by the press as if he himself were a public official. He was followed when he went to London ("he said he cannot reveal the identity of the people he will meet with there, because he was asked to preserve their anonymity"), and when he returned ("Atty. Amnon Zichroni said yesterday upon his return from London that his visit there was 'interesting'"). He was mobbed by reporters when he visited his client in prison ("Atty. Amnon Zichroni went into the prison yesterday and spent 55 minutes there. When he came out he said to *Ha'aretz*'s correspondent: 'I do not confirm that Vanunu is here'"), and when he came to court. Soon, this constant visibility in the press became a news item in and of itself:

> Atty. Amnon Zichroni has become the most recognizable Israeli lawyer overseas these days. He has turned into a true 'media star,' with the interviews he grants, some by satellite, broadcast throughout the world 24 hours a day. The phone in his office never stops ringing, and foreign and local journalists frequent the office in order to glean any crumbs of information on the affair that has caught the interest of the world media today.[20]

Zichroni's use of the media was also functional in a more general sense. He utilized the curiosity aroused by espionage cases not only to serve his clients' interests, but also to prevent the security services from hiding prisoners away in secret dungeons without justification. Although the public knew very little about the Levinson affair, for instance, he made sure that it remained in the headlines. After Levinson's conviction in the longest internal security trial in the history of Israel, about which hardly any details were leaked, Zichroni granted an interview to *Hadashot* in which he stated that his client was a nice, straightforward, and honest person, with health problems and a wonderful family:

> Yes, a wonderful family indeed. It is truly moving. A family that finds itself in such a situation and yet mobilizes the spiritual strength to so warmly support the father and husband caught up in this problem.[21]

When the arrest of Yosef Amit was revealed in 1993, Zichroni hinted at his motives in more interviews:

> The state tends to want a cloak of secrecy for security reasons, because it fears the adverse effects on foreign relations, or because of its reluctance to disclose the operational tactics of the intelligence services. On the other hand, there are cases in which the accused also agrees to a cloak of secrecy in order to maintain his privacy and avoid injury to his family. But the aspect that is forgotten is the right of the public to know. We live in a democratic state, in which the principle of public trials is sacred and must be carefully upheld.[22]

The Amit case brought the importance of public trials to public attention, and represented a turning point in the campaign waged by civil rights activists against the conducting of espionage and treason trials in secrecy. In the words of legal commentator Moshe Negbi, these trials were "an ugly stain on our democracy."[23] He did not dispute that certain cases must be kept secret for reasons of state security, but added that it was hard to believe that reasons of security could justify imprisonment and concealment for long periods of time. After the Amit affair, the chairman of the Knesset's constitutional committee called on the parliament to reconsider the interdiction on information concerning the imprisonment of spies, as it was inconceivable that a person could disappear and be brought to trial without public knowledge.

On the other hand, the same case also raised the question of excessive and unsubstantiated information. Rather than satisfying the public's right to know, interviews and news items that conceal more than they reveal about a matter of internal security simply create confusion. This problem became particularly acute in 1988, when Zichroni began a series of secret international contacts to free Israeli prisoners, with the press occasionally printing items that sparked baseless rumors. That year, the Soviet Union made another attempt, as it had done throughout the Cold War era, to get Klingberg back in a spy exchange. Soviet and Israeli representatives met several times, with both sides regularly utilizing the services of lawyers in these contacts. Zichroni was involved in the negotiations as the attorney for Kalmanowich, who was drawn into the deal despite the fact that he was probably just a small-time operator. Through these negotiations, Zichroni was introduced to East German attorney Wolfgang Vogel, who suggested he might be able to arrange for the release of Ron Arad, the Israeli navigator whose plane was shot down over Lebanon in 1986, in return for Klingberg. An agreement was signed between Zichroni and Vogel, and Zichroni managed to obtain a picture of Ron Arad, but the deal never went through.

While these negotiations were going on, the Israeli and international press were continually spreading rumors about convoluted spy exchanges.

In East Berlin, Kalmanowich's lawyer is negotiating the possibility of a prisoner exchange. . . . Reliable sources in the United States relate: Atty. Amnon Zichroni met with Atty. Wolfgang Vogel, who specializes in the exchange of prisoners between the East and the West, asking him to include him in such a deal. The meeting took place with the tacit approval of the Israeli government. Atty. Amnon Zichroni refused to comment.[24]

Some of the items were true: in 1978, at the request of Prime Minister Begin, Zichroni successfully negotiated the release of the Israeli soldier Avraham Amram from an Arab prison, and the attorney's connections with the PLO were used in 1991 to obtain information about the hostages in Lebanon. Many other items, however, were premature, raising high expectations before any actual results were achieved. When Israel has no clue about its MIA's in Lebanon, and some foreign agent claims to be able to provide information or set up an exchange, policymakers tend to give a green light to pursue the lead, even if it is unlikely to bear any fruit. Throughout the world, there are characters—some of them reliable but most of them not—who engage in the prisoner exchange business. The less reliable they are, the more they inflate the supposed deals they can arrange. What is more, security services and governments often take advantage of such ersatz negotiations in order to give the impression that they are continuing their efforts to secure the release of prisoners when there is actually nothing they can do. Consequently, during Zichroni's negotiations with Vogel, the involvement of half a dozen different countries in the venture was reported in the world press:

> *Die Welt:* The possibility of a comprehensive spy exchange in which 9 countries will participate, including the United States and the Soviet Union, is being examined. . . . The release of a spy named Prof. Glinberg is being discussed. . . . The West German paper does not indicate what Israel will get in return. Last week, the "Spy Releaser," East German attorney Wolfgang Vogel, visited Israel on a specially-arranged visa. The release of Scheransky [a Jewish activist who was in a Soviet prison at the time] is being mediated. MK Eliav to the newspaper's correspondent: 'Can't say anything.' Amnon Zichroni, attorney for Kalmanowich: 'The information has no foundation." . . . A comprehensive spy exchange with the participation of Israel, the Soviet Union, the United States, Great Britain, the two Germanys, South Africa, Norway, and Iraq is about to be concluded.[25]

During this period, Zichroni's name featured in many similar items relating to the exchange of spies, prisoners, and hostages, and it was invariably hinted that he was operating with the "tacit approval" of the Israeli government. Indeed, some of his past associates began to eye him suspiciously:

> For many years, Zichroni has done nothing to lift the smoke screen. Sometimes it even seems he enjoys the mystery surrounding him. . . . In fact, in the activities of Atty. Amnon Zichroni, the hidden exceeds that which meets the eye. It is unclear where he is flying off to, in whose service, who is footing the bill, and who he has to report to.[26]

Although as a private lawyer, Zichroni was not obliged to report to anybody, left-wing activists began to associate him with the "establishment," viewing him as a comrade who had betrayed them and gone over to the other side:

> The fact that Zichroni is acting on behalf of the state is interpreted by many as identification with the establishment, the same establishment

he rebelled against for so many years and in whose shade he now rests. A former friend states: 'Zichroni's rebellion has long been over . . . when, as a lawyer, you begin to work with the state, you become a party to its secrets, and when you are a party to the secrets, you become a party to the ideology, and then also the goals. Anyone who does not preserve the boundaries, may find himself in all kinds of dark corners.[27]

This is an interesting comment because it reveals a misunderstanding of the role of the civil rights lawyer. It assumes, in line with political sociology of the early twentieth century, that the state is composed of a ruling elite and a militant opposition, and that the democratic process consists of the ideological struggle of the opposition to change the government and take it over. This position ignores the existence of a civil society which continues to maintain a certain autonomy, even though it operates in conjunction with the sphere in which the government and opposition wage their ideological battles. Nor does this attitude recognize the role of the professional lawyer as mediator between the civil society and the political state. Many of Zichroni's colleagues in the peace camp attempted to confront him with an ultimatum: you are either with us or with the establishment. They never entertained the possibility that a private lawyer could operate in close contact with the government in order to protect norms that derive from the civil society, such as a spy's right to a fair trial. By appearing so often in the media and remaining secretive, Zichroni was seen to be behaving like one of "them":

Last week, in his appearance on [the newscast] Mabat in reference to Amit, Zichroni, the former draft dodger, revealed himself in such a state-like security-like light. No, he responded to his interviewer with the intonation of a government minister, he could not go into detail, and this is obvious enough; but not one word of condemnation issued from the mouth of the lawyer who has gained the full trust of the security branches in recent years.[28]

What this criticism missed was the fact that Zichroni had always operated within the framework of the systems into which he was born and in which he lived. Although he adopted an autonomous stance toward these systems, he invariably took advantage of the procedures available to the individual within them. As a conscientious objector he wrote letters, as secretary of the

Third Force he handed out fliers, as Avnery's aide he operated in the legislature, and as a lawyer he defended his clients in court. In this sense, he was always an outsider to the Israeli left, whose members perceived their task as ideological opposition to the regime. Thus, any action taken on behalf of that regime was defined as betrayal. Zichroni was particularly criticized whenever he took upon himself the defense of an "enemy." In 1988 he defended none other than Avraham Shapira, the ultra-orthodox chairman of the Knesset's finance committee, in a failed plea before the District Court, and later the Supreme Court, to forbid publication of an unfavorable biography by journalist Arie Avnery. In 1991 he pleaded for former GSS official Yossi Genossar's right to carve the date according to the Gregorian calendar, rather than the customary Jewish date, on the tomb of his son who fell in battle in the Gaza Strip, and in 1993 he again represented Genossar when his appointment as General Secretary of the Housing Ministry was rescinded because of his involvement in the 300 Bus Affair. Many people considered it unforgivable for Zichroni to provide this service to, and maintain a friendship with, one of the principal GSS agents pardoned in the questionable deal which ended that affair, and one publication even printed the news under the headline: "Dr. Zichroni and Mr. Genossar."[29] The headline was coined by peace activist Maxim Ghilan, who believed that Zichroni agreed to defend Genossar because he considered him a political dove who might be useful to the peace process then underway between Israel and the Palestinians. But this was not good enough for Ghilan:

> Zichroni was, in his youth, a pacifist and a war-resister. At a time when fighting was of the essence, and the Israel Defense Forces were more concerned with defense than nowadays, Zichroni went to jail in order not to serve in the army. Now he has changed. He believes expediency should cleanse all guilt—if the guilty do, later on, something politically useful for peace. Zichroni believes—at best, and if we give him the benefit of the doubt concerning his real intent—the situation to be so bad that the main thing is to change Israeli policy. At whatever moral cost.[30]

What ideologues of the extreme left like Ghilan did not realize is that purposeful action in the service of civil society, in contrast to symbolic acts such as singing sad songs and releasing doves into the air at peace demonstrations, is often conducted by professionals who may have to establish contacts with those on the other side of the fence in order to advance their cause. In the Vanunu case, this led to such mistrust that Zichroni was fired. Although the main reason for his dismissal was most likely an argument over the attorney's fees, the press reported that Vanunu objected to the close relationship between his lawyer and the security services, and complained that Zichroni did not identify with his actions either privately or publicly.

This intriguing contention was voiced not only by Vanunu, the self-declared ideologue, but also by Zichroni's former associates in the peace camp. It is intriguing because it is true; Zichroni never showed any sign that he identified with the sale of Israel's atomic secrets to the *Sunday Times*. Nor did he intend to bolster his client's case by delivering ideological speeches on Israel's atomic strategy on the steps of the courthouse. Several groups in Great Britain and Australia were interested in turning the Vanunu trial into an exposé of Israel's nuclear capability, a motive hinted at by Vanunu's brother, Meir. According to one press report, he demanded that Zichroni take a more aggressive approach and fight to have the trial held in open court.[31] Although noted for his advocacy of the principle of public trials, Zichroni saw it as his job to defend his client rather than allow him to star as the hero in a show trial. He therefore opted for a two-fold strategy. In his public appearances he emphasized the broad ideological issues, stressing the need to demilitarize the Middle East and turn it into a nuclear-free zone. In court, however, he sought to prove that the material that Vanunu had handed over to the paper contained nothing that had not previously been published. This distinction between the ideological and the professional aspects of the trial was invaluable for the defense attorney, but it did not satisfy the Vanunu family or, for that matter, Zichroni's critics.

Zichroni strongly objected to nuclear weapons. In Geneva in September 1987, he devoted his talk at the fourth NGO meeting organized by the United Nations to this issue, which few Israelis, including his critics on the left, had ever raised before. He argued that possession of nuclear weapons by any country, including the superpowers, should be regarded as "a war crime as well as a war against humanity in the tradition of the Nuremberg Tribunal and the Geneva Conventions."[32] Aware that passing a resolution to this effect was totally unfeasible, he turned his attention to the Middle East, which, he declared without hesitation, had become a nuclear weapons zone, thereby posing a threat not only to the inhabitants of the region but to the whole world. He stated that Israel could no longer avoid open discourse on the issue, not even for bogus security reasons (which may have been the major impact of the *Sunday Times* article and Vanunu's pictures). He described the two strategies advocated in Israel—a policy of vagueness whereby the existence of nuclear weapons was not admitted, and an open declaration that Israel had the bomb—and explained that, interestingly enough, the debate between them did not line up along the left–right continuum. Finally, he proposed that the only viable strategy was a third one—declaring the Middle East a nuclear-free zone. Unlike the superpowers, he contended, the countries of the Middle East were small, so that a nuclear attack would annihilate a whole country. There would be no opportunity for a second strike because of the utter destruction caused by the first, in which millions would die, and he added:

> As we can see, the future looks rather dreary; we need to dismantle the nuclear weapons programme and create a Nuclear-Weapons-Free Zone in the Middle East. The NGOs of the world have increasing power, and it is up to all of us to mobilize world public opinion for a non-nuclear Middle East.[33]

Although Zichroni was attacked in Geneva by Vanunu's brother Meir, who had come there to mobilize public opinion to his brother's cause, he distributed documents proving that Vanunu's disclosures made no difference and that details of Israel's nuclear capability had previously appeared in the world press. Even after he was dismissed by Vanunu, he continued to speak out against nuclear proliferation and the arms race in the Middle East. He claimed that the decision to amass a nuclear arsenal in Israel was taken by the founding fathers at a time when the Holocaust was still clear in their minds, and they therefore thought of the Arab–Israeli conflict in terms of total war. After 1967, however, things changed, and Israel was now strong enough to allow itself to modify its nuclear policy. In an article in *Globes*, he maintained that it was in the interest of both Israel and the U.S. to perpetuate the arms race because it was good for American industry, and called for a halt to it:

> The Middle East has turned into a massive arms dump. Israel is currently one of the most important accelerators of this process. The most important

limit to this process could be—limitations imposed by the USA on its arms exports. This would really slow down the race. But it is quite reasonable to assume that the American arms lobby will do all it can to avoid such limitations, and it is equally reasonable to assume that it will succeed.[34]

Still, there is a difference between ideology and professional action. Television courtroom dramas are often constructed around a decisive moment when defendants or their lawyers deliver a moving speech that sways the judge and jury and turns everything around. In real courtrooms, however, or at least until recently when cameras where allowed in, the defense must rely on legal arguments that generally have little to do with ideology. For example, when Vanunu was kidnapped, Minister of Defense Yitzhak Rabin issued a decree suppressing certain evidence on the grounds that it could jeopardize state security, especially information about the manner in which Vanunu was seized. According to Israeli law, the decree would be valid only if it was approved by a Supreme Court justice. The ensuing hearing occupied ten court sessions. Judge Gabriel Bach's final ruling to admit certain evidence in defiance of the Minister of Defense did not stem, as far as one could tell, from any ideological rhetoric more appropriate in speeches delivered in city squares, but from the legal arguments presented by Zichroni and Feldman, who replaced him as Vanunu's attorney. The question was not whether the evidence might endanger state security, but whether that risk should be taken in order to assure the defendant's right to a fair trial. The conditions imposed by Bach on the manner in which the evidence could be presented in court were not to the liking of the Vanunu family, who hoped to influence public opinion, but they seemed quite reasonable from the perspective of the balance between law and security. Vanunu was allowed to describe how he was arrested, how long and under what conditions he was held, and his feelings and fears. However, the judge would not allow him to reveal the name of the country in which he was seized (although he wrote "Rome" on his hand and held it up to the window of the police car that brought him to court for the journalists to see) or the means of transportation employed by the agents to bring him back to Israel, details that did not seem relevant enough to the defense arguments to justify their revelation.[35]

We can learn something about the effectiveness of ideological arguments in the courtroom from Vanunu's 1990 appeal to the Supreme Court to reduce the 18-year sentence imposed by the district court. In response to defense attorney Feldman's argument that Vanunu had acted for purely ideological reasons, two of the judges in the original trial termed this mere rationalization. Although the third judge accepted the defense contention, he still concurred with the majority on the grounds that ideological motivation had no bearing on the nature of the crime. The district court thus ruled that "people in a democratic society are entitled to disseminate information, but not confidential information obtained illegally. Even if a person has a number of motives, some of which are legal and some which are not, he may be found guilty on the basis of one of them, whatever his dominant motivation was."[36]

In the appeal, Feldman argued that the majority opinion had not understood Vanunu's motive and had interpreted the evidence of it subjectively and one-sidedly. Justice Meir Shamgar, who presided over the panel of judges, had this to say about ideological motives:

> A motive, however innocent, does not strip the prohibited act of its nature as a crime, as determined by criminal law. . . . The view that the goal or motive justifies the means and provides an a priori exemption from criminal responsibility is the antithesis of democratic rule, which is rooted in honoring the law and the rule of law rather than in the power and arbitrariness of individuals seeking to implement their ideas without considering the essence of their actions. This is a blueprint for anarchy, and its victims are all those individuals whom it is right and proper to protect from the devices and aspirations of those who place their faith in the truth of their own ideas beyond any law. The victims are the innocent citizens who become guinea pigs for the criminal for the realization of his ideology.[37]

Shamgar stressed the price that might have to be paid by the victims of those who reveal state secrets for ideological reasons, a consequence which in his opinion called into question the morality of the ideologically motivated act. In other words, he expressed a view to which Zichroni appears to have subscribed throughout his life: Israeli democracy, severely challenged by security constraints, might benefit less from ideological speeches on street corners, of the kind he himself had expounded as a disciple of Mordechai Stein in the 1950s, and more from the professional activity of civil rights lawyers who see to it that even in trials conducted behind closed doors, the rights of the defendant are protected. Nothing is worse for a democracy than when people accused of internal security crimes vanish into secret dungeons. In order to prevent such things from happening, lawyers must act responsibly and professionally to maintain the balance between the right of the state to ensure its existence and the right of the civil society, and the individuals and groups composing it, to a life of liberty. It was to this task that Amnon Zichroni devoted most of his life.

Notes

1. Quoted in Jehudith Karp, Report of the Commission appointed by the attorney general to investigate the GSS affair, December 20, 1986, 30.

2. Jehudith Karp, "Finding an Equilibrium," *Israeli Democracy* (Fall 1990): 30.

3. See Ian Black and Benny Morris, *Israel's Secret Wars: The Untold Story of Israel's Intelligence* (London: Hamish Hamilton, 1991); Dan Raviv and Yossi Melman, *Every Spy a Prince: The Complete Story of Israel's Intelligence Community* (Boston: Houghton Mifflin, 1990).

4. According to Jehudith Karp, Report of the Commission.

5. *Ha'olam Ha'ze*, May 2, 1984.

6. Amnon Zichroni to Chief of Staff Moshe Levy, letter, April 19, 1984.

7. Amnon Zichroni to Professor Zamir, letter, May 29, 1984.

8. George Kennan, "Totalitarianism in the Modern World," in *Totalitarianism*, ed. Carl Friedrich (New York: Grosset and Dunlap, 1964).

9. See Gilbert Marcus, "The Veil of Secrecy in South Africa," *International Commission of Justice Review* 29 (December 1982): 56–60.

10. See Garth Nettheim, "Open Justice and State Secrets," *Adelaide Law Review* 10 (September 1986): 281–317.

11. See Graham Zellick, "Spies, Subversives, Terrorists and the British Government: Free Speech and Other Casualties," *William and Mary Law Review* 31 (1990): 773–821.

12 "Landau Commission Report," excerpts published in *Israel Law Review* 23 (Spring–Summer, 1989).

13. *Al Ha'Mishmar*, November 10, 1986.

14. *Ha'aretz*, November 10, 1986.

15. *Ma'ariv*, November 10, 1986.

16. *Ma'ariv*, November 20, 1986.

17. *Ma'ariv*, November 11, 1986.

18. Na'omi Levitzki, "Ha'ish Se'vanunu Somech Alav" [The man Vanunu trusts], *Koteret Rashit*, November 12, 1986.

19. Levitzki, "Ha'ish Se'vanunu Somech Alav," *Koterét Rashit*, November 12, 1986.

20. Aya Ornstein, "Vanunu Megadel Zakan Ba'kele: Bikesh Mi'praklito Shokolad" [Vanunu grows a beard in prison: asked his attorney for chocolate], *Ma'ariv*, November 12, 1986.

21. *Hadashot*, September 3, 1993.

22. *Ha'aretz*, June 4, 1993.

23. Moshe Negbi, "Ketem Al Ha'demockratia" [A stain on democracy], *Ma'ariv*, August 24, 1994.

24. *Ma'ariv*, June 8, 1988.

25. *Ma'ariv*, September 7, 1989.

26. Eli Kamir, "Amnon Zichroni: Ha'mitos Ve'hametzi'ut" [Amnon Zichroni: The myth and reality], *Ma'ariv,* June 11, 1993.

27. Kamir, "Amnon Zichroni," Ma'ariv, June 11, 1993.

28. Gideon Levy, "Ne'edarim Bi'dey Ko'hotenu" [Missing and kept by our own forces], *Ha'aretz*, June 6, 1993.

29. Maxim Ghilan, "Dr. Zichroni and Mr. Genossar." *Israel and Palestine Political Report*, 171 (April 1992), 1.

30. Ghilan, "Dr. Zichroni and Mr. Genossar," 2.

31. *Ha'aretz*, March 8, 1987.

32. Statement delivered by Amnon Zichroni at the Fourth United Nations International NGO meeting on the Question of Palestine, September 7–9, 1987. Palais des Nations, Gebeva. Background paper no. 5, 1.

33. Statement, Zichroni, 2.

34. Amnon Zichroni, "The Arms Race Has a Price," *Globes* article reprinted in *Israel and Palestine Political Report, Paris.*

35. Mordechai Ben Shlomo Vanunu v. State of Israel, Supreme Court 64/87, August 12, 1987.

36. Quoted in Supreme Court Convened as Court of Appeals 172/88, P.D. 84, vol. 44, section 3, 1991, 265–66.

37. Quoted in Supreme Court Convened as Court of Appeals 172/88, P.D. 84, vol. 44, section 3, 1991, 265–66.

CHAPTER ELEVEN

The Advocate of Civil Society

In a study on lawyers and politics in France, Lucien Karpik shows how nineteenth century lawyers represented the civil society. Since the Napoleonic era, the public constituted a sovereign force that could be called upon to defend or attack the state, and one which both government and opposition were anxious to appease. And it was the lawyers who represented it, for "this collective, impersonal figure speaks only through mediators."[1] The lawyers were thus the spokespersons for the collective, impersonal, amorphous public which, in return, ennobled them. According to Karpik, this relationship persisted until the politicized twentieth century, when the rise of revolutionary discourse on the one hand, and technical expertise on the other, stripped the lawyer of the role of advocate of the public. Consequently, lawyers today are associated either with the state or with the market. And yet, although public wisdom (and experience) casts them as agents of the state and manipulators of the market, their professional norms coincide in principle with the civil society—the plurality of groups operating in relative autonomy from either of these two sectors.

The willingness of legal professionals in recent history to serve the most authoritarian states,[2] and their often brazen pursuit of material interests,[3] have blinded us to the fact that the rise of the legal profession, like that of other liberal professions, was accompanied by norms of liberty. Professionalism, that is, the application of systematic knowledge, can not flourish for any length of time within a restrictive environment. However unaware some lawyers may appear to be of their calling's association with norms of any kind, the development of the professions over time required a relatively predictable setting in which truth was not contingent upon state or market interests, and dialogue was not controlled by hegemonic political or economic forces.[4]

This personal history thus serves as a reminder of the oft-forgotten relationship between lawyers and civil society. We have traced the career of one attorney, Amnon Zichroni, noting his twenty-three-day-long hunger strike as a conscientious objector, the activities of the splinter groups of political dissenters he joined, and the crucial restraining role they played in the young State of Israel through such actions as disclosing information about the 1956 massacre in Kfar Kassem. We have considered the seminal court cases in which he challenged the definition of citizenship according to nationalist criteria, opposed the construction of settlements in the West Bank, and acted to protect the freedoms of the press, association, and religion. We have followed his efforts to defend Palestinian leaders in the occupied territories, to defend the right of the Progressive List for Peace to run for election, to provide legal aid to persons imprisoned under a veil of secrecy, and to expose the cover-up in the 300 Bus Affair. We have joined him in the secret meetings between Israelis and PLO officials beginning in the late 1960s, and in acts of civil disobedience in defiance of the law banning these meetings.

In most of these instances, Zichroni acted as a lawyer committed to the formal procedures of the law and the institutions of the state. In his private law practice, he also competed in the marketplace. At the same time, his life story is the biography of an advocate of civil society—a role that stemmed neither from "revolutionary discourse" nor from "technical expertise," to use Karpik's terms, but from a professional attitude that championed the liberty of the individual and the autonomy of the voluntary group. As a result of both his personality and his upbringing in the "civil circles," Zichroni placed himself directly on the intersection between the civil society and the state. By occupying this position, he sometimes came into conflict with the state, but also engaged in its activities in the pursuit of individual freedom and group autonomy.

In a new state struggling to uphold democratic principles within severe security constraints, this was no easy task, particularly as there was no acknowledgment of the civil society. Especially after 1967, when political discourse in Israel was politicized to the degree that people were forced to choose sides on virtually every issue, notably the Palestinian question that dominated the public sphere after the Six Day War, civil society did not have many advocates. The individual seeking freedom from religious coercion and political domination, the minority seeking national self-determination, and the voluntary group preoccupied with its own well-being rather than the fate of the nation-state, had to fight hard, primarily in the courts, and generally with limited success. The role of advocate of civil society differs from the conventional image of the civil rights lawyer, however, because neither the government nor the market is defined as the enemy. On the contrary, the civil rights lawyer fights to secure a place for the individual citizen within these systems.

One important lesson to be learned from this personal history is that the lawyer's mediating role between the civil society and the state and market involves a self-aware professionalism. While intellectuals such as writers, artists, and philosophers have developed a self-awareness of their societal role, professionals have not.[5] Ever since the Dreyfus affair at the end of the nineteenth century, which brought intellectuals out into the public arena, the image of Emile Zola crying out "*J'accuse*" has been a role model for free thinkers encountering social, political, military, or religious injustice.[6] Although certain professionals have also occasionally spoken out against such ills, there appears to be little consciousness of their role as guardians of civil society among lawyers, engineers, physicians, academics, and the members of other liberal professions. While they often speak of social responsibility when asked to address the graduating classes of their alma maters, it is only in rare cases that such responsibility has, in fact, become part of their creed.[7]

Moreover, in modern times professional expertise has largely been mobilized by the nation-state. It would be hard to imagine Israel's survival as a nation, for instance, without the recruitment of professional know-how into the service of state security. With the loosening of the hegemonic hold of the state, market forces began to determine the enlistment and behavior of professionals, affecting such trends as the changeover from public to private medicine, the status of teachers, etc. Over the years, the number of professionals in all public and private enterprises has burgeoned. The operation of any contemporary organization today requires computer programmers, social workers, public relations consultants, marketers, organizational psychologists, strategic experts, and so on. As the numbers of these professional people have grown, individual advocates of civil society such as Zichroni have become less visible. But whether they realize it or not, the nurturing of civil society largely depends on professionals. More than ever before, when individuals and groups confront the strong forces of the state and the market, they need the mediation of those responsible for the production, distribution, and application of knowledge.

I am not talking about the involvement of professionals in civic activities in their spare time. What I am suggesting is the correlation between a thriving profession and political liberty. It is in the professional's interest per se to ensure an environment in which knowledge can evolve and be applied. Totalitarianism placed severe restraints on knowledge, enlisting it to its needs for a limited period but not allowing it to flourish over time. It was not by chance that it was knowledge developed by the democratic powers that won World War II, for effective professionalism requires liberty.[8] It is my contention that journalists have a vested interest in freedom of speech, social workers in a fair distribution of resources, and lawyers in the rule of law. "Self-aware professionalism" refers to the understanding that these social norms are the vested interests of professionals, and therefore worth fighting for in the political arena. The prescriptive model I am proposing calls for the social and political involvement of the professional in maintaining these norms in the face of the ever-growing force of the state and market. While this involvement alone may not ensure the autonomous space necessary for an active society, it might be an important beginning if lawyers, for example, set themselves up as advocates of the rule of law. Zichroni's objection to a double standard in the way the law was applied within Israel and in the occupied territories derived, above all, from a self-aware professionalism, which in turn became a social and political asset.

This attitude requires refinement of the common image of the civil rights lawyer as a sheriff confronting a villainous regime. The Zichroni story demonstrates that the advocate of civil society is not a lone lawman riding into town to save the day, but rather a guerrilla fighter. The protection of civil rights in the cases we have considered here depended less on the lonely fighter than on the support that fighter could enlist in the community at large. This was true when 18-year-old Zichroni won broad public support during his hunger strike as a conscientious objector, when he turned a small political party into a significant parliamentary force, when he focused public attention on the landmark cases he fought in matters of principle, such as the Tamarin case, the Elon Moreh case, or the 300 Bus Affair, and in his battle against the 1986 amendment infringing on the freedom of Israelis to meet with PLO officials. The last of these is an excellent example of a "guerrilla operation," in that Zichroni and Feldman relied on the support of the wider community of legal professionals. However reluctant these people were to take sides over the outlawing of free contact between Israeli citizens and PLO officials, and however apolitical they chose to remain, Israel's jurists realized that the amendment posed a threat not only to civil rights, but to professional norms as well. The discourse on the amendment was largely devoted to the principles dictated by their professional, and not necessarily civic, conscience. While enhancing the effectiveness of their argument, this attitude also furthered the cause of civil society, and hence of democracy. The focus on professional matters, such as the need to distinguish criminal from political offenses, prevented the government's political opponents from being defined as criminals, injected into the public arena a terminology that held in check a heated political debate which could easily have led to the breakdown of the democratic dialogue, restrained flagrant violations of the law in the name of civil disobedience, and mediated between the state and the "family of nations" by championing notions that prevail in other democratic communities.

While the model of the lone sheriff is easy to grasp, the complex system of guerrilla-like operations is harder to describe. We would have to know the conditions for instituting such a system, under what rules it would operate, and what its chances of success would be in an environment unamenable to civil rights. Although constructing a theoretical model that addresses these questions is beyond the scope of a biographical study, one prescriptive conclusion can be drawn: in a country like Israel, where democracy is in constant danger and the tension between law and security is always at issue, the protection of civil rights depends on a large professional community willing to draw a line in the sand. Whenever that line is crossed, whenever professional norms, such as the journalist's freedom of speech or the lawyer's ability to adhere to a predictable law, are infringed upon, political involvement is justified. This does not mean that professionals should become politicians, but that they should be aware that in addition to the material demands that organizations such as the

Israeli Bar Association are always willing to make, there are fundamental conditions for the survival of every profession for which they also have to be ready to fight.

For professionals to protect civil society, they need to abandon the conventional wisdom that professionalism must remain politically neutral. Doctors, lawyers, engineers, and programmers often speak a language that has little relevance to the issues on the public agenda, so that not surprisingly the university where most of them are trained is known as "the ivory tower." Similarly, economic advisers, strategic experts, and other professionals called upon to advise governments often maintain the distinction between goals, which are set by the government, and means, which are supplied by the professional. This approach, however, is not only dangerous, as it allows knowledge to be recruited into the service of malevolent causes, but it is also wrong. No profession can be defined as ethically or politically neutral. The survival of every profession rests on a set of demands which require a political awareness similar to that of any other social or political group in society.

Professionals can not be expected to readily agree on how to act to ensure their demands. Journalists differ on what constitutes freedom of expression, social scientists on the nature of their endeavors, and lawyers on the definition of the rule of law. In Israel, this disagreement led to silence over the treatment of the inhabitants of the occupied territories. As a group, Israeli journalists displayed little solidarity with their colleagues in East Jerusalem when newspapers were censored, university professors were silent when universities in the West Bank were closed, and most jurists said nothing when two separate systems of law were implemented on either side of the Green Line. Their silence was not only morally wrong, but professionally dangerous, as the infringement of norms across the Green Line impacted on their status within Israel.

The main impact was felt by civil society. As we have seen, whereas a civil society began to emerge after the end of the Ben-Gurion era, when mobilization of the citizenry for national imperatives gave way to a sense of individualism and voluntarism, after 1967 the country was pervaded by an attitude of escapism. Life continued as if there were no occupation: merchants bought and sold, teachers taught, clerks worked at their desks, musicians played music, and young people were drafted into the army. Civil society—that viable force whereby an empowered public determines its own fate—yielded to the power of the state and the market, whose concern for the populace or the consumer exceeded their concern for the right of individual citizens—Jews and Arabs alike—to life, liberty, and the pursuit of happiness. One wonders who if not the professional, for whom liberty is a condition of survival, could function as advocate of civil society. As Karpik states, the public speaks only through mediators. When professionals forsake their mediating role, civil society surrenders to the might of the state and the market. Indeed, just like democracy itself, civil society has many enemies and few friends.

Notes

1. Lucien Karpik, "Lawyers and Politics in France, 1814 - 1950: The State, the Market and the Public," *Law and Social Inquiry* 13 (Fall 1988): 727.

2. See Konrad H. Jarausch, *The Unfree Professions: German Lawyers, Teachers and Engineers, 1900–1950* (New York: Oxford University Press, 1990); Patricio Silva, "Technocrats and Politics in Chile: From the Chicago Boys to the CIEPLAN Monks," *Journal of Latin American Studies* 23 (May 1991): 385–410.

3. See Margaret Brazier et al., "Falling from a Tightrope: Doctors and Lawyers between the Market and the State," *Political Studies* 41 (June 1993): 197–213.

4. See Michael Keren, *Professionals against Populism: The Peres Government and Democracy* (Albany: SUNY Press, 1995.

5. See Arthur Isak Applbaum, *Ethics for Adversaries: The Morality of Roles in Public and Professional Life* (Princeton, N.J.: Princeton University Press, 1999).

6. See Jeffrey C. Goldfarb, *Civility and Subversion: The Intellectual in Democratic Society* (Cambridge: Cambridge University Press, 1998).

7. See Steven Brint, *In an Age of Experts: The Changing Role of Professionals in Politics and Public Life* (Princeton, N.J.: Princeton University Press, 1994).

8. See Peter Drukier, *Post-Capitalist Society* (New York: Harper, 1993).

Bibliography

Abramowitz, Amnon. "Amnon Zichroni Ba'derech Le'ei Sham" [Amnon Zichroni on the way to somewhere]. *Hotam*. June 27, 1980.

Abrams, Kathryn. "Lawyers and Social Change Lawbreaking: Confronting a Plural Bar." *University of Pittsburgh Law Review* 52 (Summer 1991): 753–83.

Adeleke, Tunde. "Black Biography in the Service of a Revolution: Martin R. Delany in Afro-American Historiography." *Biography* 17 (Spring 1994): 249–67.

Al-Asmar, Fauzi. *Li'hiot Arvi Be'israel* [Being an Arab in Israel]. Jerusalem: Dr. Israel Scha'hak Publications, 1975.

Allan, T. R. S. "Citizenship and Obligation: Civil Disobedience and Civil Dissent." *Cambridge Law Journal* 55 (March 1996): 89–121.

Applbaum, Arthur Isak. *Ethics for Adversaries: The Morality of Roles in Public and Professional Life*. Princeton, N.J.: Princeton University Press, 1999.

Arian, Asher. *Politics in Israel: The Second Generation*. Chatham, N.J.: Chatham House, 1989.

Avnery, Uri. *Israel without Zionists: A Plea for Peace in the Middle East*. New York: Macmillan, 1968.

Barber, Benjamin R. *Jihad vs. McWorld: How Globalism and Tribalism Are Reshaping the World*. New York: Ballantine Books, 1996.

Beilin, Yossi, et al. *Israel's Foreign Policy and Human Rights*. Herzliya, Israel: Friedrich-Ebert Stiftung, 2001.

Ben-Gurion, David. "Hok Sherut Bita'hon (Misspar 2), Tav Shin Yod Bet." *Hazon Vaderech* 4. Mapai Publications, 1953.

———. *Israel: A Personal History*. New York: Funk & Wagnalls, 1971.

———. *Like Stars and Dust: Essays From Israel's Government Year Book*. Sede Boquer: The Ben-Gurion Heritage Center, 1997.

Benveniste, Eyal. *Legal Dualism: The Absorption of the Occupied Territories into Israel*. Boulder, Colo.: Westview, 1990.

Beres, Louis Rene. "Civil Disobedience, Jewish Law and the Middle East Peace Process." *Outpost* (April 1996): 7.

Bernstein, Barton J. "The Oppenheimer Loyalty-Security Case Reconsidered." *Stanford Law Review* 42 (July 1990): 1383–1484.

Bing, Anthony G. *Israeli Pacifist: The Life of Joseph Abileah.* Syracuse: Syracuse University Press, 1990.

Bisharat, George E. "Courting Justice? Legitimation in Lawyering under Israeli Occupation." *Law and Social Inquiry* 20 (Spring 1995): 349–405.

———. "Land, Law and Legitimacy in Israel and the Occupied Territories." *American University Law Review* 43 (Winter 1994): 467–561.

Bracha, Baruch. "Judicial Review of Security Powers in Israel: A New Policy." *Stanford Journal of International Law* 28 (Fall 1991): 39–102.

Brazier, Margaret, et al. "Falling from a Tightrope: Doctors and Lawyers between the Market and the State." *Political Studies* 41 (June 1993): 197–213.

Brint, Steven. *In an Age of Experts: The Changing Role of Professionals in Politics and Public Life.* Princeton, N.J.: Princeton University Press, 1994.

Butovsky, Yaron. "Law of Belligerent Occupation: Israeli Practice and Judicial Decisions Affecting the West-Bank." *Canadian Yearbook of International Law* 21 (1983): 217–34.

Capizzi, Joseph E. "Selective Conscientious Objection in the United States." *Journal of Church and State* 38 (Spring 1996): 339–63.

Carter, April, "Liberalism and the Obligation to Military Service." *Political Studies* 46 (March 1998): 68–81.

Chase, Anthony. "Lawyers and Popular Culture: A Review of Mass Media Portrayals of American Attorneys." *American Bar Foundation Research Journal* 2 (September 1986): 281–300.

Cohen, Jean L., and Andrew Arato. *Civil Society and Political Theory.* Cambridge, Mass.: MIT Press, 1992.

Colas, Dominique. *Civil Society and Fanaticism: Conjoined Histories.* Stanford: Stanford University Press, 1997.

Cossins, Anne. "Revisiting Open Government." *Federal Law Review* 23 (September 1995): 226–76.

Cowan, Lindsey. "The Lawyer's Role in Civil Disobedience." *North Carolina Law Review* 47 (1968–1969): 587–97.

Crick, Bernard. *In Defense of Politics.* London: Weidenfeld and Nicolson, 1962.

Dahl, Robert A., ed. *Political Oppositions in Western Europe.* New Haven, Conn.: Yale University Press, 1966.

Dahrendorf, Ralf. *Reflections on the Revolution in Europe.* London: Chatto & Windus, 1990.

Dalton, Russell J. *Citizen Politics in Western Democracies: Public Opinion and Political Parties in the United States, Great Britain, West Germany, and France.* Chatham, N.J.: Chatham House, 1988.

Dalton, Russell J., and Manfred Kuechler. *Challenging the Political Order.* New York: Oxford University Press, 1990.

Davis, Spencer E. Jr. "Constitutional Right or Legislative Grace? The Status of Conscientious Objection Exemptions." *Florida State University Law Review* 19 (Summer 1991): 191–208.

Dayan, Moshe. *Avney Derech.* Tel Aviv: Dvir, 1976.

Dees, Morris. *A Season for Justice: The Life and Times of Civil Rights Lawyer Morris Dees.* New York: Macmillan, 1991.

Doherty, Maura C. "Fearless Counsel: Being an Attorney for the Civil Disobedient." *Notre Dame Journal of Law, Ethics and Public Policy* 5 (Winter 1991): 1043–1968.

Dori, Latif. "Interview with Dori." *Al Awdah* 73 (November 16, 1986): 6.

Drukier, Peter. *Post-Capitalist Society.* New York: Harper, 1993.

Dworkin, Ronald. *Taking Rights Seriously.* Cambridge, Mass.: Harvard University Press, 1977.

Edel, Leon. *Writing Lives: Principia Biographica.* New York: Norton, 1984.

Edelman, Martin. *Courts, Politics and Culture in Israel.* Charlottesville: University Press of Virginia, 1994.

Englard, Izhak. "Law and Religion in Israel." *The American Journal of Comparative Law* 35 (1987): 185–208.

Epstein, Alek D. "For the Peoples of the Promised Land: Intellectual and Social Origins of Jewish Pacifism in Israel." *Journal of Israeli History* 19, no. 2 (Summer 1998): 5–20.

Feinberg, Rachel. Megilat Dubova. Toldo Ir Sh'e'avra u'vatla Min Ha'olam [The tale of Dubova: history of a town that disappeared from the face of the earth]. Tel Aviv: La'am, 1940.

Feller, S. Z. "Ha'hok Sh'emevaze Et Diney Ha'onshin" [The law that scorns the criminal code]. *Davar* (August 8, 1986): 17.

———. "Ideologia She'hithapssa Le'mishpat" [An ideology masquerading as law]. *Halishka* 6 (April 1989): 24.

Ferguson, James R. "Government Secrecy After the Cold War: The Role of Congress." *Boston College Law Review* 34 (May 1993): 451–91.

Franks, C. E. S., ed. *Dissent and the State.* Toronto: Oxford University Press, 1989.

Fuchs, Esther. *Encounters with Israeli Authors.* Marblehead, Mass.: Micah, 1982.

Galson, Miriam. "Taking Aristotle Seriously: Republican Oriented Legal Theory and the Moral Foundations of Deliberative Democracy." *California Law Review* 82 (March 1994): 329–99.

Gelber, Yoav. Toldot Ha'hitnadvut. Vol. 2. Jerusalem: Yad Ben-Zvi, 1981.

Gibson, Dale. "Civil Disobedience and the Legal Profession." *Saskatchewan Bar Review* 31 (December 1966): 211–24.

Ginger, Ann Fagan. *Carol Weiss King: Human Rights Lawyer 1895–1952.* Niwot: University of Colorado Press, 1993.

Goldfarb, Jeffrey C. *Civility and Subversion: The Intellectual in Democratic Society*. Cambridge: Cambridge University Press, 1998.

Habermas, Jürgen. *The Structural Transformation of the Public Sphere: An Inquiry into a Category of Bourgeois Society*. Cambridge, Mass.: MIT Press, 1992.

Hajjar, Lisa. "Cause Lawyering in Transnational Perspective: National Conflict and Human Rights in Israel/Palestine." *Law & Society Review* 31 (1997): 473–504.

Hall, John A., ed. *Civil Society: Theory, History, Comparison*. Cambridge: Polity Press, 1995.

Hall, Mark, and George Klosko. "Political Obligation and the United States Supreme Court." *Journal of Politics* 60 (1998): 462–80.

Halliday, Terrence C. *Beyond Monopoly: Lawyers, State and Professional Empowerment*. Chicago: Chicago University Press, 1987.

Hart, H. L. A. "Positivism and the Separation of Law and Morals." *Harvard Law Review* 71 (February 1958): 593–629.

Heidenheimer, Arnold J., et al., eds. *Political Corruption: A Handbook*. New Brunswick, N.J.: Transaction Press, 1989.

Herzl, Theodor. *The Jewish State*. New York: Herzl Press, 1970.

Hockins, Barbara Ann. "What Lies in the Public Interest? A Legal History of Official Secrets in Britain." *Queensland University of Technology Law Review* 9 (1993): 31–60.

Hofshi, Nathan. *Belev Va'nefesh*. Publication by the author's friends, undated.

Hurka, Thomas. *Perfectionism*. New York: Oxford University Press, 1993.

Ignazi, Piero. "The Silent Counter-revolution: Hypotheses on the Emergence of Extreme Right-wing Parties in Europe." *European Journal of Political Research* 22 (1992): 3–34.

Isaac, Jean Rael. *Party and Politics in Israel: Three Visions of a Jewish State*. New York: Longman, 1981.

Ismuzik, D. "Ein Do'eg" [Nobody takes care]. *Haaretz*. 19 Nissan, 1932. Aviezer Yelin Archive of Jewish Education in Israel and the Diaspora, Tel Aviv University, Container 4.59.

Jarausch, Konrad H. *The Unfree Professions: German Lawyers, Teachers and Engineers, 1900–1950*. New York: Oxford University Press, 1990.

Jennings, Jeremy, and Anthony Kemp-Welch, eds. *Intellectuals in Politics*. London: Routledge, 1997.

Johnston, Michael. "Right and Wrong in American Politics: Popular Conceptions of Corruption." *Polity* 18 (Fall 1986): 367–91.

Kagan, Robert A. "Do Lawyers Cause Adversarial Legalism? A Preliminary Inquiry." *Law and Social Inquiry* 19 (Winter 1994): 1–62.

Karpik, Lucien. "Lawyers and Politics in France, 1814–1950: The State, the Market and the Public." *Law and Social Inquiry* 13 (Fall 1988): 707–36.

Keren, Michael. *Ben-Gurion and the Intellectuals: Power, Knowledge and Charisma*. DeKalb: Northern Illinois University Press, 1983.

——. *The Pen and the Sword: Israeli Intellectuals and the Making of the Nation-State.* Boulder, Colo.: Westview, 1989.

——. "Law, Security and Politics: An Israeli Case Study." *International Journal of the Sociology of Law* 21 (1993): 105–20.

——. *Professionals against Populism: The Peres Government and Democracy.* Albany: SUNY Press, 1995.

——. "Biography and Historiography: The Case of David Ben-Gurion." *Biography* 23 (Spring 2000): 332–51.

Klein, Claude. "The Defense of the State and the Democratic Regime in the Supreme Court." *Israel Law Review* 20 (1985): 397–417.

Kolinsky, Eva, ed. *Opposition in Western Europe.* London: Croom Helm, 1987.

Kremnizer Mordechai. "Mi Shenoge'a Be'ashaf" [Whoever touches the PLO]. *Koteret Rashit* (September 19, 1985): 48–49.

Lahav, Pnina. *Judgment in Jerusalem: Chief Justice Simon Agranat and the Zionist Century.* Berkeley: University of California Press, 1997.

Lehring, Percy B. "Toward a Multicultural Civil Society: The Role of Social Capital and Democratic Citizenship." *Government and Opposition* 33 (Spring 1998): 221–42.

Lippman, Matthew. "Towards the Recognition of the Necessity Defense for Political Protesters." *Washington and Lee Law Review* 48 (Winter 1991): 235–51.

Luban, David. "Conscientious Lawyers for Conscientious Lawbreakers." *University of Pittsburgh Law Review* 52 (Summer 1991): 793–813.

Lustick, Ian. *Arabs in the Jewish State: Israel's Control of a National Minority.* Austin: University of Texas Press, 1980.

——. "Israel and the West Bank after Elon Moreh: The Mechanism of De Facto Annexation." *The Middle East Journal* 35 (1981): 557–77.

Major, Marie-France. "Conscientious Objection and International Law: A Human Right?" *Case Western Reserve Journal of International Law* 24 (Spring 1992): 349–78.

Manusco, Maureen. "The Ethical Attitudes of British MPs: A Typology." *Parliamentary Affairs* 46 (April 1993): 179–91.

Marcuse, Herbert. *One-Dimensional Man.* Boston: Beacon, 1964.

Marcus, Gilbert. "The Veil of Secrecy in South Africa." *International Commission of Jurists Review* 29 (December 1982): 56–60.

McMorrow, Judith A. "Civil Disobedience and the Lawyer's Obligation to the Law." *Washington and Lee Law Review* 48 (Winter 1991): 139–63.

Mill, John Stuart. *On Liberty.* Indianapolis: Bobbs-Merrill, 1956.

Minow, Martha. "Breaking the Law: Lawyers and Clients in Struggles for Social Change." *University of Pittsburgh Law Review* 52 (Summer 1991): 723–51.

Moorhead, Caroline. *Troublesome People: The Warriors of Pacifism.* Bethesda, Md.: Adler & Adler, 1987.

Mosse, George L. *Fallen Soldiers: Reshaping the Memory of the World Wars*. New York: Oxford University Press, 1990.

Muller-Rommel, Ferdinand, ed. *New Politics in Western Europe: The Rise and Success of Green Parties and Alternative Lists*. Boulder, Colo.: Westview, 1989.

Nettheim, Garth. "Open Justice and State Secrets." *Adelaide Law Review* 10 (September 1986): 281–317.

Nordav, Max. *Morals and the Evolution of Man*. London: Cassell, 1922.

Norris, Pippa, ed. *Critical Citizens: Global Support for Democratic Government*. Oxford: Oxford University Press, 1999.

O'Brien, Patrick K. "Political Biography: A Polemical Review of the Genre." *Biography* 21 (Winter 1998): 50–57.

Peretz, Don. *The Government and Politics of Israel*. Boulder, Colo.: Westview, 1983.

Peri, Yoram. "Israel: Conscientious Objection in a Democracy under Siege." In *The New Conscientious Objection: From Sacred to Secular Resistance*. Edited by C. Moskos and J. C. Whiteclay. New York: Oxford University Press, 1993.

Philip, Mark. "Defining Political Corruption." *Political Studies* 45 (Special Issue 1997): 436–62.

Putnam, Robert D. *Bowling Alone: The Collapse and Revival of American Community*. New York: Simon & Schuster, 2000.

Rabinowitz, Victor. *Unrepentant Leftist: A Lawyer's Memoir*. Urbana: University of Illinois Press, 1996.

Radai, Frances. "Religion, Multiculturalism and Equality: The Israeli Case." *Israel Yearbook on Human Rights* 25 (1995): 193–241.

Ramras-Rauch, Gila. *The Arab in Israeli Literature*. Bloomington: Indiana University Press, 1989.

Rawls, John. *A Theory of Justice*. Oxford: Oxford University Press, 1973.

Raz, Joseph. *The Authority of the Law: Essays on Law and Morality*. Oxford: Clarendon Press, 1979.

Reshef, Shimon. Zerem Ha'ovdim Ba'hinuch [The workers' educational stream]. Tel Aviv: Ha'kibutz Ha'me'u'had, 1980.

Russell, Peter H. "The Politics of Law." *The Windsor Yearbook of Access to Justice* 11 (1991): 127–42.

Salmond, John A. *The Conscience of a Lawyer: Clifford J. Durr and American Civil Liberties 1899–1975*. Tuscaloosa: University of Alabama Press, 1990.

Sarat, Austin, and Stuart A. Scheingold, eds. *Cause Lawyering: Political Commitments and Professional Responsibilities*. New York: Oxford University Press, 1997.

Sartori, Giovanni. *Parties and Party Systems: A Framework for Analysis*. Cambridge: Cambridge University Press, 1976.

———. *The Theory of Democracy Revisited*. Chatham, N.J.: Chatham House, 1987.

Saunders, Frances Stonor. *Who Paid the Piper? The CIA and the Cultural Cold War*. London: Granta Books, 2000.

Schedler, Andreas. "Anti-Political-Establishment Parties." *Party Politics* 2 (July 1996): 291–312.

Shamir, Ronen "'Landmark Cases' and the Reproduction of Legitimacy: The Case of Israel's High Court of Justice." *Law & Society Review* 24, No. 3 (1990): 781–805.

Shavit, Yaacov. *Jabotinsky and the Revisionist Movement 1925–1948*. London: Frank Cass, 1988.

Sher, George. *Beyond Neutrality: Perfectionism and Politics*. Cambridge: Cambridge University Press, 1997.

Shils, Edward, "The Virtue of Civil Society." *Government and Opposition* 26 (Winter 1991): 3–20.

Shimoni, Gideon. *The Zionist Ideology*. Hanover, N.H.: University Press of New England; Waltham, Mass.: Brandeis University Press, 1995.

Shoham, Uri. "The Principle of Legality and the Israeli Military Government in the Territories." *Military Law Review* 153 (Summer 1996): 245–73.

Silva, Patricio. "Technocrats and Politics in Chile: From the Chicago Boys to the CIEPLAN Monks." *Journal of Latin American Studies* 23 (May 1991): 385–410.

Swift, James. *Civil Society in Question*. Toronto: Between the Lines, 1999.

Talmon, J. L. *Political Messianism: The Romantic Phase*. New York: Praeger, 1960.

Thompson, Dennis F. *Political Ethics and Public Office*. Cambridge, Mass.: Harvard University Press, 1987.

Thompson, Dennis F. "Mediated Corruption: The Case of the Keating Five." *American Political Science Review* 87 (1993): 369–81.

Thoreau, Henry D. "Civil Disobedience." In *Civil Disobedience: Theory and Practice*. Edited by Hugo Adam Bedau. Indianapolis: Pegasus, 1969.

Walzer, Michael. *Obligations: Essays on Disobedience, War and Citizenship*. Cambridge, Mass.: Harvard University Press, 1970.

Walzer, Michael. "The Civil Society Argument." In *Theorizing Citizenship*. Edited by Ronald Beiner. Albany: SUNY Press, 1995.

Ware, Alan. *Political Parties and Party Systems*. Oxford: Oxford University Press, 1996.

Wickman, Gary. "Knowing Law, Knowing Politics." *International Journal of the Sociology of Law* 18 (February 1990): 31–44.

Wolf, Joseph M. "National Security v. the Rights of the Accused: The Israeli Experience." *California Western International Law Journal* 20 (Winter 1989): 115–51.

Zamir, Yitzhak. "Rule of Law and Civil Liberties in Israel." *Civil Justice Quarterly* 7 (1988): 64–74.

Zellick, Graham. "Spies, Subversives, Terrorists and the British Government: Free Speech and Other Casualties." *William and Mary Law Review* 31 (Summer 1990): 773–821.

Zichroni, Amnon. *1 against 119: Uri Avnery in the Knesset*. Tel Aviv: Daf Hadash, 1969.

———. "Ha'va'ada Lo Hikpida Al Ekronot Mishpat Besisi'im" [The commission did not consider basic legal principles]. *Davar*. June 14, 1974.

———. *The Israeli Invasion of Lebanon, 1982.* Tokyo: Sanyusha, 1983.

———. "Equal, Less Equal, Not Equal at All. . . ." *Al Awdah* (May 4, 1986).

———. "Politically Motivated Ban on Meetings with PLO Officials.: *Al Awdah* (October 26, 1986): 14.

———. "Ezra'h Lamrot Shlilat Heruto" [Citizen despite his imprisonment]. *Biton Sherut Bate'i Ha'sohar.*

Zinn, Howard. "Law, Justice and Disobedience." *Notre Dame Journal of Law, Ethics and Public Policy* 5 (1991): 920.

Zweig, R. W., ed. *David Ben-Gurion: Politics and Leadership in Israel.* London: Frank Cass, 1991.

Index